The Complete Book of

HANDCRAFTS

The Complete Book of
HANDCRAFTS

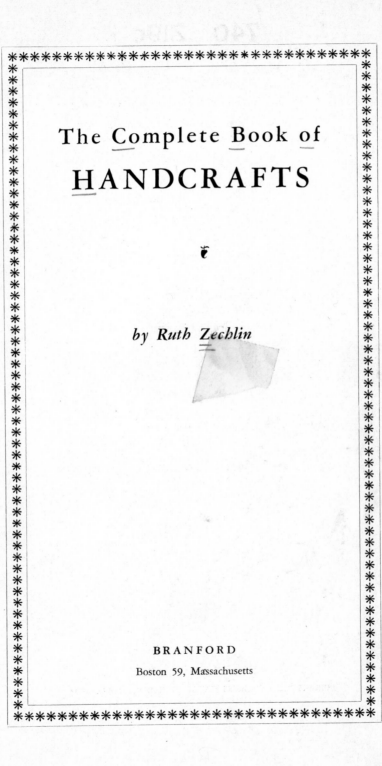

by Ruth Zechlin

BRANFORD

Boston 59, Massachusetts

ⓒ 1959

Published in cooperation with Otto Maier Verlag

English language Edition first published 1959

Translated

by

PETER GORGE

and

F. SYLVIA WESTON

Knitting section edited

by

JAMES NORBURY

LIBRARY OF CONGRESS CATALOG CARD-NUMBER 58-13665

Made and printed in the Netherlands by
Internationale Uitgeverij Duphare, Amsterdam

Foreword

It has become clear to me beyond any doubt that man is formed more by the things he makes than by anything else. (Pestalozzi)

It is indeed a great joy to handle a beautiful object and to see it grow into something new in our hands. So many of us have had to miss this experience, because the machine has replaced most handcrafts. Vast fields of human activity therefore lie fallow, and many important talents are unexploited. Mechanisation has come to rule us increasingly and chokes the very faculties we now need more than ever. Men have felt this for a long time and have realised that something precious, an essential part of their inheritance, is escaping them; they have resisted it and have tried to hold and even to recapture it.

But these faculties are still alive in our children and we would like to keep and develop them. Indeed, we would also like to cultivate them in ourselves. How often do we find that a person who has done nothing with his hands for years suddenly has an opportunity to use them again and feels this to be a kind of liberation. I can still see before me a young student, who carved a Christmas Crib with loving care. She had not done anything like it since her childhood, and when she had finished, she stood before her work and exclaimed happily: "I could shout with joy and gratitude". Whether we carve or weave, embroider or make a toy, we always feel the same: first the joy of creating, then the satisfaction with the finished work; finally, we are also happy if it can give pleasure to someone dear to us.

Indeed, the pleasure in making things grows all the time. That is beyond doubt the most gratifying aspect of handwork. We need this pleasure in creating, more than ever today, for it touches our innermost nature.

Since this volume appeared for the first time twenty-five years ago, handwork has gained many friends and the crafts have been practised more widely. This was helped by the aims of many educationists, and, to a large degree, by the shortages of our time, for handwork is no mere substitute, but can produce something entirely original. We only have to think of the uses of straw, rushes and other materials. The book has been enlarged considerably, in view of so many new projects. Its text has grown threefold since the first editions, the number of illustrations even more. This edition - the twenty-first, - in particular, has been extended considerably and given new form. Many photographs - since we have much higher standards today than twenty-five years ago - have been replaced. The chapters on Batik, Metalwork and Simple Pottery are new. The sections on carving from branches and natural wood in the chapter on Woodwork have been enlarged. The chapter on Embroidery was greatly inspired by the work of Swiss friends, while an invitation to the United States and my visit to schools in the Red Indian reservations at Cherokki, N.C. and Santa Fe, New Mexico, enabled me to extend the chapter on Raffia and Plaiting.

I have attempted throughout the book to make the reader thoroughly conversant with the nature of the material and its appropriate technique. These very fundamental matters are always discussed at the beginning of each chapter. Examples, showing the different uses of the material, follow but, although I have described the making of these examples in every detail, I did not intend them as patterns, to be followed mechanically. The aim of this book is rather to inspire and to encourage the reader to work out his own original ideas. It therefore gives simple and basic interpretations, for we cannot learn too much from simple forms and techniques. But the joy in the first, tentative efforts has often led to a longing to devote more time to a particular craft, indeed even to make it a vocation. Also, everybody who has ever bound a book or done some woodwork will have new eyes for the beauty of a well-made, hand-bound book and will see the difference between a cheap, dolled-up piece of furniture and a piece that is well made by a craftsman. Personal experience with the material and striving for form make us appreciate all craftsmanship.

This book of crafts aims to make us enjoy the work of our hands and to encourage a creative use of leisure. It may even influence the choice of a practical vocation. Adolescents must know the different materials and work with them, before they can decide on their future careers. Having covered so much ground, our book can give young people an opportunity to develop their gifts in many spheres. Indeed, they may even find the proper field for their own particular talents.

Contents

		page
FOREWORD		V
ACKNOWLEDGMENT		XIV
THE SIGNIFICANCE OF HANDWORK AND RULES WE MUST		
OBSERVE		XV
NEEDLEWORK		1
KNITTING		1

I.	ABC of Stitches		2
	1 Basic Principles		2
	2 Stitches	Charts A and B	
	3 Styles for Simple Knitting	Charts C and D	
	4 Tension and Knitting to a Pattern		6
	5 Correct finish to Portions of a Garment		7
	6 Gloves		13
	7 Socks		17

II.	Patterns		19
	1 Simple Patterns in Knit and Purl		19
	2 Pleats		20
	3 Dropped Stitch		20
	4 Brioche Knitting		20
	5 Bound Stitch		22
	6 Simple Lace Stitch		23
	7 Coloured Knitting		28

III.	Simple Designs for Children		29
	1 Baby's Matinée Coats		29
	2 Kiddy Pants		34
	3 Baby's Bootees and Mitts		36
	4 Romper Suit		38
	5 Sports Stockings, Socks, Ski-socks and Gloves		39
	6 Jackets and Waistcoats		41
	7 Stoles		42

CROCHET		44
Crochet Stitches	Charts E and F	
Simple Crochet		45

VII

Stole, Shoulder Nets, Rucksack, Shoes for a Baby, Child's Jacket,
Two Borders   45-48
Tunisian Coloured Crochet   48
Hairpin Work   49

EMBROIDERY   51

Embroidery in colours   52
Cross Stitch and other Embroidery Stitches   52
A Child's Frock, Tablecloth, Mitts, Coffee Cosy, Borders with
coloured braid   54-56
Swiss Drawn Threadwork   56
Inlaid Threadwork   56
Tulle   57

     Christening Robes   60
     Appliqué   60

SEWING   67

With Needle and Cotton   67
ABC of Sewing   68
     I.   *The Most Common Stitches*   68
     II.   *Different Seams*   68
     III.   *Hems*   69
     IV.   *Gathering and Setting on a Band*   70
     V.   *Binding, Bias Binding, Facing*   70
     VI.   *Mitred Corner*   71
     VII.   *Let-in Buttonholes*   71

Sewing dolls' clothes   71
Children's Clothes of Simple Cut (Chart M)   73
Smock   76
     VIII. *Openings*   77
     IX.   *Buttonholes and Loops*   78

Simple practical patterns for Sewing   79
For Travelling, Camping and the Beach   81
How to Sew Slippers   83

NETTING, KNOTTING   87

Filet Network   87
Macramée   92
Cording   95
Chinese Plait   96
Accessories, Knots and Fringes   96
Beadwork   97

WEAVING   99

Explanation of Weaving Terms   100
Types of Fabric   101

page

Cardloom Weaving   101
Weaving with a Heddle Reed   103
Tablet or Card Weaving   106
Weaving on a Loom and Making our own Loom   112
Making a Loom   112
The Warp Threads   118
Mounting a Short Warp   118
Mounting a Long Warp   120
Weaving   122
Materials and Patterns   124

PLAITING IN RAFFIA. RUSHES AND STRAW   129

Materials and their Preliminary Treatment   129
Plaiting   132
Straw Plait   135
Shoes from Raffia and Maize, or Corn, Straw   137
Winding with Raffia   140

Using a Soft Base   140
Raffia Winding on a Hard Base   146

Knotting with Maize (Corn) Leaves   146
Netting with Raffia   148
Raffia Weaving and Raffia Fabric   149
Simple Toys   155

BASKETRY   159

Cane and Reeds   159

Tools and Materials   159
Preparing the Cane   160
First Steps (Base and Table Mat)   160
Techniques   162
The Base   163
Raising and the Sides   164
Borders   165-167
Handle and Ring   168
Various Baskets   168-171

Baskets with a Wooden Base   172-173
Baskets from Brown Willow Rods   174
Shopping Baskets   176

LEATHERWORK   179

The Material   180
Tools   180
Cutting   181
Lining   181
Joining   183

	page
Buttons and Fastenings	183
Simple Articles	184
Shoes and Gloves	189
SILHOUETTES	194
LINO CUTTING AND FABRIC PRINTING	197
Lino Cutting	197
Tools and Material	197
Designs	197
Making the Block	199
Taking a Print	199
Fabric Printing	200
Materials and Equipment	200
The Design	200
Printing	201
Uses	202
BATIK	205
Tools and Material	206
Applying the Wax	208
Dyeing	208
COILING - FIRST STEP IN POTTERY	211
Tools and Raw Material	211
Working Processes	212
Drying and Surface Treatment	213
Firing	214
Slip, Glazes, Majolica Colours	214
PAINTING ON PORCELAIN	217
History	217
Painting under and over Glaze	219
Tools and Materials	219
Painting	219
METALWORK	220
The Materials	220
Filigree Techniques	222
Heating and Hardening	222
Bending	222
Making a Brooch	222
Surface Treatment	223
Hammered Work	224
Tools	224

Blocking	224
Annealing	224
Finishing	224
Box Work	225
Soldering with ready-made Solder	227

PAPERWORK	227
Transparencies	227
Paper Sculpture	228
Folding Paper	234

COLOURED PAPERS	238
Paste, Marbled, Sized, Batik, Mottled Papers	238-240

CARDBOARD	242
Materials	242
Tools	244
Simple Folders	245
Mounting Maps	246
Elements of Bookcrafts	247
Warping	248
The Grain	248
Cutting and Covering Boards	249
Time-table, Calendar, Leporello Photo-Album	249
Adjustable Folder	250
Reading Case	250
Cutting the Materials	250
Different Types of Spine	251
Corners, Bound Edges	252
Useful Folders	253
Photo-albums and Portfolio	253
Portfolios and an Album	254
Guest-book, Diary, and Folder with side flaps	255
A Composite Box	256
Assembling, Reinforcing, Covering, and Lining	258
Box with a Flat Hinged Lid	258
Portfolio with a Fitted Box	260

BOOKBINDING	262
Tools and Materials	262
Working Processes	263-270

LAMPS AND LAMPSHADES

page

271

Lampshades 271

Simple, elegant forms 271
Ceiling and Desk Shades 271
Renewing an old shade 273
Pleated Shades 273
With Simple Pleats 273
Hanging, with Pleats 275

Types of Lamps 276

Lamp made from a Chianti Bottle 276
Table Lamp with Pleated Shade 277

Attaching the Flex or Electric Cord 277

WOODWORK 279

Wood 280

Structure 280
As a Living Substance 280
Most important Woods 280

The Technical Aspect 281

Essential Tools 281
Saws, Drills 282
Chisels, Measuring, Rasp, File and Sandpaper 283
Shooting Board and Plane 283
Glue 284
Sawing and Finishing Parts 284
Joints 284
Basic Joints (Chart O) 286
Finishing the Surfaces 286

Examples 288

1 *Carvings from Bark and Roots* 288
2 *Twigs (Chart P)* 290
3 *Carvings from Firewood* 290
4 *Coconut Shells* 290
5 *Small figures and Dolls' Heads* 292
6 *Decorative Carving* 292
7 *Carving moulds for Cakes and Cookies* 294
8 *Bowls* 294
9 *Toys from scraps of Wood (Chart Q)* 296

DOLLS AND ANIMALS 302

Dolls 302
Woollen Animals 307

		page
MASKS		309
Various Masks		309
Heads for Dolls and Marionettes		311
CHRISTMAS CRIBS AND DECORATIONS FOR THE CHRISTMAS TREE		317
Stars		317
Candleholders		319
Christmas Cribs		322
INDEX		325

ACKNOWLEDGMENT

PHOTOGRAPHS

Jeannine le Brun: 62, 274, 278, 279, 283, 408, 491, 588, 1216. — Sigrid von Carlowitz: 1213
Van Hauen: 70—72, 74, 75, 86—88, 90, 91, 113—116, 122, 123, 137, 194, 422, 662, 663, 672—676, 696, 701, 708, 882, 1254
Gabriele Hauck: 409
Foto-Kabus: 3—6, 64, 66, 67, 73, 76, 77, 80—85, 93, 100—104, 107—110, 112, 118, 127, 129, 134, 136, 140, 141, 144—148, 189, 273, 275, 276, 284—289, 351, 352, 376, 421, 561, 571, 572, 586, 589, 644, 645, 652, 697, 762, 764, 765, 785, 847, 853—860, 876, 886, 890, 940, 941, 991, 992, 1022, 1030, 1137, 1152, 1185, 1195, 1257
Lendvai-Dirksen: 126
Studienrat Michel: 833
Els-Schall: 128, 139, 196, 281, 282, 350
Franz Stoedtner: 1
Photo-Umbo: 1196
Foto Wizig: 277
Ruth Zechlin: 68, 69, 94—99, 105, 106, 111, 117, 119—121, 122, 124, 125, 144, 145, 150, 197, 199—201, 407, 506—508, 510, 525—530, 537—540, 570, 584,, 585, 601, 605, 618, 633, 637, 643, 664, 695, 702, 703, 727, 728, 769, 770, 778, 780—784, 790—793, 806—808, 815, 819, 821, 835, 842—844, 879—881, 936—939, 956, 957, 961, 966—969, 985, 1006, 1007, 1015, 1021, 1055, 1056, 1059, 1131, 1133—1136, 1146, 1147, 1149—1151, 1182, 1183, 1211, 1212
Aus Büchern des Otto Maier Verlages:
Kallmann, Weben: 562, 566—568
Morf, Papparbeit: 997, 999, 1000, 1003, 1004, 1020
Pesch, Lederarbeiten: 794, 795, 816

WORK ILLUSTRATED

Akademie der Bildenden Künste, Stuttgart, Abt. Prof. Karl Hils: 845 a, b
Hedwig Bleek, Bonn: 1136
Humanistisches Gymnasium, Weiden/Opf., Abt. Studienrat Erwin Schörner: 833 a, b
Maria Kegel-Maillard, Meersburg: 286, 287
Firma Walter Kircher, Marburg: 541, 542, 543
Edeltraud Klein, Ravensburg: 940
Traute Krukenberg-Zechlin, Singen: 538—540, 958
Landesgewerbeamt Baden-Württemberg (Menzel): 195
Landwirtschaftl. Päd. Inst. Giessen, Abt. Ruth Zechlin: 644
Lohelandwerkstätten in der Rhön: 490, 814
Irmela Maier, Ravensburg: 2, 140, 1152
Katja Maillard, Stuttgart: 842
Liesel Metzger: Überlingen: 129
Oberschule Goslar, Abt. Studienrat Karl-Heinz Leidreiter: 846, 877
Oberschule Stuttgart, Abt. Studienrat Otto Klauss: 840
Päd. Hochschule Braunschweig, Dozent Willi Ebert: 1197
Päd. Institut Weilburg/Lahn, Abt. Dozent Werner Bähr: 844, 1134
Päd. Institut Weilburg/Lahn, Abt. Dozentin Ruth Zechlin: 76—85, 93, 100, 128, 134, 136, 139, 141, 144, 145, 147, 148, 194, 196, 273—276, 281, 282, 284, 285, 421, 422, 570—572, 584—586, 588, 633, 652, 663, 672, 674, 676, 697, 701, 702, 708, 762—765, 769, 770, 785, 847, 854, 860, 876, 882, 886, 890, 941, 991, 992, 1022, 1030, 1137, 1183, 1195, 1257
Päd. Institut Weilburg/Lahn, Abt. Sozialpraktikum Hedwig Letschert: 1055
Pestalozzi Fröbelhaus, Berlin: 1056, 1150
Renate Rhein, Hannover: 859
Rosgarten-Museum, Konstanz: 283
Schloszschule Salem, Abt. Studien-Ass. Hermann Kegel: 1147
Lina Schondelmaier, Konstanz: 127, 135
Schweizer Heimatwerk, Zürich: 277
Spielmannschule Weilburg: 853
Staatliche Höhere Textilfachschule, Münchberg, Direktor Studienrat Stephan Eusemann: 587
Volksschule Braunschweig, Abt. Edmund Schulze: 878, 887, 888, 889
Volksschule Hasselbach: 1198
Volksschule Marburg: 288
Werkakademie Kassel, Abt. Prof. Ernst Röttger: 1143, 1196
Werkkunstschule Offenbach, Abt. Prof. Maria Steudel: 409
Studienrat Bruno Zwietasch: 1206—1211

XIV

The Significance of Handwork

The craftsman's life seems happy to me; he works, as the birds build their nests, the bees their combs; - how I envy the potter at his wheel, the carpenter at his bench. (Goethe)

How many human beings would be freer and happier if they could work with their hands! For handwork brings happiness; it liberates and solves many problems in children and grown-ups.

Almost everybody has the gift to create. We are born with it, just as most of us are born with a love of music, but it must be developed and encouraged. To unfold these gifts, we use the same methods as in music. Here - as in music - we aim to develop creative ability in everyone. Not all of us can sing in opera or in concerts (it would lead to horrible dilettantism, if everybody with very modest gifts were to make such attempts) but we should all be able to sing a folksong, a simple tune, or a round. We try to do the same for the crafts. Not every layman should paint in oils, attempt great design or "improve" on the expert. We want *simple work,* but it must be genuine and it should bear a professional touch.

These faculties were quite natural to humanity in the past, but today we carry the burden of a century of rather problematic development. It was started by industrialisation, which in turn became mass-production. To form a picture of the way in which natural and healthy creative power dried up and was choked by forms and patterns - mere whims of fashion - we must look back to the time when these things took place. It was a time when industry began to come under the influence of machines, when people were drawn into the cities from the countryside and when the towns grew to a gigantic size. The needs of this expanding population were catered for by an industry that produced huge quantities of almost everything. These goods had to be got rid of as quickly as possible and made a fast-changing fashion a necessity. In consequence, forms degenerated very quickly. Cheap printed patterns killed every creative impulse. We only have to think of the embroidery patterns, with their printed instructions for colours tacked on to the canvas, with the outlines already traced - not to speak of the complete lack of taste, shown in multi-coloured yarn and similar cheap aids to effect. These things are all so horrible, because they are not produced for love of the work, but out of sheer calculation and avarice.

It is not altogether right to blame the machine for this collapse. The machine is no more than an improved tool with greater possibilities. It could have been used as a help to make things well, but we allowed it to rule us, instead of ruling it ourselves. Here we touch on the crisis that set off the "Age of the Machine". It is expressed in the stylistic development of the last hundred years and leads to the decline of handwork. The aberrations in the arts also affected the crafts-man's work down to the last and influenced the appearance of our homes.

The last decades of the nineteenth century, especially, are characteristic of the decline of all form. It was the time of mock-gothic, mock-renaissance and the "battle of the styles". The mid-Victorian age saw façades plastered with cheap stuck-on decorations and with outsize porticos. Rooms were decorated accordingly with paintings, resplendent in gilt frames, artificial flowers, plaster statuettes and all kinds of embroideries, down to newspaper-stands and match-box holders. Cha-racteristically, the original functions of things are completely disguised under the load of ornaments - mostly in imitation of more precious materials - that were meant to impress.

The Art Nouveau style followed this period and began with the entirely proper aim of putting an end to mere imitation of the past. Its followers looked for a natural "organic" style and took the plant world as their model. But since function was not considered and since industry quickly adopted the new forms, the move-ment ended in fresh confusion. Everything sprouted, blossomed and trailed, whether ink-wells, paper-knives, vases, fret- or poker-work, patterns on a carpet, a win-dow on the stair-case, plaster-work on the ceiling or tiles on the stove. The traces of Art Nouveau still survive in many houses.

Although there were several healthy movements towards regeneration after the end of the first World War, they did not touch the homes of people.

The Modern Movement - a reaction to the last century's love of ornament at any cost - first of all cleaned up. The demand for functionalism, though entirely justified, was carried to extremes and led to the rejection of all decoration. Pic-tures disappeared from the walls, cloths from the tables, furniture became clum-sy and lifeless. This purely rational approach did not allow for any feelings at all and spelt the death of handwork. It had become unnecessary. At the most, flat coloured surfaces were allowed to produce "aesthetic effects" and "subtle contrasts".

Meanwhile, architects, including the Bauhaus Group and others, continued the struggle for simplicity, genuineness and natural materials. Good craftsmanship, good handwork and better homes were the aims. Model houses and rooms were designed and young people were fired with enthusiasm for the crafts. But, un-fortunately, the aim of a return to a real popular art led to folk art as the latest fashion. After the beauty of old peasant work had come to be recognised, many shrewd manufacturers took advantage of it. Woodwork was made to look old and "hand-carved", patterns for embroidery now incorporated stags and Gothic letter-ing, red hearts appeared on plaster vases, on slippers, handbags and wherever there was room for them. Thus we saw functionalism turn into a new sentimentality.

It was heartbreaking to see beautiful forms of an old, native tradition cheapened and misused. The past cannot be revived artificially, but the originality and vigour of its art can be an inspiration. We must not make the mistake of imitating the forms of other periods, for each age has its own expression.

There are many people today who strive successfully to express our own age in sound workmanship and genuine materials. We need only think of the movements for better design in many countries, of the work of educators and architects, of the museums and of the efforts to produce better toys. But veritable orgies of shoddiness and sentimentality are still perpetrated, especially in the souvenir industry.

We must start with the simplest things of everyday life again, with the things we buy and make ourselves. Everything we use - children's toys and our immediate surroundings - must again have clear and natural forms. It will give us reverence for objects of daily use. Goethe's words will assume a new importance:

It will remain true: to limit oneself to a few possessions, to love these, to respect them and to live with them, makes the poet, the artist, the true human being.

As we realise the errors of the last hundred years, so we can also genuinely revive the tradition of a better age. We will not take the dead forms, but the spirit of authenticity that causes the form to grow organically. We must make our own way and we must find the courage to express our humanity through the crafts, however simply.

RULES WE MUST OBSERVE

Our own creative faculties will always be the decisive factor. But to produce good work, certain rules must be observed, regardless of style and taste. We cannot achieve anything without accepting such standards.

Aspects of Function.

We must always ask: What is the function of this article? An object must fulfil its intended function. The over-decorated rooms of the last century show where neglect of function leads.

But to serve a purpose is not enough. Our work should also fulfil another need. It should not merely make life easier, it should also be beautiful and give pleasure. If we only worry about function, we achieve an austere utility that leaves us unsatisfied. Neglect of function and aimless decoration lead into a world of cheap and meaningless souvenirs. We must, therefore, achieve *a harmony of beauty and function*. Material, colour and technique must be chosen from this point of view, but they must not be completely unrelated, for it is only through their relationship that anything good can be produced.

Material.

The material is of a great importance. It has its individuality, whether it be linen, wool, silk, paper, straw or clay, and will not tolerate coercion. We must learn to understand its nature.

Let us take a few examples. One substance demands a clear and simple form, another, perhaps, would like to be involved; yet another needs a very special treatment. It is the same problem in every sphere, in craftsmanship and in architecture. Since the material is so important in our work, we must develop a feeling for it - a real understanding.

Methods and Techniques.

The appropriate technique derives from a thorough knowledge of the material. Most mistakes occur because the material's essential qualities were neglected or not sufficiently known; no one remembered how paper curls, wood warps, or which way a fabric stretches. Now the wardrobe has split panels, the corners of the leather folder strive upwards, and the child's dress, embroidered with so much love and hard work, has an ugly tail. These things all happen when someone attempts a thing, whose technical nature is still a mystery. But we want work well executed, not made by dilettantes but by careful, conscientious amateurs.

We also must realise that one material should not assume the features of another. Paper should remain paper and not ape linen, leather or wood. Cardboard is not leather, and simple pine should not pretend to be mahogany or ebony.

Form and Decoration.

An object's function decides its form. The form should always be in harmony with the material. We want a certain form and we shall therefore choose a material suitable for it - or we may have the material and choose the appropriate form - otherwise everything will appear forced. Thus we shall not force raffia, cane and rushes into structures with sharp outlines; oak will be used for objects of a more solid appearance, and birch for lighter and more graceful pieces. We will not make large bags of soft leather, or use a checked fabric for anything round.

Sometimes the beautiful form alone is a source of delight and decoration would only spoil it. We need only think of a fine, smooth vase, a handsome basket, a turned wooden bowl or a well-made leather case. We must therefore be careful and restrained when we decorate.

There must be a close connection between form and ornament. The ornament must be adapted to the form. We can embroider the most beautiful border, but if it is not in harmony with the form it is merely wasted effort, for the work gives no satisfaction.

Technique and ornament also belong together. A hem in sewing can often be made a decorative feature. This applies to the way an entire piece is made, as we can observe in a hammered bowl, a plaited basket, a piece of weaving or some smocking.

Ornament and material must be similarly related. Let us take cross stitch. In Fig. 197 the crosses have been embroidered into the run of the threads of the linen in the traditional manner. They form a unity with the fabric, and are in sharp contrast to cross stitches of embroidery patterns, where the ornament is often printed on any fabric without regard for its weave, or where the pattern is simply ironed on and embroidered afterwards. The relationship between ornament and fabric is destroyed. The result is a painful picture of a struggle between the threads of the fabric and the embroidery, and shows why the ornament of really good work is closely related to function and material.

Colour.

Colour is part of decoration. Most embroidery patterns today also have printed instructions for colours, with exact details of shades and even the manufacturer's numbers of the different yarns. The embroiderer merely assembles, and does no more than someone who is busy with a jig-saw puzzle. Multi-coloured yarn, with its thread changing from yellow to orange to brown and, again, to yellow, etc., is even worse. The pattern becomes quite accidental, wherever the thread happens to run.

It is essential to escape from such techniques and to develop a healthy sense of colour. For this reason, we restrict ourselves in this book - at least at the beginning - to a few simple and clear colours. Those who have not given much time or thought to colour should take a heap of coloured yarns and bits of material and should experiment. We can observe such a lot! Who would have thought that red could be so different in silk, in wool, in cotton, chenille or knitting wool?

And how different this pure yellow looks now, when we hold it next to some red, instead of dark blue, as we did a moment ago. A black velvet, covered with white tulle, seems no longer black and white, but grey. Such experiments can lead to the most remarkable harmonies and discoveries.

Colours have different effects. Shades of red seem warm, shades of blue cold. These tones must be harmonised and special attention must be given to the right proportion, as well as to contrast - the basis of all colour arrangement. It cannot be stressed too often, that colours are only harmonious if they stand in a certain relation to each other. A lot of blue, a little white and a little red can give a very happy effect. The same colours, used in equal quantities, look as if they were fighting to dominate each other.

All these problems must be considered. But knowledge and skill are nothing without a creative imagination, without love and devotion. We must have our heart in our work.

2 The oldest
extant picture
of knitting,
dating from about
1400. A detail
from the altar
painting by Master
Bertram at Buxtehude

3 (right) shows
an example of
knitting with
handspun sheep's
wool

NEEDLEWORK

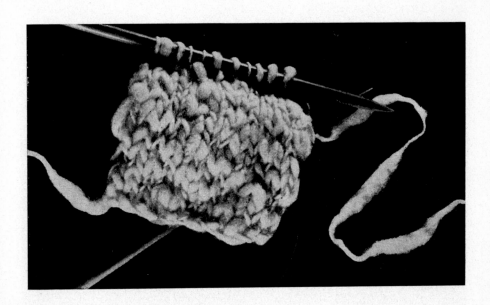

KNITTING

Very little is known about how knitting began. Evidences point to the craft being a household one among the nomads in North Africa and historical records prove that it was well established in England by the reign of Edward IV. France had established itself as the centre of lace knitting by the reign of Henry VIII, and in Germany and Holland embossed and cabled knitted fabrics can be traced to the late 16th and early 17th centuries. The homely appeal of knitting lies in its simplicity. All that is needed are needles and yarn, a thorough grasp of a few very simple principles, and a modicum of patience that is the common demand of any craft.

In the following pages you will find the basic principles of knitting; the application of those principles to the creation of delightful fabrics and patterns that can be easily knitted by you once you are adept in the use of needles and yarn.

ABBREVIATIONS.

K.	- knit	w.o.n.	- wool on needle	w.ft.	- wool front
P.	- purl	w.r.n.	- wool round needle	rep.	- repeat
sl.	- slip	tog.	- together	w.b.	- wool back
st.	- stitch	p.s.s.o.	- pass slip stitch over	alt.	- alternate
w.f.	- wool forward	patt.	- pattern		

1

The needles quoted for the patterns are English gauge. The following table shows you the comparative sizes in English and American knitting pins.

ENGLISH.   1 2 3 4 5 6 7 8 9 10 11 12 13 14 15 16 17 18 19 20

AMERICAN.   8 9 10 11 12 13 14 15 16 17 18 19
              Sets of four steel needles numbered as English.
16 15 14 13 12 11 10 9 8 7 6 5 4 3 2 1
       Pairs of needles numbered as Continental.
              No. 7 is the same size in each method of numbering.

I. ABC of knitting (see also Charts A and B)

4 Garter Stitch

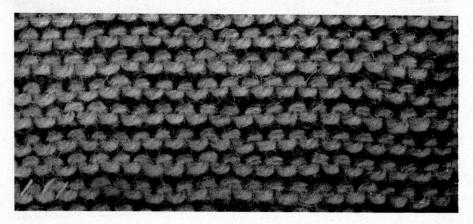

1. BASIC PRINCIPLES

Flat Knitting	*Circular Knitting*	*Casting on*
Worked on two needles throughout.	Worked on sets of four or five needles with points at both ends or on a circular needle where sweaters, skirts and dresses are knitted in the round.	Various methods (See Chart A).

Edges of Fabric

For babies' garments and underwear a knitted edge is always used. To make a knitted edge, simply knit the first and last stitch on every row. A chain edge is made by knitting the first and last stitch on every knit row and purling the first and last stitch on the purl row; that is, knitting and purling these stitches on every alternate row.

Garter Stitch (4)
Worked on two needles, every row knit. Worked in rounds on four needles:
1st round - Knit.   *2nd round* - Purl.
Repeat these two rounds throughout.

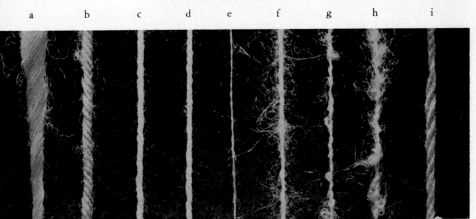

6 Different Yarns. (a) Handspun sheep's wool. (b) Camping wool. (4 ply sports wool). (c) Stranded wool. (4 ply). (d) Baby wool. (4 ply). (e) Fine French Mohair wool. (f) Angora. (g) Friska (Turkish). (h) Coarse mohair. (i) Sports wool. (Double thickness)

Stocking Stitch (Sometimes called "Smooth fabric"). Worked on two needles:
1st row - Knit.   *2nd row* - Purl.

These two rows worked throughout the fabric. Worked on four needles in rounds. Every round knit.

Ribbing

Used for cuffs, welts on pullovers and as all-over patterning in sports garments.
(a) K1, P1 rib. Cast on an even number of stitches and work every row K1, P1. The same principle applies when knitting in rounds on four needles.
(b) K2, P2 rib. Cast on a number of stitches divisible by four and K2, P2 on every row or round.

Patternings

(a) Solid fabrics are produced by an interchange of knit and purl stitches (101-104).
(b and c) Lace fabrics. Created by using the "over principle" followed by the K2 tog. The "over principle" is the w.f., w.o.n., or w.r.n. (114-122). Lace patterns can also be created by dropping stitches (100, 144).
(d) Cable fabrics. (111, 112).
(e) Colour knitting.

Increasing Stitches in the fabric

1st Method. Knitting or purling into the front and back of one stitch thus making two stitches out of one (24).
Second Method. Picking up the loop that lies between the stitch just worked and the following stitch (23).
Third Method. Increasing to three stitches from one by knitting into the front and back and then the front again of the same stitch (25).
Fourth Method. Double increase at end of row. Make one as second method in the stitch before the last stitch on the row, and on the next row increase in the made stitch using first method.
Fifth Method. Mainly used for buttonholes, casting on stitch or looping wool on needle (36, 37).

Decreasing stitches in the fabric

First Method. Knitting two stitches together (26).
Second Method. Slipping one stitch, knitting next stitch and passing the slip stitch over the knitted stitch (27).
Third Method. Decreasing two stitches by slipping one, knitting the next two stitches together and passing the slip stitch over the stitch formed by the two knitted together (28).
Fourth Method. K3 tog. by knitting three stitches together thus forming one stitch (29).

Joining wools or threads

New wool or thread should always be joined at the end of the row.

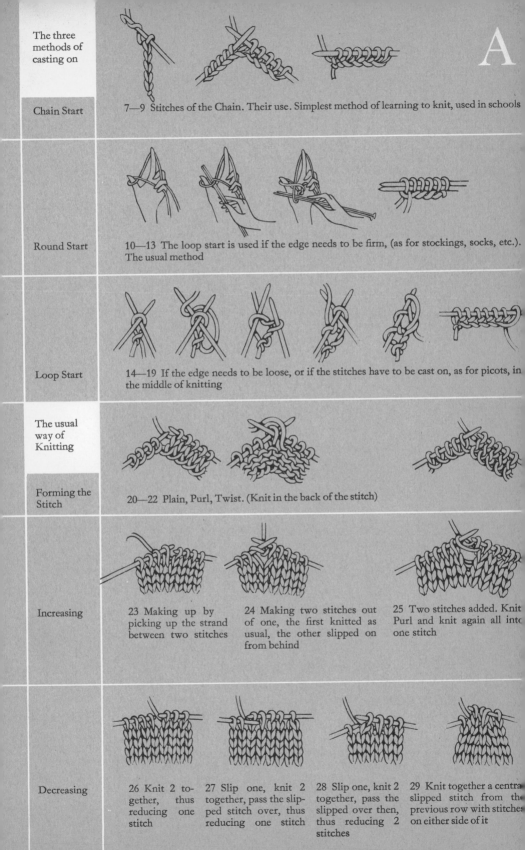

| The three methods of casting on | |
| Chain Start | 7—9 Stitches of the Chain. Their use. Simplest method of learning to knit, used in schools |

A

| Round Start | 10—13 The loop start is used if the edge needs to be firm, (as for stockings, socks, etc.). The usual method |

| Loop Start | 14—19 If the edge needs to be loose, or if the stitches have to be cast on, as for picots, in the middle of knitting |

| The usual way of Knitting | |
| Forming the Stitch | 20—22 Plain, Purl, Twist. (Knit in the back of the stitch) |

| Increasing | 23 Making up by picking up the strand between two stitches | 24 Making two stitches out of one, the first knitted as usual, the other slipped on from behind | 25 Two stitches added. Knit Purl and knit again all into one stitch |

| Decreasing | 26 Knit 2 together, thus reducing one stitch | 27 Slip one, knit 2 together, pass the slipped stitch over, thus reducing one stitch | 28 Slip one, knit 2 together, pass the slipped over then, thus reducing 2 stitches | 29 Knit together a central slipped stitch from the previous row with stitches on either side of it |

B

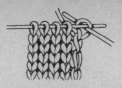

30 Firm knotty edge. The first stitch on the plain row is purled

31 Slip the first stitch and purl the last

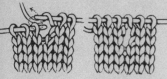
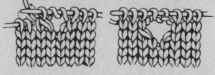

32—33 Small hole. On one row wind the wool round, over the needle, then decrease. On the second row treat the made loop as a stitch

34—35 Larger hole. On one row knit 2 together, wind the wool over twice, and knit 2 together again. On the second row knit and purl into the loop

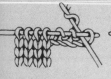
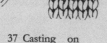

36 Casting on by knitting on

37 Casting on with loops

38/39 Casting off

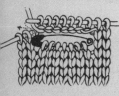
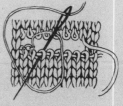

40 Thumbhole

41/42 Horizontal Buttonhole. On one row cast off stitches. On the return row make fresh stitches and knit them again as usual

43 Buttonhole from Released Stitches

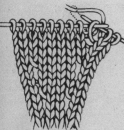
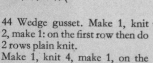

44 Wedge gusset. Make 1, knit 2, make 1: on the first row then do 2 rows plain knit.
Make 1, knit 4, make 1, on the fourth row then do 2 rows plain again. Make 1, knit 6, make 1 on the seventh row, thus adding 2 stitches between the made stitches on every third row

45/46 Grafting: joining two lots of knitting together invisibly
45 Plain grafting
46 Rib grafting

47 Round knitting. Beginning. Make a loop with the thread in a ring round the index finger then pick up stitches to the front and to the back of it from the main thread

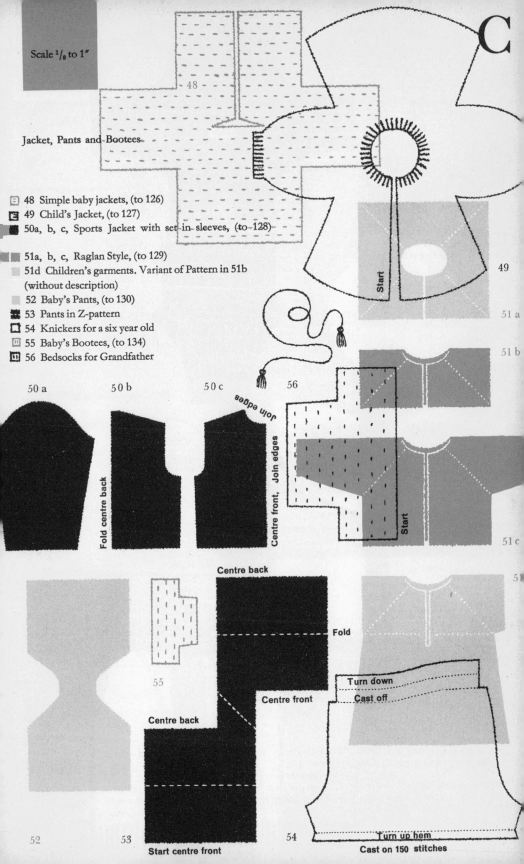

Scale ¹/₈ to 1"

Jacket, Pants and Bootees

48 Simple baby jackets, (to 126)

49 Child's Jacket, (to 127)

50a, b, c, Sports Jacket with set-in sleeves, (to 128)

51a, b, c, Raglan Style, (to 129)

51d Children's garments. Variant of Pattern in 51b (without description)

52 Baby's Pants, (to 130)

53 Pants in Z-pattern

54 Knickers for a six year old

55 Baby's Bootees, (to 134)

56 Bedsocks for Grandfather

C

48

49

51 a

51 b

51 c

5

50 a   50 b   50 c   56

Fold centre back

Centre front, Join edges

Join edges

Start

55

52   53

Centre back

Centre front

Centre back

Start centre front

Fold

Turn down

Cast off

54

Turn up hem

Cast on 150 stitches

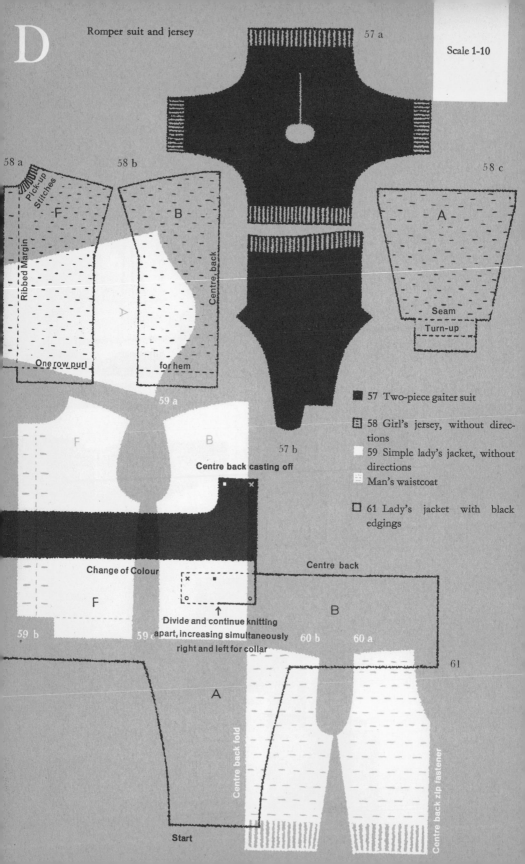

D

Romper suit and jersey

57 a

Scale 1-10

58 a

Pick-up Stitches

F

Ribbed Margin

One row purl

58 b

B

Centre, back

for hem

59 a

58 c

A

Seam

Turn-up

F

B

Centre back casting off

57 b

Change of Colour

F

59 b

59 c

Divide and continue knitting
apart, increasing simultaneously
right and left for collar

Centre back

B

60 b   60 a

61

A

Centre back fold

Start

Centre back zip fastener

■ 57 Two-piece gaiter suit

⊞ 58 Girl's jersey, without directions

☐ 59 Simple lady's jacket, without
directions

⊡ Man's waistcoat

☐ 61 Lady's jacket with black
edgings

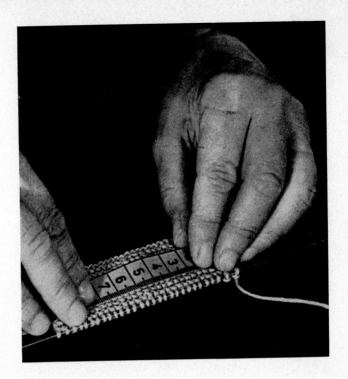

62 Before we start the main work we make a little test of the stitches

Casting off

Always cast off at the same tension as the knitted fabric. In ribbed and patterned fabrics cast off in pattern.

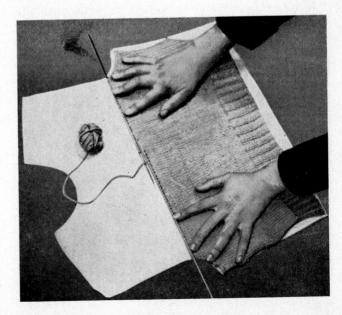

63 The work should be placed frequently upon the pattern

4. TENSION OF KNITTING

The tension of knitting is the number of stitches and number of rows to the square inch knitted in stocking stitch. The following table gives the basic tensions for 2-, 3-, 4-ply and double knitting.

Needles. Size	2-Ply Sts.	Rows.	3-Ply Sts.	Rows.	4-Ply Sts.	Rows.	Double knitting Sts.	Rows.
1	—	—	—	—	—	—	$3\frac{3}{4}$	$4\frac{1}{2}$
4	5	7	$4\frac{1}{2}$	$6\frac{1}{2}$	4	6	$4\frac{1}{2}$	$5\frac{1}{2}$
5	$5\frac{1}{2}$	$7\frac{1}{2}$	5	7	$4\frac{1}{2}$	$6\frac{1}{2}$	$4\frac{3}{4}$	6
6	6	8	$5\frac{1}{2}$	$7\frac{1}{2}$	5	7	5	$6\frac{1}{2}$
7	$6\frac{1}{2}$	$8\frac{1}{2}$	6	8	$5\frac{1}{2}$	$7\frac{1}{2}$	$5\frac{1}{4}$	7
8	7	9	$6\frac{1}{2}$	$8\frac{1}{2}$	6	8	$5\frac{1}{2}$	$7\frac{1}{2}$
9	$7\frac{1}{2}$	$9\frac{1}{2}$	7	9	$6\frac{1}{2}$	$8\frac{1}{2}$	$5\frac{3}{4}$	$7\frac{3}{4}$
10	8	10	$7\frac{1}{2}$	$9\frac{1}{2}$	7	9	6	8
11	$8\frac{1}{2}$	$10\frac{1}{2}$	8	10	$7\frac{1}{2}$	$9\frac{1}{2}$	$6\frac{3}{4}$	9
12	9	11	$8\frac{1}{2}$	$10\frac{1}{2}$	8	10	$7\frac{1}{4}$	10
13	$9\frac{1}{2}$	$11\frac{1}{2}$	9	11	$8\frac{1}{2}$	$10\frac{1}{2}$	—	—
14	10	12	$9\frac{1}{2}$	$11\frac{1}{2}$	9	11	—	—

KNITTING TO A PATTERN

Paper patterns may be used as the basic shapes for knitted garments, the shapings being worked by the increasing and decreasing principles already given. The pieces should be slightly smaller than the paper pattern to allow for the elasticity of knitted fabric. The knitted fabric should be placed on the paper pattern from time to time to check the shaping (63).

Ribbing for welts, cuffs, neckbands etc.

Ribbing should always be worked on needles two sizes finer than the needles used for the remainder of the garment.

65 Chain stitch

64 Stitching up parts with lacing stitch

66 Border of garter stitch   67 Increase with Raglan style

Steaming and pressing knitted fabric

The pieces of the garment should be pinned out to shape, wrong side uppermost and then lightly pressed using a warm iron and a damp cloth. Never press the ribbed portions of a garment. If the whole garment is in ribbing, pin out the pieces and *very lightly press* using a warm iron and a wet cloth.

Making up garments (64, 65)

First Method. Used for garments with a knit stitch edge. Simply oversew the edge stitches together.

Second Method. Back stitch seam. This is an ordinary back stitch and gives a tailored line to the garment.

Third Method. Chain stitch edge (65). Where the edges of the fabric are uneven they should be lightly joined together and then chain stitch worked on the right side of the fabric up the seam.

5. CORRECT FINISH TO VARIOUS PORTIONS OF A GARMENT

Commencing of garment

Where a garment is worked in stocking stitch, as the edge of stocking stitch curls, the first section of the fabric should be in garter stitch or ribbing. In babies' matinée coats and cardigans the garter stitch or ribbing is carried up the front border, the width being ascertained by the type of garment being knitted.

Separate Borders

These can be knitted in rib or moss stitch. Another method is to knit up the stitches along the edge of the front and round the neck, work in stocking stitch for double the width required, cast off and then knit the cast-off edge to the knitted-up edge on the wrong side, forming double border.

Picot Edge (68, 69)

Cast on an odd number of stitches and work eight rows in stocking stitch. On the next row K1, + w.f., K2 tog. to end of row. Work nine more rows in stocking

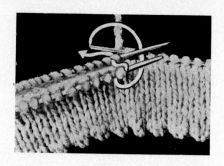

68 and 69 Picot work. How to work a picot edge

70 Increases worked on diagonal edge

71 Decreases worked on diagonal edge

72 Diagram showing armhole shaping

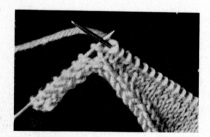

73 Diagram showing shaping on top edge of knickers

74 Diagram showing turns in shaping shoulders

75 Diagram showing working of V neck

76 Centre of V neck band

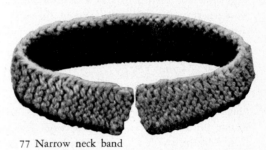

77 Narrow neck band

78

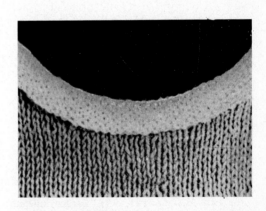

79

78 and 79 Round neck with double band

80 Simple roll collar

stitch. On completion of garment turn up at holes to form picot and flat-stitch on wrong side to form hem.

A similar hemmed border without picots is shown on the stockings in Fig. 137.

Diagonal Edges (70, 71)

Diagonal edges to a piece of fabric are worked by knitting the first two stitches on the row, increasing one stitch in the last stitch but one on the row, working the decreases and increases on alternate rows throughout.

Shaping upper edge of knickers (73)

The method used here is to work to within an inch of the end of the row, turn, then work back to an inch at the end of the next row, turn again. Continue working in this manner, turning half an inch in from the last turn on every row.

Shoulder Shaping (74)

Shoulder shaping is worked in the same way as shaping the upper edge of knickers, but here the number of stitches on the needle is divided by three, work to one third of the stitches, turn, work back slipping the first stitch. Work to two thirds of the stitches on the needle, turn, and work back, again slipping the first stitch. Now work back. Cast off.

Shaping Armholes (72)

Armholes are shaped by casting off groups of 4, 3 stitches on first row of armhole shaping and following alternate row, then decreasing at armhole edge on every alternate row until shaping is completed.

Buttonholes

First Method. K2 tog., w.f., K2 tog. at point where buttonhole has to be made. On the next row work into the front and the back of the w.f. thus making two stitches out of one. Complete by buttonholing round hole.

Second Method. (41, 43). Larger buttonholes can be made by casting off two or three stitches on the first row and casting on the same number of stitches on the next row, thus completing the buttonhole.

Third Method. Horizontal buttonholes can be made by cutting one stitch, letting it drop for two or three rows. Now draw the wool from the right and left, pick up the free loops with a darning needle and fasten off. Buttonhole stitch round buttonhole.

V Neck, Round Neck, Neckband and Collar

a) V Neck. (71)

Divide at centre, casting off centre stitch if there are an odd number of stitches on the needle. Work graduated decreases up each side of the neck.

Neckband (75, 76)

Join shoulders. Using set of four needles, knit up even number of stitches round neck, knitting one up at centre V. Work in rounds of K1, P1 rib, decreasing one stitch at each side of stitch knitted up at centre V on every round.

b) Round Neck (78, 79)

Cast off approximately a third of the number of stitches used for the complete neck, at centre. Work on each group of stitches, decreasing one stitch on every alternate row until shoulder width is reached.

Separate Neckband (77)

This is knitted as a separate straight piece in garter stitch, moss stitch or ribbing and stitched into the neck hole with join at centre back.

Knitted-up Round Neck (78, 79)

Join shoulders. Knit up stitches as for V neck. Work in rounds of K1, P1 rib.

Knitted-up Front Band (81)

Knit up stitches round front edge, work in garter stitch for single band and stocking stitch for hemmed band.

Pockets

Straight Pocket (82)

When position for pocket is reached, knit to and fro in garter stitch for width of pocket, thus forming pocket top. Cast off. Now cast on the same number of stitches and continue until piece of knitting is completed.

The pocket lining is worked by picking up the stitches cast on and working for the depth of the pocket in stocking stitch, then casting off.

Flat-stitch edges of pocket on right side and all round lining on wrong side to complete.

Pocket with patent opening (83)

Work across number of stitches for width of pocket in stocking stitch for 1¼ inches. Now work in reverse stocking stitch for another 1¼ inches. Cast off. Complete as above.

Pocket in Brioche Knitting (84)

The pocket here is knitted sideways by knitting to and fro across stitches to point where pocket top is placed on garment. Break off wool. Now work to and fro on

82 Simple square pocket

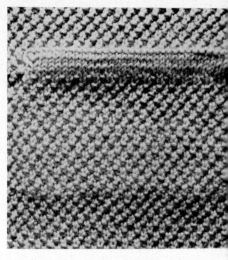

83 Simple moss stitch pocket

84 Pocket for parallel knit jacket

85 Oblique pocket

86 Knitting in of gussets

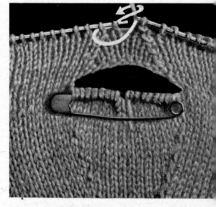

87 Thumb-hole and insert

remainder of stitches for same number of rows. Join up work again in one piece. Complete as previous pockets.

Slanting Pocket

Knit to commencement of slanting edge of pocket. Now decrease one stitch at slanting edge on every alternate row to depth required, finishing at slanting edge. Re-join wool to remaining stitches and increase one stitch on every alternate row to match decreases. Re-join wool and continue until piece of knitting is completed.

The pocket edge has been worked in garter stitch by knitting up stitches along slanting edge, then working in garter stitch every row knit, increasing one stitch at lower edge of pocket opening and decreasing one stitch at upper edge for depth required. Cast off.

The pocket lining is knitted separately and is an oblong piece of stocking stitch that is flat-stitched down on the wrong side of the work.

6. GLOVES

Mittens without gussets

Using the four-needle method, casting on three needles and working in rounds, cast on the number of stitches required for the cuff of the mitten. This will vary between 48 and 72 stitches according to the ply of wool and size of needle used.

Work in ribbing (K1, P1, or K2, P2) for the depth of the cuff, approximately 2½ inches. Now continue in rounds of stocking stitch until the mitten measures up to the base of the thumb. At this point the thumb hole is made by slipping the number of stitches required for half the thumb (between 10 and 14) on to a safety pin. Cast on the same number of stitches on the next round and continue in rounds until sufficient has been worked to reach the top of the fourth finger. Now divide the stitches in half, the thumb hole lying at the front about half an inch from the side, and, still working in rounds, shape the top by decreasing at each end of the two sets of stitches until sufficient to reach the tip of the middle finger has been worked. Graft the two sets of stitches together at the top of the mitten.

The thumb is knitted by picking up one stitch for each of the cast-on stitches, one stitch at each side of the thumb hole and then the stitches on the safety pin. Work in rounds until the shaped top of the thumb is reached. Divide stitches in two and shape off as for top of mitten.

Another method of making a thumb hole (90), is to knit in a strand of a different coloured thread across the stitches at the base of the thumb instead of putting them on a safety pin. When the mitten has been completed the coloured thread is carefully pulled out. The released stitches are picked up and a stitch at each side of the thumb hole as above. Complete thumb as above.

Pockets can be knitted by the same method.

Mittens with Gussets

Work the cuff as on the first mitten. Work in rounds of stocking stitch for half an inch. To make the thumb gusset, increase in the first and second stitch on the first needle on the next round. Work two rounds without increases. On the next

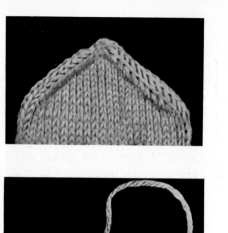

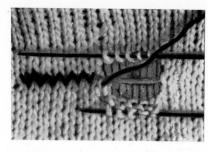

90 Thumb hole without gusset
(Removal of auxiliary thread)

88 Glove tip (left, upper)

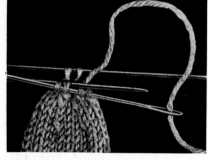

89 Casting off for finger tips

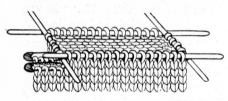

91 and 92 The lay-out for the fingers

round increase in first stitch on first needle, K2., increase in next stitch, work to end of round. Work two more rounds without increases.

On the next round increase in first stitch on first needle, K4, increase in next stitch, knit to end of round. Continue increasing in this manner on every third round until the gusset is a third of the total number of stitches that were cast on for the cuff, working two plain rounds after the last increase.

Thumb Hole and inset

Transfer the gusset stitches to a safety pin. Cast on from 5 to 7 stitches to close up thumb hole and continue in rounds, shaping top of mitten as first mitten (26 and 27). (See also 88).

Work thumb as for first mitten, decreasing one stitch at each side of the cast-on stitches on first and third rounds. Continue without further decrease until top of thumb is reached. To shape the top, on the first round K2 tog., K2 all round. Work two rounds. On the next round K2 tog., K1, all round. Work one round. There should now be between 6 and 8 stitches on the needle. Draw a thread through these stitches and fasten off securely.

Gloves (91 and 92)

Work as for mitten with thumb gusset and thumb until base of fingers is reached. Work out division of stitches for fingers. To do this divide number of stitches in round by 4, giving you the approximate number of stitches for each finger. Taking two less stitches for the little finger, work across these stitches, cast on 2, work in

93

rounds on these stitches for length of finger. Shape top as thumb on mitten with gusset.

Picking up two stitches through cast-on stitches and casting on two at the other side of the finger, work three more fingers in the same manner, adjusting the number of stitches according to the width of the fingers.

Figure 89 shows tips of fingers being finished.

Simple Mittens in Flecked Double Knitting Wool (93)

Materials: 3-ozs. Double Knitting wool in a Fleck shade. 5 No. 13 needles.

Tension: 7½ sts. and 9 rows to one inch.
    Cast on 36 sts, 9 on each needle.
    Work 30 rounds in K1, P1 rib.
    On the next round increase 8 evenly in the round.
    Work thumb gusset and thumb.
    Work up to base of fingers and complete as instructions for glove.

15

94 Heel with the idle stitches

95 Beginning of the decreasings

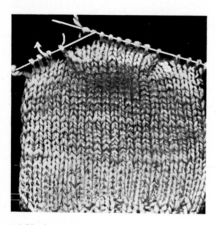

96 Heel turning

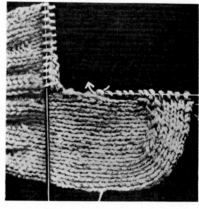

97 Connecting heel and instep
(Picking up stitches along the ankle part)

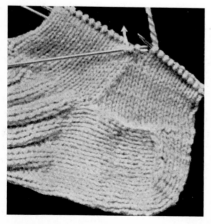

98 Ankle decreasings

99 Decreasing for the toe

7. SOCKS

Socks are knitted in rounds on four or five needles. The size of needles will vary from 11's to 16's according to the thickness of the wool or yarn used.

Cast on number of stitches required for top of the sock. Work in rounds of ribbing for 3½ to 4½ inches. Continue in rounds of stocking stitch for plain sock or pattern for patterned sock, until top of heel is reached.

The Heel (94)

Slip half the number of stitches on to one needle. Work in rows of either stocking stitch, or for a reinforced heel, on the first row, K1, sl. 1, P. the second row, sl. 1, K1 on the third row and P. the fourth row. Work in stocking stitch or as above for the reinforced heel, until the piece measures ¾ inch shorter than its width.

Turning the Heel (95, 96)

Divide the stitches on the heel needle by 3, adding any extra stitches to the centre group. Thus if there are 36 stitches, you will have 12, 12, 12; if there are 38 stitches, 12, 14, 12. Now work to the last *13* stitches, work 2 tog., turn, work to last 13 sts., work 2 tog. turn; work to last 12 sts., work 2 tog. turn; work to last 12 sts., work 2 tog. turn.

Working Instep (97)

Divide stitches remaining on heel needle into two. Pick up stitches along side of heel. Commence working in rounds again, decreasing on next and every third round at top of heel piece until the number of stitches is the same as those cast on at the commencement of the sock (26 and 27).

Continue in rounds until the toe is reached.

Shaping Toe (99)

Now decrease on the third and fourth stitches from the end of each needle on every third round three times, on every second round twice and on every alternate

101 Simple moss stitch   102 Double moss stitch

round once. Continue decreasing in this manner on every round until 8 stitches remain. The stitches are then drawn together with a darning needle and sewn up on the wrong side.

Flat Toe (88)

Divide stitches half on one needle, quarter on each of the other two. On the first needle containing half, decrease one stitch from each end on every alternate round. On the second needle, decrease one stitch in from the beginning, and on the third needle one stitch in from the end on every alternate round until 8 stitches remain . . . 4, 2, 2. Place the two sets of two on one needle, and graft the two sets of four stitches together.

II. Patterns

1. SIMPLE PATTERNS IN KNIT AND PURL

Moss Stitch (101)

Cast on an odd number of stitches and work every row
* K1, P1, rep. from * to last st., K1.

Double Moss Stitch (102)

Cast on an even number of stitches.
1st and 2nd rows - * K1, P1, rep. from * to end.
3rd row - * P1, K1, rep. from * to end. These 3 rows form the patt.

K2, P2 Rib (103)

1st and 2nd rows - * K1, P1, rep. from * to end. 3rd row - * P1, K1, sep. from *
1st. and every row or round - * K2, P2, repeat from * to end.

Grain Pattern (104)

Odd number of stitches.
1st. row - * K1, P1, rep. from * to last st., K1. 2nd row - P. 3rd row - * P1, K1, rep. from * to last st., P1. 4th row - P.

103 Mossed rib   104 Grain effect

2. PLEATS (107, 108)

Narrow Pleats. (Worked in rounds). Cast on number of stitches divisible by 3. Work every round * P2, K1, rep. from * to end of round.

Wide Pleats. Cast on number of stitches divisible by 4 plus 1.
1st and every row - * K2, P1, rep. from * to last st., P1.

3. DROPPED STITCH (5, 100)

1. Horizontal Dropped Stitch (100 left)

First Method: Use fine needle for first row and coarse needle for second row throughout. To space out dropped stitch effect, work 3, 5 or 7 rows on fine needle to every one row on coarse needle.

Second Method: Cast on number of stitches required.
1st row - K. 2nd row - P. 3rd row - *K1, w.f., rep. from * to end of row. 4th row - P., dropping w.f.'s of previous row.

If longer dropped loops are required, work the w.f. 2, 3 or 4 times round the needle, dropping these loops on the following row as above.

2. Vertical Dropped Stitch (144). This stitch is produced by dropping stitches right down the fabric at point where horizontal dropped stitch is to be worked.

For a stole, cast on multiples of 5 plus 4, work to length required in garter stitch, then drop 5th and every following 5th stitch before casting off.

A neater edge can be formed for vertical dropped stitch by working a w.f., K2 tog. at the point where stitches are to be dropped before the cast-off row.

Always drop the stitch that lies over the w.f. if this method has been used.

105

106

4. BRIOCHE KNITTING (SOMETIMES CALLED OVERLAY KNITTING)

Simple Overlay (105)

Cast on a number of stitches divisible by 2.
1st row (an increase row) - K1, * w.f., sl. 1 purlwise, K1, rep. from * to last st., K1.
2nd row - K1, * w.f., sl. 1 purlwise, K2 tog., rep. from * to last st., K1.

Repeat *2nd row only* for length required and work the following row before

107 Double overlay					108 Broad pleats

109 Net overlay (above)				110 Bound stitches (below)

casting off: K1, * K1, K2 tog., rep. from * to last st., K1. Cast off in ordinary way.

Double Brioche Stitch (106)

Cast on an odd number of stitches.

1st row - * K1, w.f., rep. from * to last st., K1.

2nd row - K1, (w.f. of previous row), wool to front of needle, slip the next st. purlwise (knitted stitch of previous row), thus the wool lies in front of the slip stitch, repeat from * to last 2 sts., K2.

Net Brioche (109)

Cast on number of stitches divisible by 2.

1st row (an increase row) - K1, * w.f., sl. 1 purlwise, K1, rep. from * to last st., K1.

2nd row - K1, w. ft., * sl. 1 purlwise, w.r.n., P2 tog., rep. from * to last st., K1.

3rd row - K1, P1, * sl. 1 purlwise (the w.r.n. of previous row) P2, rep. from * to last 3 sts., sl. 1 purlwise, P1, K1.

4th row - K1, * P2 tog., sl. 1 purlwise, w.r.n., rep. from * to last 4 sts. P2 tog., w.b., sl. 1 purlwise, K1.

5th row - K1, w.r.n., P2, * sl. 1 purlwise (the w.r.n. of previous row), P2, rep. from * to last st., K1.

Rows 2 - 5 inclusive form the patt.

5. BOUND STITCH (110)

Cast on number of stitches divisible by 4 plus 2. Purl all across for foundation row. Proceed as follows:

1st row - K1, * bring wool to front of work, sl. 2., take wool to back of work, K2, rep. from * to last st., K1.

2nd row - Purl.

3rd row - Knit.

4th row - Purl.

5th row - K1, * K2, w.ft., sl. 2, w.b., rep. from * to last st., K1.

6th to 8th rows - As 2nd to 4th.

These 8 rows form the patt.

Cable Pattern knitted in rounds (111)

Cast on multiple of 6 sts.

1st and 2nd rounds - * P2, K4, rep. from * to end of round.

3rd round - P2, sl. next 2 st. on cable needle and leave at front of work, K2, K2 sts. from cable needle, repeate from * to end of round.

4th to 6th rounds - Repeat first round 3 times.

Cable and Rib Pattern (112)

Worked in rounds. 9 stitches are needed for each pattern.
1st and 2nd rounds - * K1, P1, K6, P1, rep. from * to end of round.
3rd round - * K1, P1, sl. next 3 sts. on cable needle and leave at front of work, K3,
K3 sts. from cable needle, P1, rep. from * to end of round.
4th to 6th rounds - Repeat 1st round 3 times.

6. SIMPLE LACE STITCH

Ladder Stitch, worked in rounds (113)
Cast on multiple of 4 sts.
1st round - * K2, w.f., K2 tog., rep. from * to end of round.
2nd round - K.
These 2 rounds form the patt.

Eyelet Foundation. Knitted in rounds (115)
Cast on multiple of 2 sts.
1st and 2nd rounds - K.
3rd round - * w.f., K2 tog. rep. from * to end of round.
These 3 rounds form the patt.

Oblique Lace Stitch, worked on 2 needles (116)
Cast on a multiple of 2 plus 1.
1st - 5th rows - K.
6th row - K1, * w.f., K2 tog., rep. from * to end.
7th row - P.
8th row - K2, * w.f., K2 tog. rep. from * to last st., K1.
9th row - P.
10th row - As 6th.
These 10 rows form the patt.

Bead Chain Pattern, worked in rounds (114)

Cast on number of stitches divisible by 4.
1st and 2nd rounds - * P2, K2, rep. from * to end.
3rd round - * P2, w.o.n., sl. 1, K1, p.s.s.o., rep. from * to end of round.
These 3 rounds form the patt.

Spider Web Pattern, worked on 2 needles (118)

Cast on a multiple of 6 sts. plus 2.
1st row - K1, * w.r.n., P1, w.r.n., P3 tog., sl. 1, K. into front and back of next st.,
rep. from * to last st., K1.
2nd row - K.
3rd row - K1, * P3 tog., w.o.n., P1, w.o.n., sl. 1, K. into front and back of next
st., rep. from * to last st., K1.
4th row - K.
These 4 rows form the patt.

112 Cable with intervening rib

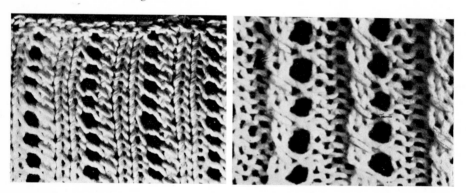

113 Ladder holed work

114 Bead chain work

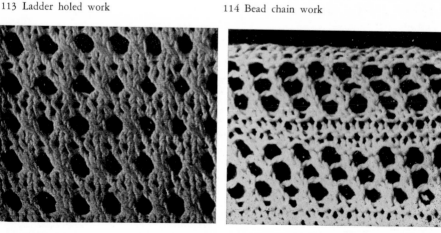

115 Holed foundation

116 Oblique holed rows

Manikin Pattern, worked on 2 needles (119)

Cast on odd number of stitches.
1st to 3rd rows - K.
4th row - P.
5th row - K1, * w.f., K2 tog., rep. from * to end.
6th row - P.
These 6 rows form the patt.

Herringbone Pattern, worked on 2 needles (117)

Cast on number of stitches divisible by 6
1st row - * P2, K2 tog., w.f. K2, rep. from * to end.
2nd row - P2 tog., w.r.n., P.2, K2.
These 2 rows form the patt.

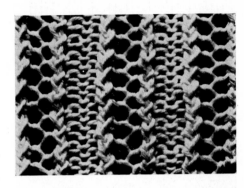

117

Network Pattern, worked on 2 needles (100, on Right)

Cast on even number of stitches.
1st and every row - K1, * w.f., sl. 1, K1, p.s.s.o., rep. from * to last st., K1.

Lozenge Pattern, worked in rounds (120)

Cast on number of stitches divisible by 8.
1st round - * K5, w.f., K3 tog., w.f., rep. from * to end of round.
2nd and every alt. round - K.
3rd round - * w.f., sl. 1, K1, p.s.s.o., K1, K2 tog., w.f., K3, rep. from * to end of round.
5th round - * K1, w.f., K3 tog., w.f., K4, rep. from * to end of round.
7th round - * w.f., K3, w.f., sl. 1, K1, p.s.s.o., K1, K2 tog. repeat from * to end of round.
8th round - K.
These 8 rounds form the patt.

Scales Pattern, worked on 2 needles (121)

Cast on number of stitches divisible by 11 plus 2 edge stitches.
1st and all odd rows - (wrong side facing) * K2, P9, rep. from * to last 2 sts., K2.
2nd row - * P2, K1, w.f., K2, K3 tog., K2, w.f., K1, rep. from * to last 2 sts., P2.
4th row - * P2 K2, w.f., K1, K3 tog., K1, w.f., K2, rep. from * to last 2 sts. P2.
6th row - * P2, K3, w.f., K3 tog., w.f., K3, rep. from * to last 2 sts., P2.
8th row - * P2, w.o.n., K3, K3 tog., K3, w.r.n., rep. from * to last 2 sts. P2.
These 8 rows form the patt.

Laurel Leaf Pattern, worked on 2 needles (122)

Cast on number of stitches divisible by 12 plus 1.
1st row - K1, * w.f., sl. 1, K1, p.s.s.o., K7, K2 tog., w.f., K1, rep. from * to end.
2nd and every alt. row - P.

25

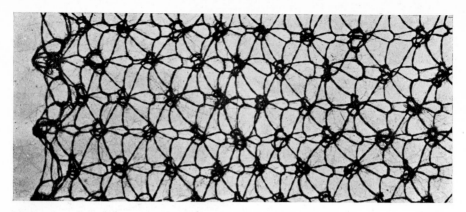

118 Spider web work

119 Manikins

120 Lozenge pattern

121 Scales

26

3rd row - K1, * w.f., K1, sl. 1, K1, p.s.s.o., K5, K2 tog., K1, w.f., K1, repeat from * to end.

5th row - K1, * w.f., K2, sl. 1, K1, p.s.s.o., K3, K2 tog., K2, w.f., K1, repeat from * to end.

7th row - K1, * w.f., K3, sl. 1, K1, p.s.s.o, K1, K2 tog. K3, w.f, K1, repeat from * to end.

9th row - K1, * w.f., K4, sl. 1, K2 tog., p.s.s.o., K4, w.f., K1, repeat from * to end.

11th row - K1, * K3, K2 tog., w.f., K1, w.f., sl. 1, K1, p.s.s.o., K4, repeat from * to end.

13th row - K1, * K2, K2 tog., K1, w.f., K1, w.f., K1, sl. 1, K1, p.s.s.o., K3, repeat from * to end.

15th row - K1, * K1, K2 tog., K2, w.f., K1, w.f., K2, sl. 1, K1, p.s.s.o., K2, repeat from * to end.

17th row - K1, * K2 tog., K3, w.f., K1, w.f., K3, sl. 1, K1, p.s.s.o., K1, repeat from * to end.

19th row - Sl. 1, K1, p.s.s.o., * K4, w.f., K1, w.f., K4, sl. 1, K2 tog., p.s.s.o., * repeat from * to * ending sl. 1, K1, p.s.s.o., on last 2 sts.

20th row - P.
These 20 rows form the pattern.

7. COLOURED KNITTING

Colour knitting is generally worked in stocking stitch, one row knit, one row purl, the work being carried out from charts on squared paper. The colour not in use is either carried across the back of the work (this is called stranding), or twisted round the colour in use (this is called weaving the colours). The simplest way to work in two colours is to hold one colour in the right hand and one in the left, bringing the colour into work according to the sequence of squares on the graph paper.

An important point to remember is that the wool should be allowed to flow loosely across the back of the fabric, otherwise the finished pieces of work will have a "puckered" appearance. When we are stranding a colour, we should never strand over more than five stitches as this would cause the coloured strands at the back to be too long. The method when working over five stitches or more is to twist the colour not in use round the colour in use at every fourth stitch.

Where a colour is only used for a single motif, or if a supplementary colour is only introduced very rarely into the pattern, it is much simpler to use a short length of wool simply working across pattern stitches in the colour and weaving the colour where it joins the main colour to avoid gaps in the work. Designs in colour knitting can be worked from cross-stitch patterns and there is an endless variety of these from all countries in Europe. Figure 123 shows you various patterns in colour knitting.

These can quite easily be charted out from the photograph on to a sheet of graph paper. Fig. 124 shows the back of the fabric with the strands of wool lying across the back of the work, and Fig. 125 shows the front of a piece of fabric on which a simple chequer pattern has been worked.

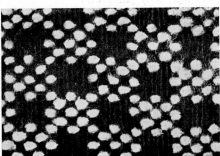

124 and 125

III. Simple designs for children (charts C and D)

1. BABY'S MATINÉE COATS

A baby's coat for a one-year old will need approximately 3 - 4 ozs. of Baby Wool. The knitting of a coat, such as the one shown in Fig. 126, is quite simple.

If we work on size 9 needles the tension will be approximately 7 sts. to the inch. The width of the coat is 11 ins. (22 ins. all round), so we cast on 77 sts. Work in garter st. for 6½ ins, now cast on at beginning of the next 2 rows sufficient stitches for the length of sleeve required. Continue on all these sts. until the edge of the sleeve measures 3½ ins. Now cast off the centre 19 sts. for the back of the neck. Work on the first set of sts. for ¾ of an inch, then increase at the neck edge by

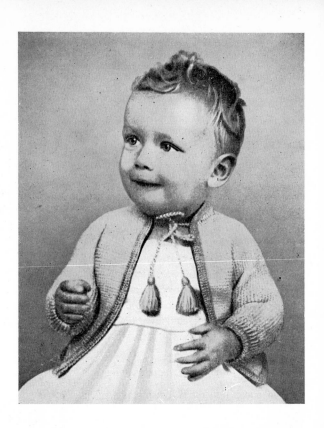

126 Simple baby jacket with coloured edgings

casting on two sts. on every alternate row until 10 sts. in all have been cast on. Continue straight until the end of the sleeve measures 7 ins. Now cast off the sleeve sts. and continue on remaining stitches until front matches length of back. Cast off. Complete the other half in the same manner. Using No. 11 needles, pick up the sts. along the edge of the sleeve and working in self colour or contrast in K1, P1 rib, work for 1¼ ins. Cast off. Using the No. 11 needles, knit up sts. round front edges and neck and work in rib as on cuff for 1¼ ins. Fold the edge round the front and neck at the centre to the wrong side of the work and flat stitch to form double edge. To complete the coat, crochet two chains 9 ins. long, adding tassels to ends of chains (465 - 468). Stitch ends of chain to wrong side of front edges of neck, join side seams and sleeve seams and lightly press work on wrong side.

Baby's Coat and Bonnet (127)

Materials: 3-ply Baby Wool. Two No. 10 needles. Set of No. 10 needles.

Tension: 7½-sts. to one inch.
(See Chart C).

Coat. Commencing at front edge, cast on 78 sts. Knit 21 rows.
Proceed as follows:
1st row - P. to last 9 sts., turn.

2nd row - K. to end.
3rd to 6th rows - K. all across.
Repeat rows 1 to 6, 9 times more, then repeat rows 1 to 5.
Next row - Work across 39 sts., cast on 39 for sleeve.
Working in patt:

127 Child's jacket and bonnet

1st row - P. to last 9 sts., turn. 2nd row - K. to last 6 sts., turn.

3rd row - K. to end. 4th row - K. all across.

5th and 6th rows - K. all across.

Repeat rows 1 to 6, 15 times more thus finishing at sleeve edge.

Next row - Cast off 39, knit up sts. remaining on needle from front and continue in patt. until 5th row of 20th patt. on Back has been worked.

Next row - Work across 39 sts., cast on 39.

Work 2nd sleeve to match first. Work 2nd Front to match first. Cast off. Crochet picot edge all round coat and round edges of sleeves.

Bonnet. Commence at Front by casting on 90 sts. Work 21 rows in garter stitch. Proceed as follows:

1st row - P. to last 6 sts., turn.

2nd row - K. to last 6 sts., turn. 3rd row - K. to end.

4th to 6th rows - K. all across.

Repeat these 6 rows six times more.

Divide sts. on to 3 needles, 30 to each needle.

Proceed in rounds as follows:

1st Round - K. 2nd Round - (K8, K2 tog.) 9 times. (90 sts.)

3rd Round - K. 4th Round - (K7, K2 tog.) 9 times.

5th Round - K. 6th Round - (K6, K2 tog.) 9 times.

Continue decreasing on every alternate round in this manner until 18 sts. remain.

Next Round - K. Next Round - K2 tog. to end of round. (9 sts.)

Run wool through sts., draw up and fasten off securely on wrong side. Work picot edge, turn back front of bonnet. Stitch ribbon or cords with tassels to corners.

Child's Jacket (128)

Materials: 5-oz. Ground Shade. 1-oz. Contrast, 4-ply wool. 2 No. 10 needles.

Tension: 7 sts. to the inch.

Back. Using Contrast, cast on 85 sts. Knit 12 rows. Change to Ground Shade and continue in garter stitch, every row K., working shapings from paper pattern.

Front. Working 12 rows in garter stitch in Contrast and remainder in Ground Shade, proceed as for Back working shaping from paper pattern throughout.

Sleeves. Using Contrast, cast on 46 sts. Work 12 rows.

Continue in garter stitch in Ground Shade working shaping from paper pattern as before.

Border. Using Contrast, cast on 8 sts. Knit 4 rows.

Next row - K4, cast off 2, K. to end.

Next row - K4, cast on 2, K. to end.

Continue in garter stitch working buttonholes as on last 2 rows until 5 buttonholes evenly spaced have been worked, the last buttonhole being just below the neck edge, then continue in garter stitch until there is sufficient to go all round Front and neck slightly stretched. Make up with flat seams.

Child's Raglan Jacket (129)

Materials: 6-ozs. Double Knitting. 2 No. 6 needles. Set of No. 6 needles.

Tension: 5 sts. to the inch.

Commence at neck edge by casting on 76 sts.

128 Sports jacket with sleeves let in

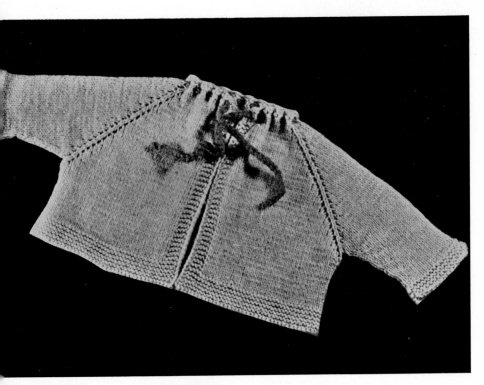

129 Child's jacket in Raglan style

K. 4 rows. Next row - K3, * w.f., K2 tog., K2, rep. from * to last st., K1.
Next Row - K.
Shape raglan as follows: 1st row - K19, w.f., K5, w.f., K28, w.f., K5, w.f., K19.
2nd row - K5, P. to last 5 sts., K5.
3rd row - K20, w.f., K7, w.f., K30, w.f., K7, w.f., K20.
4th row - As 2nd.
5th row - K21, w.f., K9, w.f., K32, w.f., K9, w.f., K21.
6th row - As 2nd.
Continue increasing in this manner until 23 sets of increases in all have been worked.
Next row - Work all across, leaving 51 sleeve sts. on length of wool. Slip remaining sts. on to one needle. Keeping 5-st. border correct, work 20 rows in stocking stitch. K. 10 rows. Cast off.
Slip 51 sts. for sleeve on three needles, the first needle being the point where the sleeve joins side of coat. Work 25 rounds in stocking stitch, decreasing one stitch at each side stitch where sleeve joined front and back. (39 sts.)
Next round - P. Next round - K. Repeat these 2 rounds 3 times more for cuff. Cast off. Thread ribbon through holes at neck. Fig. 51D shows child's frock to match.

2. KIDDY PANTS (131, 132)

These pants are knitted in baby wool, using size 11 needles at a tension of 8 sts. to the inch. Using No. 11 needles, cast on 60 sts. for four-month old, 90 sts. for one-year old and 110 sts. for two-year old.
Work in K2, P2 rib for 8 rows.

Next row - P2, * w.r.n., P2 tog., P3, rep. from * to last 3 sts., w.r.n., P2 tog., P1.
Continue in stocking stitch until a complete square has been worked. Work 12 rows in K2, P2 rib. Cast off.
Work second piece in same manner.

Gusset.

Cast on 25/29, 33/sts. Work a square in stocking stitch. Cast off.
Make up as shown. (132)

Simple Panties (130). See also Bathing Suit (52).

Materials: 3 ozs. 3-ply Baby Wool. 2 No. 11 needles.
Tension: 8 sts. to the inch.

Commence at Back by casting on 74 sts. Work 4 rows in rib.

Next row - Rib 2, * w.o.n., work 2 tog., rib 2, rep. from * to end.
Work 4 rows more in rib.
Proceed in garter stitch until work measures 6-ins. from beginning. Decrease 1 st. at both ends of next and every alt. row until 48 sts. remain, then every following 3rd row until 28 sts. remain. K. 16 rows.
Now increase 1 st. at both ends of next and every alt. row until there are 50 sts. on the needle, then cast on 2 sts. at beginning of every row until there are 74 sts. on needle. Continue on these sts. until work matches Back to lower edge of ribbing.

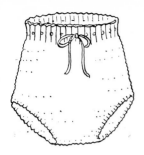

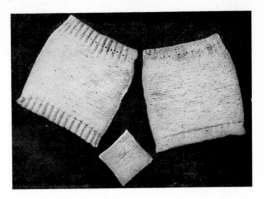

130 Simple baby pants
133 Toddler's knickers with straps

131 and 132 Separate three parts ready for kiddy pants

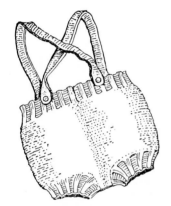

134 Baby's bootees and mitts as examples of simple knitting

Work ribbing and eyelets to match Back. Cast off. Join side seams. Using set of 4 needles, knit up 66 sts. round leg hole, work 7 rounds in K1, P1 rib. Cast off in rib.

Boy's Trousers

The basic shape is shown on Chart C. The trousers should be knitted in stocking stitch throughout.

"Z" Shape Pants

The measurements given on Fig. 55 are for a baby's size. 3-ply Baby Wool would be the most suitable yarn to use working on No. 10 needles that will give you a tension of 7½ sts. to the inch. The width at the top is 9½ ins., the work is done on two needles in garter stitch, shaping according to the pattern. Fold the finished piece of knitting at the partition lines and stitch the edges together. Hem the top edge to form a slot for the elastic.

Boy's Pants with Braces (133)

For the first piece, using 4-ply wool and No. 11 needles (tension 7½ sts. to the inch), cast on 80 to 90 sts. according to the measurement just above the waist. Work in K2, P2 rib for 2 ins., using No. 13 needles. Change to the standard size needles, No. 11, and work the back gusset as follows:

1st row - K. to last 40 sts., turn. 2nd row - K. to end.
3rd row - K. to last 32 sts., turn. 4th row - K. to end.
5th row - K. to last 24 sts., turn. 6th row - K. to end.

Continue turning in this manner until the row "K.8, turn" has been worked. On the next row, K. to the end, then K. right across.

Continue in garter stitch until the top of the leg is reached, then decrease one st. at both ends of next and every following 10th row until 3 sets of decreases have been completed. Continue until work measures 1½-ins. shorter than total length of leg. Work in K2, P2 rib for 1½-ins. Cast off. Knit a second piece in the same manner.

The gusset piece is knitted by casting on 2-sts. then increasing at both ends of 3rd and every following 4th row until there are 16 sts. on the needle, then decreasing at both ends of every following 4th row until 2 sts. remain. Work 3 rows. Cast off. The Braces are 2 straight pieces of K2, P2 rib with buttonholes at one end. Make up as (133).

3. BABY'S BOOTEES AND MITTS

Baby's Mitts (134)

Materials: Approx. ½-oz. 3-ply Baby Wool. Set of No. 11 needles.

Tension: 8 sts. to the inch.

Cast on 36/42 sts. working in rounds of K1, P1 rib for from 1¼ to 1½-ins. In the next round make holes by working * w.f., K2 tog., K4, repeat from * to end of round. Continue in rounds of stocking stitch (every round K.) until work measures 1½ to 1¾-ins. from top of ribbing.

Shape top as follows:

Next round - * K4, K2 tog., rep. from * to end of round. Work 2 rounds plain.
Next round - * K3, K2 tog., rep. from * to end of round.
Work 2 rounds plain.
Continue in this manner until 16 sts. remain, then after next two plain rounds, K2 tog. on next round all across needle. Work one round. Draw wool through remaining sts. and fasten off securely, on wrong side of work. Thread cord or ribbon through holes at wrist.

Easy-to-Knit Bootees (134)

Materials: 1-oz. 4-ply wool. Two No. 11 needles. *Tension:* 7½ sts. to the inch.

Cast on 42 sts. and K. 12 rows. Cast off 9 sts. at beginning of the next 2 rows then K. 18 rows on remaining 24 sts. On next row K2 tog. all across.
Next row - P. Next row - K2 tog. all across (6 sts.). Next row - P.
Break off wool. Draw sts. together with needle and wool and stitch up into shape as shown on Figure 134. Fold over top and thread cord through just below fold. Bedsocks (56) and Doll's Shoes can be made in a similar manner.

135

Baby's Bootees (135)

Materials: 1-oz. 2-ply wool. Set of No. 12 needles.
Cast on 52 sts., 18, 17, 17, on three needles.
Work in rounds of K2, P2 rib for 2½ ins.
Next round - * w.f., K2 tog., P2, rep. from * to end of round. K6 rounds.
Proceed for the upper toe by working on the 18 sts. on the first needle as follows:
1st row - K. 2nd row - P. 3rd and 4th rows - As 1st. and 2nd. - 5th to 8th rows - K.
Repeat these 8 rows until work measures 2 ins. Now pick up the sts. along the edge of the toe piece, work across sts. on two needles then pick up sts. along second side of toe piece. Now work three rounds purl, three rounds knit, three rounds purl.
Mark 18 sts. at centre back for heel and 18 sts. at centre front for toe. Continue in rounds of stocking stitch, every round knit, decreasing at the beginning and end of these 18 sts. on next and every round until there are only 2 sts. left of the marked 18. Now place the sts. on to two needles, the one stitch from the toe and heel being at each end of each needle and graft the sts. together.

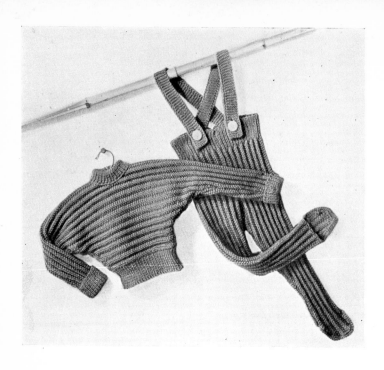

4. ROMPER SUIT (136)

The basic pattern for this design is shown in Fig. 57 and the sizing is for a child between one and two years. 4-ply wool would be the most suitable for the design that should be worked on a size 10 needle.

Pullover. This is worked in pleated knitting (108). The tension of the 4-ply will be 7 sts. to the inch. Cast on the required number for the width according to the pattern, adding approximately 40 sts. for each of the sleeves.

Cuffs: These are worked in K1, P1 rib and can be either knitted up along the edge of the sleeve or worked separately and stitched on.

Neck: Divide the work, knitting the collar in two halves.

Waistband and Collar: (80). These are worked in garter stitch and a zipper fastener stitched in for the opening.

Trousers.

Commence at the top by casting on 58 sts. Work in K1, P1 rib for 2 ins. Work gusset at centre back as follows:

1st row - K30, turn. 2nd row - K. to end. 3rd row - K24, turn. 4th row - As 2nd.

Continue in this manner working 6 sts. less until "K6, turn, work to end" has been completed. Continue all across sts. working increases and decreases according to pattern. Complete second piece in same manner, reversing position of gusset. Stitch two parts together. Crochet round flaps. Knit two straps in garter stitch. Fix them at the back and fasten with buttons and buttonholes at the front. Block and press when completed.

5. SPORTS STOCKINGS, SOCKS, SKI-SOCKS AND GLOVES

Sports Socks (137)

Double Knitting wool and set of four size 11 needles are used.

Cast on from 72 to 90 sts. according to width of leg. Work in rounds of stocking stitch for 2½ ins.

On the next round, make hem all across all but last 6 sts. by knitting together one st. from needle and one st. from cast-on edge. Now proceed in cable patt. the basis being "K4, P2, K1, P2" all round for 10 rounds. On the 11th round, work a cable across the 4 sts. (see Fig. 111). When the leg measures 8¾ ins., work calf decreases at centre back on every 10th round until 9 decreases have been worked. Work straight for another 4½ ins. Turn heel. Continue cable patt. down front of foot. Work toe as shaping at top of mitts (88).

Child's Shoes (138)

Worked in 4-ply wool on set of four size 12 needles.

Using Light, cast on approximately 40 to 60 sts. according to width of leg. Work in rounds of K2, P2 rib for 2 ins. On the next round, increase the total number of sts. by a third, making sure that they are a multiple of 4 sts. Using Light for Ground

137 Sportswear socks in cable pattern

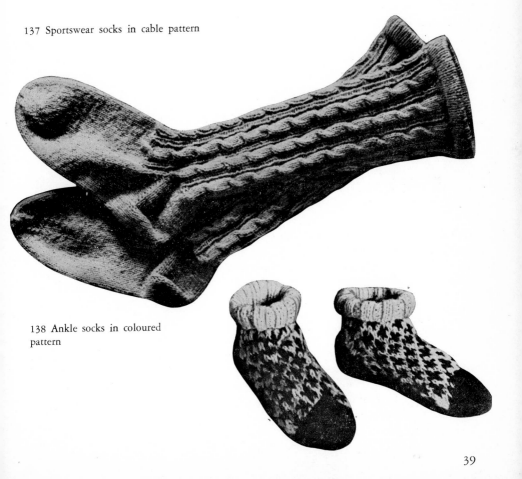

138 Ankle socks in coloured
pattern

139 Mitts with Norwegian design

Shade and Dark for pattern, working rounds of stocking stitch, work the diamond pattern as on Fig. 138. (Fig. 123c shows the design of the bootees).

Cut out leather soles and join to tops using small blanket stitch.

Ski-Socks for Adults

These are worked in Double Knitting wool, using size 11 needles, and are basically the same as the child's pattern outlined above.

Norwegian Pattern Gloves

Materials: 3 ozs. Dark, 2 ozs. Light Double Knitting wool. Set of No. 11 needles.

Tension: 6½ sts. to the inch.

Using Dark, cast on 48 sts. Work 26 rounds in K1, P1 rib, using Light for the 9th, 10th and 11th rounds and 16th, 17th and 18th rounds.

The simplest method to work the back and palm is first of all to draw up the design on squared graph paper. Work the Van Dyke pattern, continue until 32 rounds have been worked. On the 33rd, 35th, 37th, 39th and 41st rounds, increase for thumb gusset, working pattern from prepared chart.

Now place 13 sts. of thumb gusset on safety pin. Cast on 9 sts. for the thumb hole, continue in rounds until top shaping is reached, shape top (88).

Thumb. Pick up 9 sts. from cast-on sts., one st. at each side of 13 sts. of thumb gusset, work in rounds, shaping top of thumb as Fig. 89.

6. JACKETS AND WAISTCOATS

See basic pattern on Chart D.

Man's Waistcoat in Angora/Wool Mixture (140)

Materials: 8½-oz. balls Angora/Wool Mixture. 2 No. 11 needles.

Tension: 8 sts. to the inch.

The waistcoat is worked to the basic plan on Fig. 60.

The stitches used are K2, P2 rib for the lower band and stocking stitch for the remainder of the garment. Work pieces, shaping to paper pattern. At the front edge there should be a knit st. on every row as this gives a firm edge for stitching in the zip.

Lady's Jacket with Collar (141)

Materials: 16 ozs. Light, 3 ozs. Dark, Mohair in a Double Knitting weight. Two No. 6 needles.

Basic pattern as on Chart D. Using Light, commence at cuff. Knit 4 rows. Proceed in stocking stitch, shaping according to pattern on Chart D. When neck is reached divide for back and front. Work front and half of collar. Now work along

back sts. to centre of back. Work second piece in same manner. Graft at centre back and graft collar facings.

Using Dark, knit collar and front band.

Brush lightly with teazle brush to give furry surface.

Stitch collar and front band over facing and make up sleeve and side seams.

7. STOLES

Stole in Peacock's Eye Stitch (Fig. 145)

Materials: 4 ozs. fine Mohair. Two No. 4 needles.

Cast on multiple of 6 plus 1 stitches (121 sts. were cast on for the original stole). Proceed as follows: 1st to 3rd rows - K.

4th row - K1, * K1, (w.r.n.) 3 times, repeat from * to last st., K1.

5th row - K1, * (sl. 1, drop 3 w.f.'s of previous row) 6 times, there will now be 6 long loops on the needle. Working these 6 sts. together, knit and purl into them 3 times thus forming 6 sts. out of one. Repeat from * to last st., K1.

6th row - K. These 6 rows form the patt.

Continue repeating rows 1 to 6 for length of stole, then knit 2 rows for second edge. Cast off loosely.

Mohair Stole in drop stitch

Materials: 5 ozs. Mohair. 2 No. 6 needles.

Cast on 27 sts. and knit in garter stitch for length required.

Next row - K3, * drop 1, K3, repeat from * to end.

Allow dropped stitch to run right down work to form ladder.

Work 2 rows of double crochet along each end, finishing off with fringe if desired.

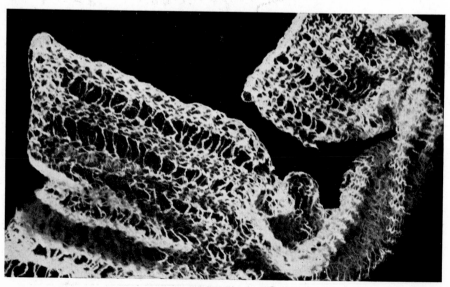

145 (opposite

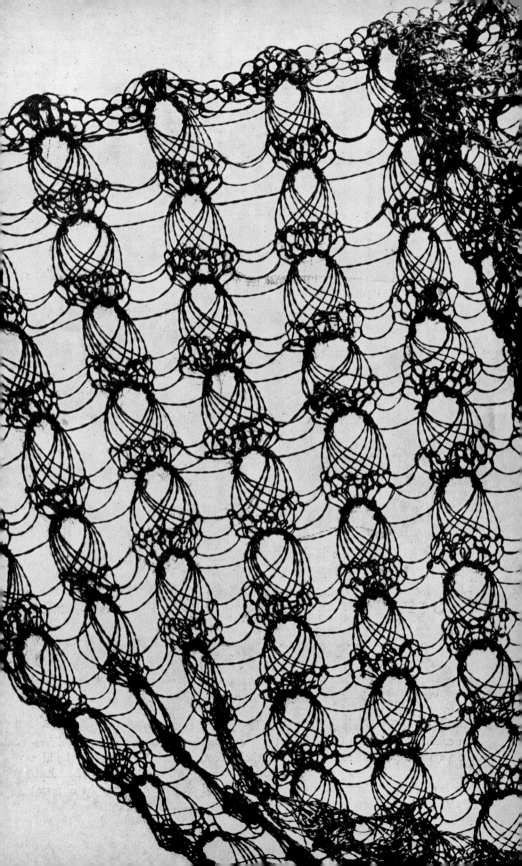

146 Two fine old crocheted edgings

CROCHET

Crochet work lends itself to various possibilities. It is not so old or basic a craft as knitting or weaving. The mesh is firmer and does not stretch as much as knitting. It uses up more material, but, on account of its firm structure, it is specially suitable for many purposes.

We can work simple practical things or work elaborate coloured designs, but we can combine the stitches from chain, treble or Tunisian crochet in very many different ways and produce rose stitch, star stitch, picot, ribwork, shellwork, or build a design in monochrome or develop a looser texture as in Fig. 147. Especially adaptable is the coloured Tunisian crochetwork described on page 48. How the different stitches are worked is shown on Charts E and F.

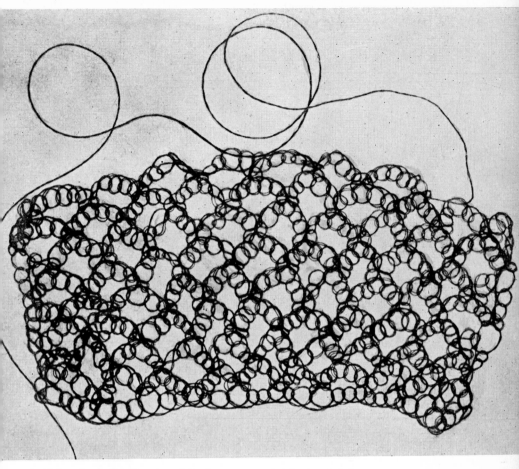

147 This stole, in fine French mohair, is easy to crochet in chn. and d.c.

SIMPLE CROCHET

Stole in Fine Mohair (147)

The whole stole is in chain and double crochet. Begin with a length of chain one d.c. into 6th chain * miss 5 chain 1 d.c. into next chain * to the end; turn with 3 chain. 2nd and following rows: 1 d.c. into 1st loop * 5 chain 1 d.c. into every loop, turn 3 chain *.

Shoulder Nets (148)

Material: A firm ring and strong cotton yarn.

We first work 15 double crochet into the ring, a curtain ring, maybe. 2nd row * five chain 1 d.c. into every d.c. *. 3rd and following rows * 6 chain 1 d.c. into every loop,

149 a.b. Start of shoulder net

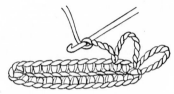

151 Start of rucksack

148 Shoulder bags are not difficult to make

work round and round until the net is big enough. When it is done, we fix rings to the final loops (152). Then we crochet or knot a thick cord about 4 feet long, put it through the rings, and then, passing it through the original ring, join both ends of the cord, and so finish the shoulder net.

Rucksack. This is worked in similar stitches, but instead of our making the beginning round, it is started with a chain 10-12 ins. long. We crochet first into one side

152 Rings are fixed thus

150

A net sack as
a practical pocket
bag or worn on
the back

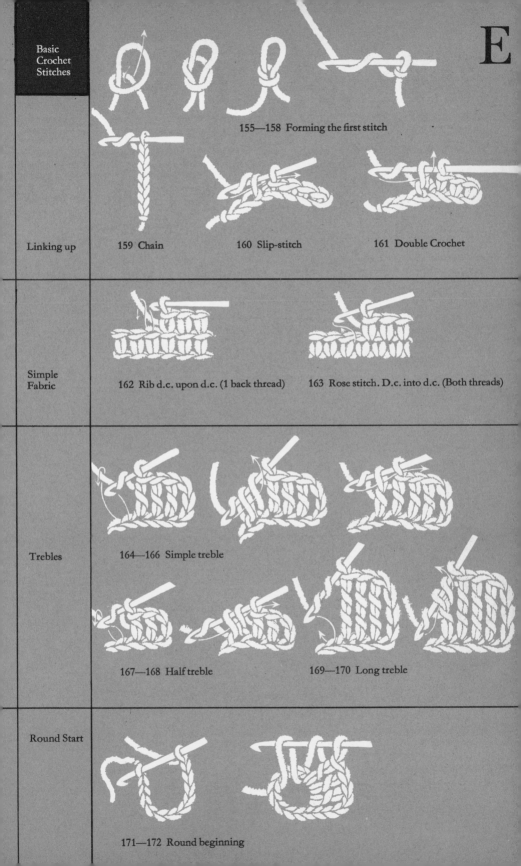

Basic Crochet Stitches

155—158 Forming the first stitch

Linking up

159 Chain   160 Slip-stitch   161 Double Crochet

Simple Fabric

162 Rib d.c. upon d.c. (1 back thread)   163 Rose stitch. D.c. into d.c. (Both threads)

Trebles

164—166 Simple treble

167—168 Half treble   169—170 Long treble

Round Start

171—172 Round beginning

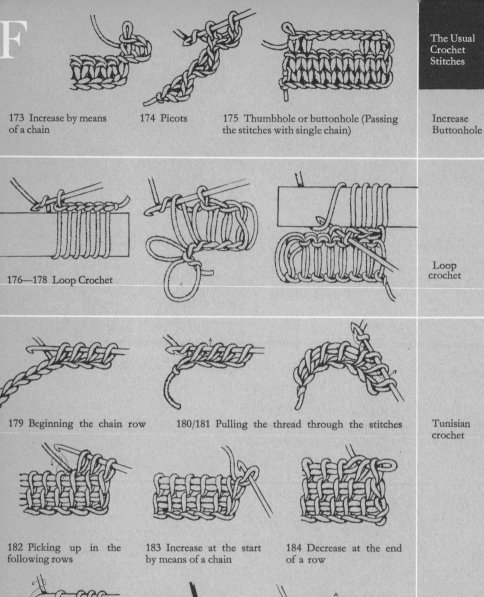

F

173 Increase by means of a chain

174 Picots

175 Thumbhole or buttonhole (Passing the stitches with single chain)

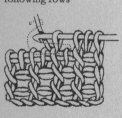

176—178 Loop Crochet

179 Beginning the chain row

180/181 Pulling the thread through the stitches

182 Picking up in the following rows

183 Increase at the start by means of a chain

184 Decrease at the end of a row

185 Tunisian Cross stitch

186 Tunisian Ribwork

187 Tunisian Purl

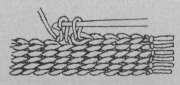

188 Bosnian Crochet

of the chain, then into the other, using the same holes, for our double crochet. (151) Further work is as for the shoulder net, going round with chain and d.c. On the bag illustrated there are 18 loops. Again, as in Fig. 152, we attach rings to the loops. (For a large rucksack two loops go to one ring). Then we knot a thick cord about 4-5 ft. long, and pull it through the rings. At the bottom, at both the corners where cord is attached we butt in a wooden knob and so the straps are added.

153 Slippers for the toddler

154 Form of a child's crocheted jacket

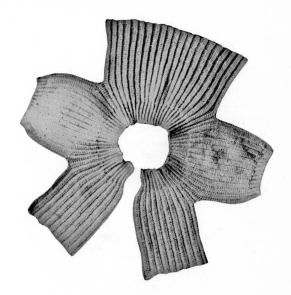

Shoes for the Baby

M a t e r i a l : 1 oz. of fairly coarse wool.

This is an especially simple design, as the upper and sole are worked in one. We begin at the bottom on the toe point with $1\frac{1}{2}$ ins. chain, and crochet all around it, putting d.c. into the stitches on both sides, but 2 in each end stitch. The sole will now be made from one side and the upper from the other. We add 1 d.c. at each end as we proceed, to make wider rings, till the shoe is the right size (4-7 rounds). After this we crochet without increase as far as the instep which begins after about $2\frac{1}{2}$ ins. We leave about $1\frac{1}{4}$ ins. across the instep and discontinue the rings, substituting to-and-fro work, till the shoe is $2\frac{1}{2}$-3 ins. long. Fastening off at one side we crochet a square for the heel $2\frac{1}{4}$ ins. across and sew it into position behind. We improve the outer edge by crocheting round it first a round of 2 chn., 1 d.c. and then a round of d.c. - or even give 2 or 3 of each. The d.c. here may be worked in a different colour. We can then twist wool to make a cord and thread it though the little holes made by the chain loops, tying into a bow in front.

Child's Jacket (154)

This jacket has a simple design so it can be either crocheted or knitted (154). Crocheting renders it closer and warmer but takes twice as much wool. A bed jacket for children or for grown-ups is just as easily done in the same manner.

We begin at the centre front with 55 chn. (medium sized wool) and crochet along it stitch for stitch (162). We give 8 double rows for the first side front, then work as follows:-

10 d.c. 45 tr. turn. 45 tr. 10 d.c. turn.

Then we work 8 double rows for the sleeves 10 d.c. 23 tr. 32 ch.-turn.

10 stitches for the band (work alternately 10 d.d. and 10 tr. here) 45 tr. 10 d.c., turn.

Back Piece. 15 double rows as for front. The second sleeve and side front are done as before. Finally we join the edges down the side and fit a draw thread at the neck, making there the necessary holes as usual.

Two Lovely Old Crocheted Borders (146)

These two crocheted borders are over a hundred years old. Above we have a foundation of white scalloped braid and we work with fine white crochet cotton upon it, roundwise.

Round 1. We put * 1 tr. 2 chn. * 7 times upon each scallop, but omit the 2 chn. between the scallops.

Round 2. 4 d.c. into each hole, except where the scallops meet.

Below Insertion Edging

We begin with 9 chn., and set a d.c. into the first one we made, do 3 chn. and set another d.c. into the same stitch, then turn. We work 5 d.c. into the first hole and 6 d.c. into the second hole, then turn. From now on we do 5 chn. then set a d.c. in the gap between the two sets of d.c., followed by 3 chn. and a further d.c. into the same place. It is easy now to continue as before.

TUNISIAN COLOURED CROCHET

In Tunisian coloured crochet we find several further changes in the hooking work. For the Tunisian ribwork we do a portion in the ordinary Tunisian stitch (179-184)

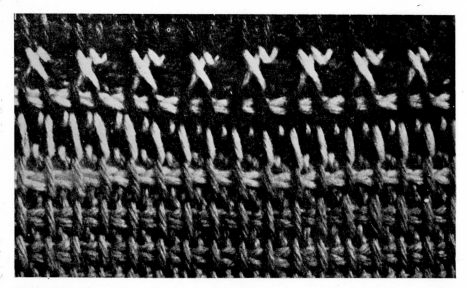

189 Tunisian colourwork

then slip the hook through a row of loops, pick up a second coloured thread and work the return stitches two at a time (186), one in each colour.

In Tunisian cross-stitch the first row with its return is worked in the usual way for Tunisian Crochet. The cross stitch is then formed throughout as we pick up the stitches two at a time on the preceding row, (185) and use the second one before the first, crossing it over. The crosses stand out especially well if a different colour is used for the return row. The return row is worked in the usual way.

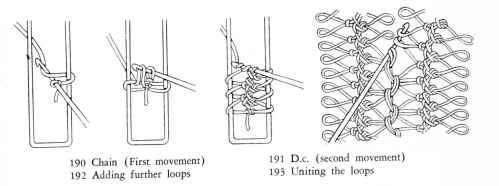

190 Chain (First movement)
192 Adding further loops

191 D.c. (second movement)
193 Uniting the loops

HAIRPIN WORK

For this work a special "hairpin" is needed besides a hook. Hairpins can be bought in different sizes. The method of working is shown in Figs. 190-193. By means of winding the thread round one side of the hairpin after each crochet stitch (and this obviously involves a clockwise rotation and change of the hook's position), we produce a broad strip whose loops are united together with d.c. and chain, or, as in Fig. 193, simply catch up the loops without using separate thread.

The loops may be arranged singly or in clusters of several taken together to resemble a sheaf.

Hairpin work is suitable for producing curtains, stoles or collars.

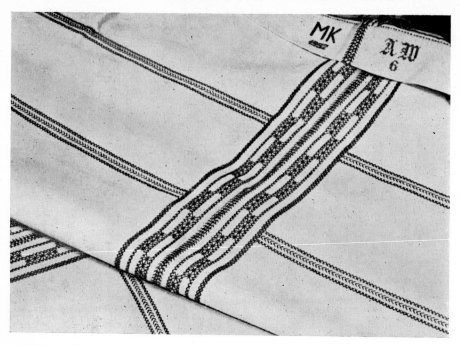

194 Tablecloth from a great-grandmother's handwoven linen cloth. On the right at the top are her monogram and that of her great-granddaughter

195 Cross stitch of the eighteenth century. This is a pleasing piece of work, not only for its particular design, but especially for its fine link up and play between light and dark

196 Table mats in bleached linen with drawn threadwork

EMBROIDERY

Women have always delighted in embroidery. To see the play of the colours on a piece of material, to watch them form into something beautiful, can be really thrilling.

But we must not overcrowd a room with quantities of bad embroidery for the sake of mere decoration. A few well-made, beautiful pieces are better than a mass of cheap rubbish determined by an all too rapidly changing fashion.

We must always ask ourselves before we start embroidering: is it worth it, will this piece really gain by our embroidery? An embroidered cushion is by no means always more beautiful than a plain one. We may have laboured on a large carpet, on a vast bedspread - indeed our work may have been most careful and conscientious - but it would have been better had we never done it, if we have used a lifeless, hackneyed pattern.

Good workmanship cannot, therefore, be the only criterion in embroidery, though naturally, we must do our best. But quite often, things are a bit difficult still, and someone not particularly good with his or her fingers might yet produce something very beautiful. We need only recall peasant embroidery and children's work which, though it often seems somewhat coarse, has a vigour and sincerity never found in a slavishly-copied pattern, however carefully and conscientiously it may have been made. A machine can do this, too, perhaps even better.

Embroidery in colours

There are many traditional stitches for decorating a piece of material: we can use the narrow cord-like stemstitch, the broader, stouter chain stitch, the vertical herringbone or the delicate horizontal herringbone, or bush stitch with its little boughs, the hemstitch that bundles in together several threads of the cloth, and very many others. We can use them individually to fix a hem, or we might introduce different decorations for borders or side patterns. Anyone who has once experimented in this work with needle, thread and different materials has always pleasure ahead. Plate H shows how the separate stitches are worked.

As our basic material we choose a linen type of fabric, e.g. coarse linen, smooth towelling or huckaback, since the threads are easily distinguished or pulled out of such material. A loosely woven damask, or a fine muslin that allows the wood of a table to shine through the cloth, has a beauty of its own. First of all we try out a sample, using an oddment of the same material, employing white threads on white material or taking two or more colours as in the examples mentioned above.

CROSS STITCH AND OTHER EMBROIDERY STITCHES

The cross stitch has been one of the most popular embroidery stitches for centuries. The crosses run across the beautiful linen vertically, horizontally, and like steps. They seem to grow out of its structure and are almost part of the fabric's very nature. Its beauty is essentially determined by the clear straight lines.

We must always think of the nature of the cross stitch when we use it, and it is therefore senseless if the pattern is printed on the material, or ironed onto it, without any regard for woof and weft. It is such a pity that so many of the beautiful old patterns, originally embroidered in really good, firm cross stitch have been degraded in this way.

As material for a piece of cross stitch embroidery we always take a good piece of linen with clear structure, such as sieved linen or huckaback, which slightly let light through their formation of holes, mercerised linen, Panama cloth, or, the finest of all, a piece of hand-woven linen.

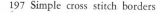
197 Simple cross stitch borders

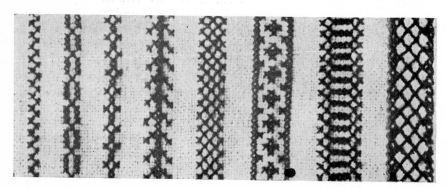

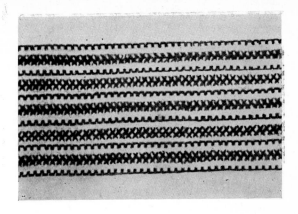

198
Section of the coloured waistband

It is possible to work simple designs such as these direct on to ordinary cloth, but it becomes easier if we transfer the design to squared paper. There we are able to visualise our design, to avoid many mistakes and to keep stitches true. Our design shows the best result if we do not mark a single thinly pencilled cross, but rather block in a complete square, since a separate stitch is also more blocklike in character. It is best to make a start with narrow borders (197), which can be used as decoration for the borders of a little child's dress. We can use coloured yarn such as red or blue on a white ground, or white on a red, blue or other dark background.

Such continuous cross stitch is very nice for a nursery bag or for the shoulder panel of a child's dress. It is easily noticed on these elongated pieces of cross stitch how the pattern is formed by the fabric underneath rather than by the crosses.

199 Child's skirt with
coloured belt

A Child's Frock in Mercerised Linen (2-3 yrs.)

The waistband (198) is in herringbone and narrow blanket stitch in red and blue. Without turnings it measures 3¼ ins. x 24 ins. It is fastened at the back with small buttons. The slightly flared skirt consists of a strip of material 18 ins. x 60 ins. This is sewn into the band.

Mitts. These have an especially easy cut, as they are made out of one piece. For the little border we first work in blanket stitch, then insert the second thread. We also work in herringbone, together with running stitches. The cloth is a white woolly material and the embroidery is in red and blue whilst the wrist has a strip of white astrakhan added (201).

Tablecloth (194)

This tablecloth has a history of its own. It was embroidered by a student who had used for the background a piece of handwoven linen, woven by her great-grandmother for her own dowry. The broad border, worked in cross stitch and star stitch, forms the centre strip. One shade of red is used. From it, narrower borders branch out. The red embroidery in a fast dye stands out against the coarse linen thread. The history of the cloth determined the emphasized centre panel, for the linen cloth had at one time been shortened in the middle. The monogram which her great-grandmother had worked is still there, and our student has added her own. In this way the cloth was transformed into a piece for festive occasions.

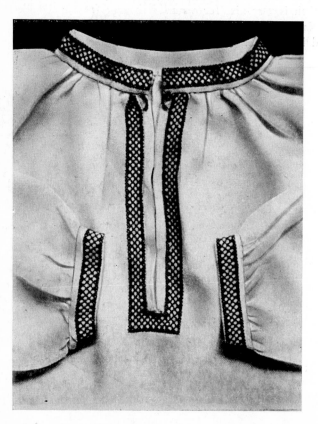

200 Toddler's smock. A slightly smaller pattern is shown in 197

54

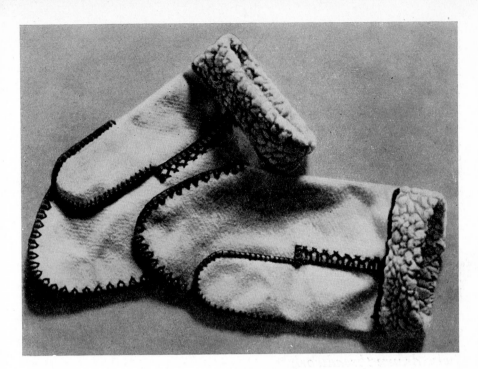

201 Mitts

202 Coffee cosy in Shantung
silk with narrow, decorative
border

A Coffee Cosy

This is composed of ten parts, fitted together, each section being somewhat fluted.
We use one piece of material for the cover (in our case natural raw silk), two pieces
of a feather-proof material for the inter-lining and a piece of silk for the actual

lining. All four parts are sewn up - first separately - and are then closed at the sides, thus receiving their final shape. The two pieces for the stuffing are then put in and are divided into ten parts, beginning at the top. Pockets will now have formed. They are filled with feathers and sewn up. The cover, decorated with strands and silks and decorative stitches, is then slipped on and sewn along the divisions. A button is sewn to the bottom of each section, so that the lining can be changed. The latter has been crocheted along the edge and has thus been given small eyelets. The lining is held in place at the top in a rather interesting way: Lining, stuffing and cover have a small hole, secured with buttonhole stitches. A hand-woven silk band, with a large button in the centre, has one end passed through the hole and tied in a bow. The button remains inside and holds the portions together.

BORDERS WITH COLOURED BRAID

A border trimming whose preparation requires very little time and which is suitable for a child's simple garment, can be worked in coloured braiding. This can be bought in several gay colours. It is washable and, combined with the different decorative stitches, produces excellent alternative designs (289).

Swiss drawn threadwork

The diagrams on pages 58 and 59 show different plans and sections of lovely tablecloths. They are inspired by traditional Swiss work. The material is the so-called crash, in which the weft and woof threads are lightly crossed. Somewhat porous, it allows the wood of a table to gleam through little holes. Colour plate "K" gives the various stitches as they appear in use. The background threads were not drawn out as they normally are for hemstitching.

Blouses

The shapes and sizes for the blouses are given on Plate M. Both are simple to make. The blouse in Fig. 281 is made from a soft white mercerised linen. The back is slit, fitted with bias binding (364), and has a button and a loop for fastening. The wide intersecting border is done in simple and zig-zag stitching combined (209, 213). The blouse shown in Fig. 282, is made of open mesh linen, embroidered in waffle stitch with one thread between the rows - all worked to correspond - and then given rows of flat stitch on the outside of the rows.

Inlaid threadwork

An especially simple handicraft which may be tackled by six- or seven- year-old children is inlaid threadwork, (278-280). First we pull one or two threads from the woven cloth, and then we catch the start of the "next-to-be-drawn" thread and attach to this end a longer different coloured thread which is drawn in as the other is pulled out. If more adjoining threads are similarly exchanged, a lovely bright border results.

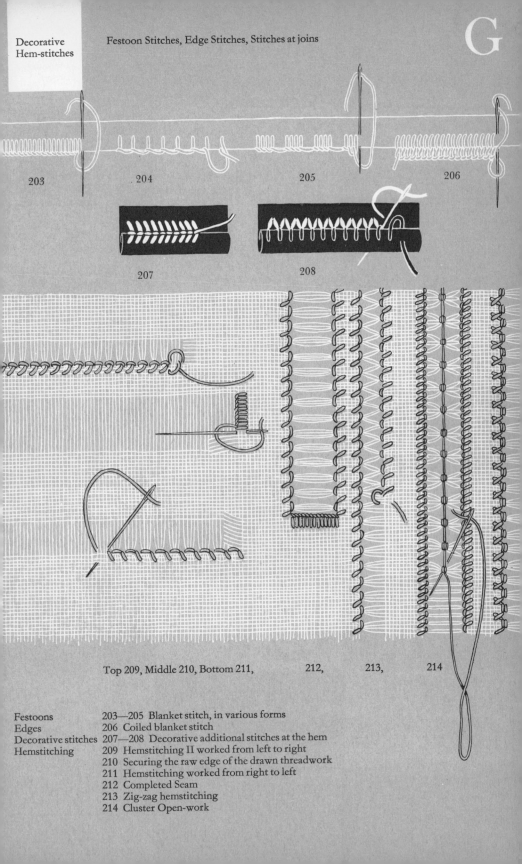

203   204   205   206

207   208

Top 209, Middle 210, Bottom 211,   212,   213,   214

Festoons   203—205 Blanket stitch, in various forms
Edges   206 Coiled blanket stitch
Decorative stitches 207—208 Decorative additional stitches at the hem
Hemstitching   209 Hemstitching II worked from left to right
                     210 Securing the raw edge of the drawn threadwork
                     211 Hemstitching worked from right to left
                     212 Completed Seam
                     213 Zig-zag hemstitching
                     214 Cluster Open-work

H

223 Half Cross stitch

215a, b, T-Stitch

232 Oblique Herringbone

216a, b, Hem Stitch

224a, b, Holbein Stitch

233 Shea
234 Chai
235 Crow

217a, b, Step Stitch

225 slap red satin stitch
226 Feather Stitch

218a, b, Vertical Herringbone

227 Cornering Stitch

236a, b, Simple Chevron Stitc
237a, b, Smocking Stitch

219a, b, Feather Stitch

228a, b, Blank- et Stitch

238a, b, Double Blanket S

220a, b, Cornering Stitch

229a, b, Tip Stitch

239 a, b, Fern Stitch

221a, b, Simple Cross Stitch

230a, b, Two-sided Cross Stitch

b

c

222a, b, c, Star Stitch

231 Simple Herringbone

240a, b, c Shadow Stitch
b Right Side
c Wrong Side

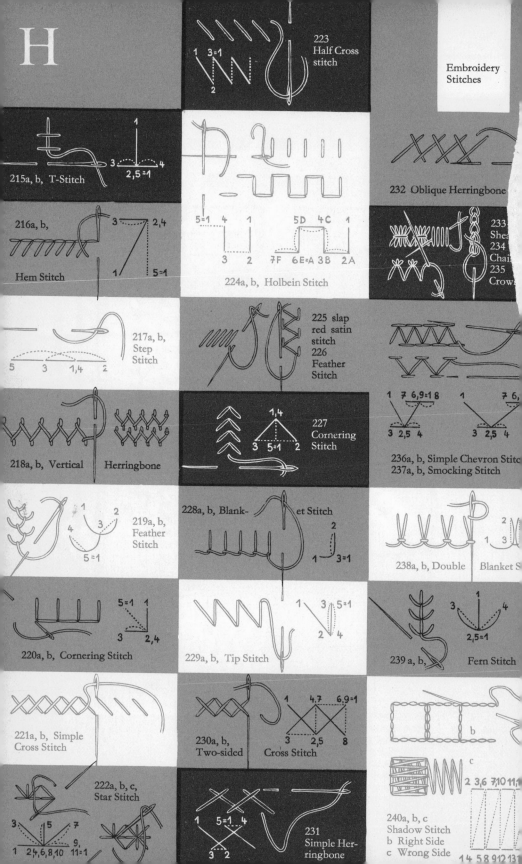

Basic Embroidery Stitches

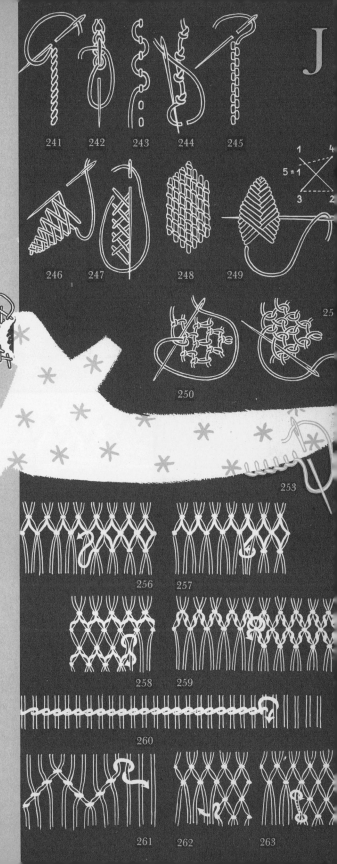

For continuous lines ●

241 Stem stitch

242 Chain stitch

243 Penetrated stitch

244 Knot stitch

245 Link stitch

246 Basket stitch

247 Closed herringbone

248 Tied Roumanian stitch

249 Fishbone stitch

250 Antwerp stitch

251 Slung blanket stitch

Basic Stitches for sewing on appliqué 252—255

Smocking stitch

256—257 Simple smocking stitch with linked thread visible

258 Smocking Stitch used in 353. (Suitable for colour work)

259 Smocking from right to left

260 Straight lacing stitch

261 Stepwise lacing stitch

262—263 Invisible connecting threads. The thread is passed behind and between the folds

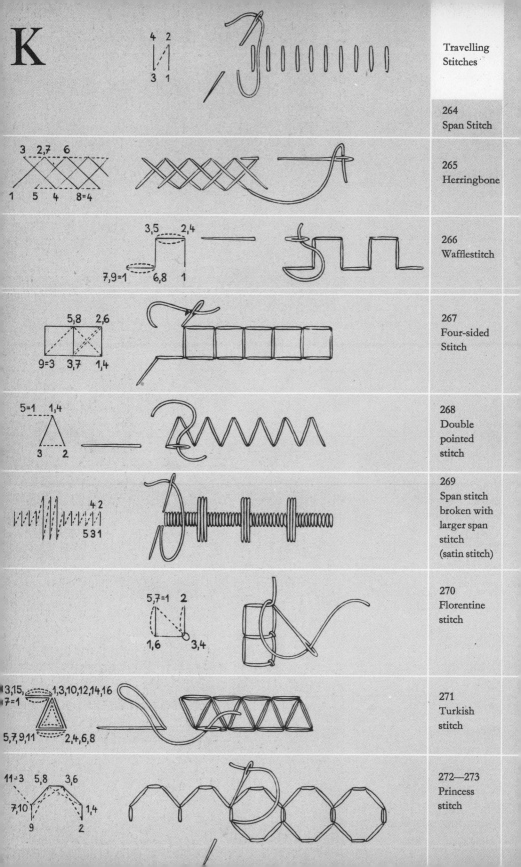

K

	Travelling Stitches
	264 Span Stitch
	265 Herringbone
	266 Wafflestitch
	267 Four-sided Stitch
	268 Double pointed stitch
	269 Span stitch broken with larger span stitch (satin stitch)
	270 Florentine stitch
	271 Turkish stitch
	272—273 Princess stitch

Tulle

The soft transparent background gives tulle embroidery its special character. It almost demands to be decorated further with threads. Even those of us who have very little time to spare for handwork will enjoy making a christening robe for a godchild or a bridal veil for a friend. We can use all kinds of stitches for tulle embroidery. The edge can be turned down and fixed in position with festoon stitches. We can also turn back the tulle at the hem to make the material more opaque. In that case we would fasten it with stem stitch, chain stitch or several rows of running stitch.

A person who has never worked in tulle should explore its possibilities on a small sample.

Figure embroidery is best made on a frame. We can also fasten the tulle to a dark piece of cardboard if necessary. The patterns emerge in the course of the work. If we do not feel quite sure, we can draw the outlines on coloured cardboard. We then

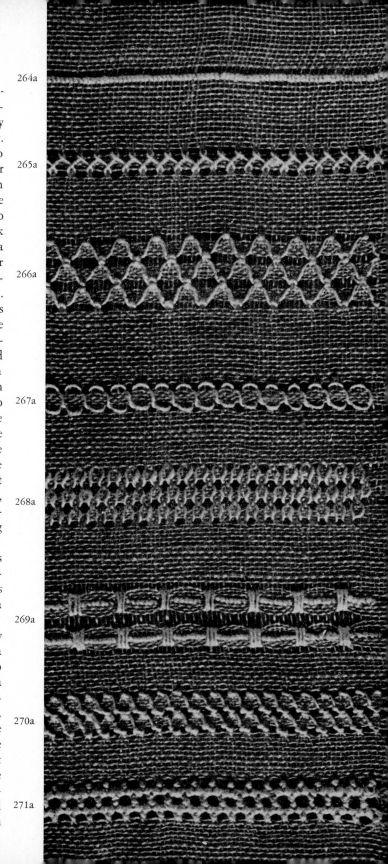

264a

265a

266a

267a

268a

269a

270a

271a

274 Section of illustration on page 51
275 Part of a cloth with waffle and span stitches

276 Part of a cloth. Princess stitch
277 Coffee cloth with travelling stitches as in 269

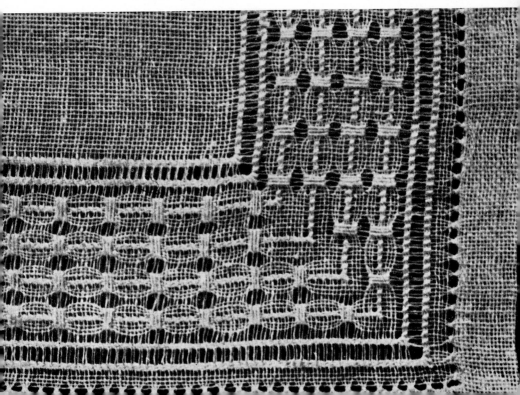

tack the tulle to it and start work. But the forms must not follow the drawing slavishly. They must do justice to the run of the tulle and must awaken a new life in the material.

Christening Robes

In Fig. 286, the decoration is stitched freely upon the tulle. The stripes in Fig. 285 are done in inlaid drawn threadwork as described on page 56, white silk twist being inserted. The bottom of the veil is hemmed.

Stranded silk, or the so-called milled yarn, serves best as material for embroidering upon the cloth, since it can be divided and we can take either fewer or more strands according to whether we like a finer or coarser effect. To take the thread through we use a bodkin which, in the U.S.A., is known as a blunt needle or an embroidery needle. It is best to give an outline to the designs in simple running stitch.

Appliqué or Sewing on to Cloth

We cut out shapes from bright scraps of material and stitch them on to a foundation fabric. Our comments on silhouettes on page 194 also apply here. The outlines must be cut from the material as simply as possible. Certain types of curtains, nursery carpets and a few other larger pieces of cloth are suitable for appliqué.

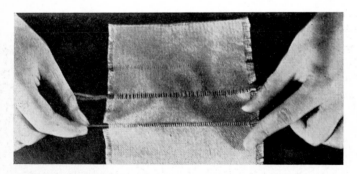

278—279 Penetrating threadwork

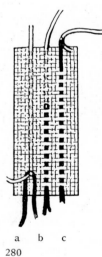

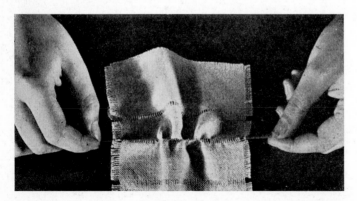

a   b   c

280

a Knotting on

b Advancing through

c Pulling through of colours

281—282 Blouses in simple cut, trimmed with travelling stitches

283 Figure embroidery. The Holy Family. From the region of Lake Constance. 1591

We cut out the shapes in paper and place them against their background to get an idea of their distribution. Then we select our pieces and put them also on their background to get an idea of the distribution of colour before we start cutting out. We then sew on the pieces we have cut out, using blanket stitch. This secures the edge so that it will not fray. Other stitches we may use are found on Chart J, Figs. 252-255

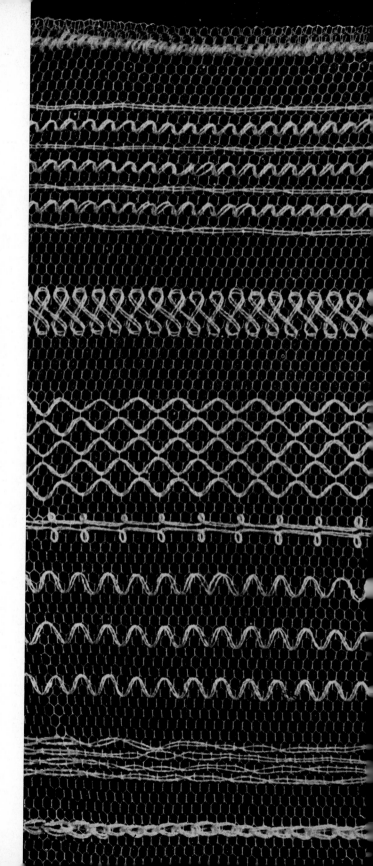

285 Christening robe in
darned stitchery

286 Christening robe in
Tulle work (opposite page)

287 Tulle work for a
cradle curtain

289 Children's clothes in simple cut

SEWING

With needle and cotton

Today we take the sewing needle for granted. We can realise how valuable to man the discovery of the needle is if we consider that, apart from its use in the house, it is the basic tool for tailors, cobblers, saddlers, bookbinders, etc. No one knows when and by whom the needle was invented, but it is believed that this outstanding invention came into existence more than 2500 years ago. The earliest needles were probably fashioned from the bones of animals and fishes, as were also the earliest safety pins used for holding together furs and skins. These are older than the sewing needle. The first formed pins used for fastening garments were of bronze, and were known as *fibulae*. Such *fibulae,* in twig shape, were found in Northern Europe and date from about 1450 B.C. Those of a simple straight form found in the South date from about 1550 B.C.

288 (page 66) Appliqué. Composition. (Work of a group of schoolchildren in Marburg)

ABC of sewing

I. THE MOST COMMON STITCHES

Running Stitch (290)

We pick up and pass over equal-sized spaces, sometimes taking two or three catches at a time, before pulling the thread through. (It is used when joins of thinnish material occur, and for bias binding).

Tacking (291)

This is like the running stitch except that we pass over a larger space, often just double the size.

Catch Stitch (292)

We take a few running stitches, then take a stitch back before we continue.

Backstitch (293)

We take up about two threads of material, then enter again where we did before, but come through again the same distance ahead, and now each time go back in the same way before advancing.

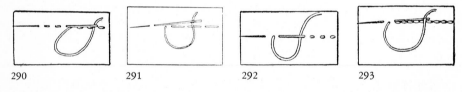

290   291   292   293

II. DIFFERENT SEAMS

Topsewing (294)

We always pierce both parts from back to front as we travel from left to right (used for joining selvedges).

Simple Seams (295)

We place together both right sides of our pieces, and unite them with running stitches. We press out and pink the edges.

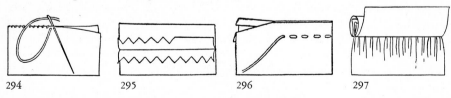

294   295   296   297

Right and Wrong or Double Seam (296)

We first of all place together both wrong sides and unite them with running stitches, then we turn right side to right side and again do running stitches.

Further Double Seam (297)

This is used particularly when we have to join a gathered piece of material to a straight piece. It is also a double seam, having two rows of stitches. The gathered piece is fitted to the plain piece and running stitches unite the two, just a little below the gatherings. Then, after turning, the second line of stitching falls in with the first.

Flat Seam (298)

We place one piece upon the other, right side to right side, so that a tiny edge will extend beyond, ready to be turned down later for a hem. Take running stitches to unite the pieces, making the hem, after opening out the work.

III. HEMS

298

Common Hems (299)

We turn down the rough edge, then turn down once more so that the rough edge lies hidden. We take the needle in at two or three threads below the hem, slanted towards the left, and out again upon the hem about the same amount from its lower edge.

Invisible Hems (300)

We take the needle horizontally from the hem itself to the material below the hem and pick up a small amount, as in running, alternately in the fold and on the cloth below it, as we go forwards.

Herringbone (301)

Here the running stitches we take are not visible on the front, as we travel from left to right, pointing our needle from right to left. This stitch is intended for a thicker material where the hem is only turned down once.

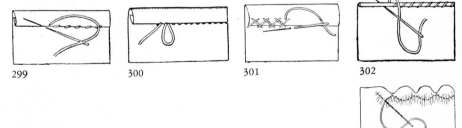

299   300   301   302

303

Rolled Hems (302)

We make a very narrow roll at the edge and stitch by hemming over and over it.

Wavy-edged Hems (303)

We take running stitches in waves going opposite to our edge, and then draw the thread up tightly.

IV. GATHERING AND SETTING ON A BAND

With cotton of adequate length we take gathering stitches, giving a further row into the same folds to ensure even distribution. By pulling up the cotton we shall be able to gather up the material in the folds to any required length (304).

If the gathered material is to be sewn to a band or singlet, both are set together, middle and ends being matched, and attached. We draw the gathering thread to the length of the band and spread out the folds evenly. We then sew them on the wrong side in with the seam, one by one, turning in about ¼ in. of the band (305, 306).

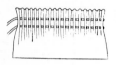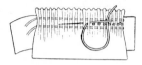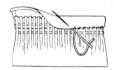

304—306

V. BINDING, BIAS BINDING, FACING

Binding with a straight band (307) and with crossway strips (308a, 308b)

We put both right sides of the material face to face, and unite them with small running stitches. Then we turn the binding up over the top and down, as a hem on the other side, hemming it so that our stitches are above the running stitches and do not penetrate to the right side (307).

To make the strips, we fold some material on the cross, snipping first along the fold and then parallel to it. To join the strips we set two at right angles, edge to edge, make running stitches across them, open out and trim the corners (308a, 308b). We apply the strips in the same way as straight bands.

For Curved Shapes (309)

We place our bias strip round the edge of a curve, such as a neckhole, take running stitches to unite the two pieces, then turn over the edge and hem down as before.

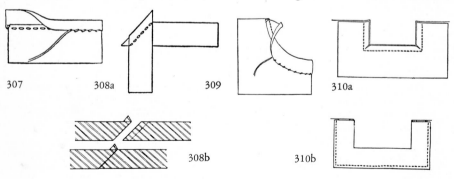

307   308a   309   310a

308b   310b

Square Yokes (310a, 310b)

We place our yoke to the neck shape and stitch both together. We snip carefully at the corners, then turn about and hem down the yoke as above. We can have the yoke showing either on the right or the wrong sides, according to whether we face right or wrong sides together when we start.

VI. MITRED CORNER 311-313

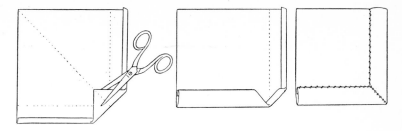

VII. LET-IN BUTTONHOLES

We put right sides of material together, then stitch round like a letter-box mouth (314). We cut a central slit, as shown, and from it we cut four further corner slits (315). The facing is pulled through the hole to the wrong side. At each end there will be a squashed fold. We stitch down the long edges so that stitches do not show on the front (316) and trim the facing side. The finished buttonhole is shown in Fig. 317.

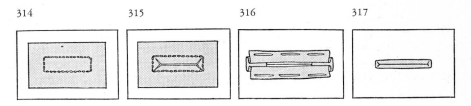

314   315   316   317

Sewing dolls' clothes

The dolls would very much appreciate a nice new set of clothes. Plenty of material is usually available, but people often wonder how to begin. Now, if it is not to be a dress with complicated cut, it is not so very difficult. We simply consult Plate L. We could make very simple garments like the tunic (318).

We take a piece of material slightly more than double the length the tunic has to be, and about as wide across as the distance from elbow to elbow. (It is best cut out with the material doubled lengthwise). We make a slit down the centre front to let the head pass through easily, and now we can have the first fitting. We mark the shape of the neck on front and back, try out the length of the skirt, and cut out for the arms and neck.

Then we start sewing. We can blanket stitch round the neck and slit, using bright colours and treat the armholes and bottom edge in a similar fashion. We make a double seam at the sides and add a little button and buttonhole at the top of the opening.

From this shape, others can be derived. A simple play suit is developed if the bottom is cut with flaps that button up (319).

For the trousers we use only the lower section of Fig. 320. Since they need not be unbuttoned here we make them with a running string or merely a hem. The top has a broad hem and is elastic threaded. Then we attach two straps. We can also sew a bib with braces and have a pocket (1152). The trousers may be made narrower at the top and wider at the bottom as Fig. 322 shows.

For a broad baggy tunic (323, 324) two squares were joined, except at the armholes, along the sides, and at the top a broad hem was given for the draw strip.

If we want a dress with a wider skirt set in, we only cut out the blouse part in this manner and take a long strip for the skirt. We join its short ends, gather it along one long side, and set it to the bodice (325, 1152).

If we want the so-called kimono style used for the milking smock, we need only cut the arm part as in Fig. 326. Fig. 327 is a longer sleeved version of Fig. 325. A jacket is cut as in Fig 328, with longer sleeves and waistband. Fig. 329 shows the cut of a loose-fitting jacket.

Figs. 330-332 show a loose-fitting jacket with shoulder seam and the turnover part allowed at the front. Sewing is done in different ways. If we use thinner material we make a double seam, but if we have thicker material we give only a single seam and pink the edges, or lightly oversew them. We bind the neck with a crossway strip of different colour, or simply with bias binding. If we face it with a similar strip, we get a stiff, stand-up collar.

Making a Pattern according to Plate L.

Here the designs stretch over four squares. We therefore take a square piece of paper and fold it in halves and quarters each way, so that, when it opens, it will contain 16 little squares. Our sheet should be four times as big as the sixteen squares on the chart. We can now easily copy the shape.

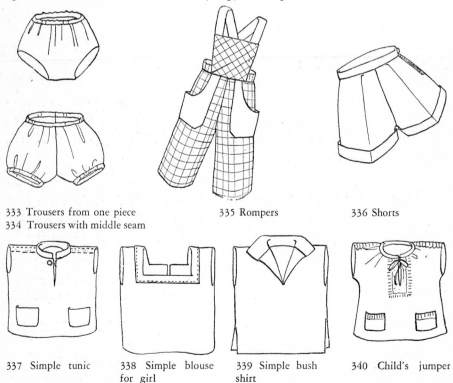

333 Trousers from one piece
334 Trousers with middle seam

335 Rompers

336 Shorts

337 Simple tunic

338 Simple blouse for girl

339 Simple bush shirt

340 Child's jumper

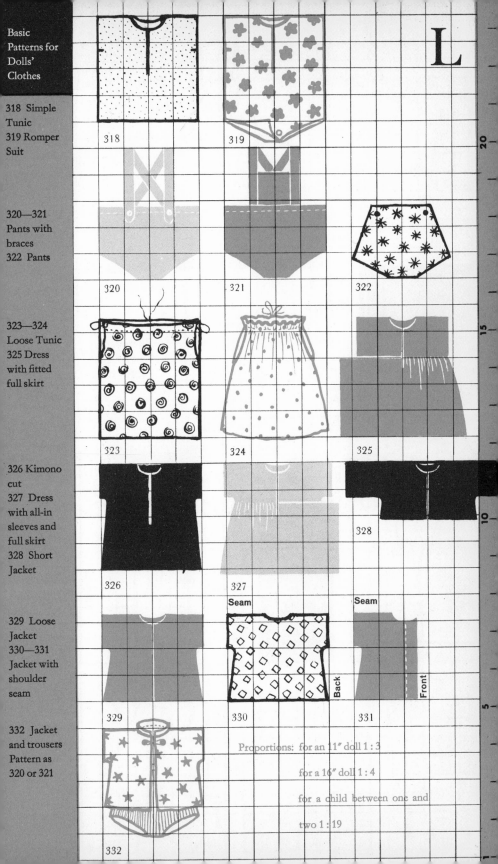

Basic Patterns for Dolls' Clothes

318 Simple Tunic
319 Romper Suit

320—321 Pants with braces
322 Pants

323—324 Loose Tunic
325 Dress with fitted full skirt

326 Kimono cut
327 Dress with all-in sleeves and full skirt
328 Short Jacket

329 Loose Jacket
330—331 Jacket with shoulder seam

332 Jacket and trousers Pattern as 320 or 321

L

318

319

320

321

322

323

324

325

326

327

328

329

330   Seam   Back

331   Seam   Front

332

Proportions: for an 11" doll 1 : 3

for a 16" doll 1 : 4

for a child between one and

two 1 : 19

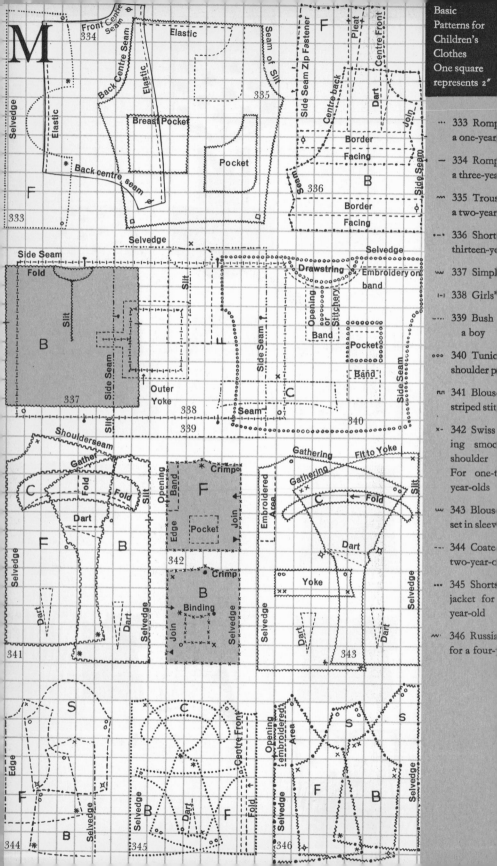

341 Blouse in Kimono cut   342 Smock with shoulder pieces   343 Blouse with shoulder pieces

344 Coatee with set in sleeves   345 Short sleeved jacket   346 Russian tunic in Raglan cut

Children's clothes of simple cut (Chart M)

When we have made the simple garment for our doll, we can readily tackle a little tunic for a godchild, or a simple blouse. Pages 72 and 73 show rows of specially simple forms to cut.

334. Panties with middle seam.

335. Trousers for a 2 year old.

336. Shorts for a 13 year old girl.

337. Simple tunic for a one-year-old child.

338. Simple blouse for a 10-12 year old girl.

This is like the tunic but has wider arm pieces and a wider collar.
The yoke at the neck is fitted to the wrong side first so that it will, when stitched and turned out, be upon the right side, where it is trimmed with stitching.

339. Simple "bush" or sleeveless shirt.

This has been given the lovely name of the ten minute shirt, because anyone is supposed to be able to make it in ten minutes.
It is cut like the tunic, the opening is as in Fig. 359. The collar is a broad oblong strip, and provides for revers.

340. Child's tunic, cut for a 4-year-old. Its collar, edged with bias binding, is given a draw cord.

341. Blouse in Kimono cut. This is illustrated in Fig. 281 and described on page 56.

342. Swiss milking smock with Shoulder Bands. For 1-3 years olds. We slit the centre front downwards from the neck and face it. The collar is made from a broad, long strip, to take a draw cord.

343. Blouse with shoulder bands. This is illustrated in Fig. 282 and described on page 56.

344. Quilted coatee. For a 2 year old. For description see below.

345. Jacket in Raglan style for a 1 year old.

346. Russian blouse in Raglan style (See Fig. 200). For a 4 year old.

347, 348, 349 Simple Bibs

344 and 350. Quilted coatee.

350. This is for a somewhat bigger child.

We use a lining of flannel or cottonwool, and therefore we must cut out our pattern three times. We need outside, inside and lining. The outer pieces are joined at the centre front, at the base and at the shoulder seams. Fig. 350 shows the corners rounded off. The lining is then attached to the shoulder and side seams to fix it to the jacket. The hem is tacked. Now the sleeves are joined, given their lining and set in the armholes. Next, the cuff facing is turned in and fixed. We make the lining, tack it in and hem it. Next we can fit a narrow piece of material to the neck, 1¾ ins. x 10¾ ins. without turnings. A loop and button, or two buttons with one loop will make the fastening.

350 Coatee

351 Linen skirt with coloured border

352 Two smocked garments in simple cut

We require about 1½ yds. of material. We join the cut sides with double seams. The selvedge is turned down for 2 ins. and sewn along except for about 2 ins. where, it must remain open for the elastic to enter. We make a row of running or back stitch about ¾ in. from the hem edge, and insert the elastic. The other selvedge has a hem.

The skirt in Fig. 351 is in Bavarian linen. It has a similar cut but is made somewhat differently. In the seam, some 9 ins. must remain open for the placket. The selvedge is not sewn but gathered along, and set in a band of corresponding length. We can add buttons and loops or a zip fastener (304-306).

The bold zig-zag is done with braid and oblique running stitches are used to sew it on.

Smock

A smock is the traditional Hungarian dress, but it was also worn by country people in England, in the eighteenth century. To "smock" means to "gather".

We like to use these loose garments today, particularly as coats, blouses and dresses for children as well as for adults.

Smocking is a decoration closely related to the cut of the garment. We can work a smock in one colour, i.e. material and silk thread both the same colour, so that its appeal rests solely upon the shadow effect produced by the folds. We can also use for the setting up of the smocking a colour differing from the material (353), and so add the colour effect to that of the shadows.

The work itself is not very difficult. First of all mark the material with a so-

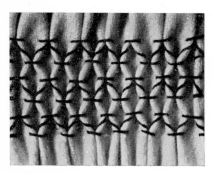
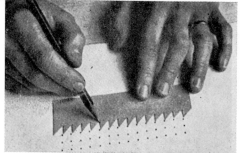
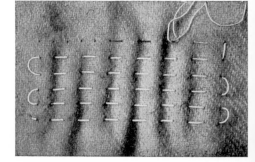

353 The coloured smocking from Fig. 258

354 Marking with the gauge

355 Putting in the auxiliary thread

called "gauge", so that we can produce even folds (354). The space between the points is about a third of an inch. We could use squared paper instead by marking from it.

We take guiding threads along these rows of dots, and in doing so we pull the material into even folds. Next we begin the actual smocking stitch which we can do in different ways. The illustration on Plate J shows the stitches generally used. The arrow shows the run of the thread.

Fig. 352 shows two smocked garments, a longer party dress and a light summer frock. Both have a very simple cut. Bodice and skirt are all in one in the party dress. (Full width of the skirt is 80 ins.). The neck and armholes are trimmed with ruching.

The summer frock is made to the pattern shown in Fig. 325. The skirt is gathered in at the centre front and centre back with smocking. The entire width of the skirt is 64 ins.

VIII. OPENINGS

Open slit (356-359)

Face the right sides together and stitch around a central line fairly closely (356). Then cut a slit, take the outer part of the facing through this slit and sew down its edges with running or hemming stitches. Fig. 359 shows the finished slit on the right side.

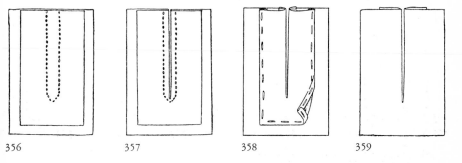

356　　　　　357　　　　　358　　　　　359

Using Crossway Strips (364)

The binding is twice as long as the slit and ¾ in. wide. Sew it around the slit, then turn it about and hem it down on the wrong side, as usual.

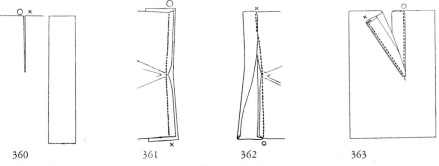

360　　　　　361　　　　　362　　　　　363

360—363 As the opening appears with the binding right across

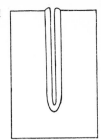

Opening with Transferred Binding (360-363)

We cut a slit and open out the edges until they form a straight line. Use material cut on the cross to bind them, passing from O to X (the two ends) (361). We keep close to the edge as we stitch, facing right sides together for outer garments, and right side to wrong for washable garments. At the centre, we go very close to the point as we stitch or give it an extra snip. Then it will set better when folded for a placket. The facing is turned about and neatly slipsewn (in outer garments).

Opening with Buttoning Placket. Polo Slit (365, 366)

Button and Buttonhole Plackets average 6 ins. x 2½ ins. and ¾ in. x 2½ ins. We sew the facing on to the wrong side and snip down to 4½ ins. Then we cut a tip at the lower end of the large part and turn the facing about. We turn in a narrow piece, place the strip in position and sew around it.

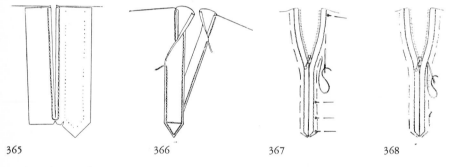

365   366   367   368

Opening with Zipper (367, 368)

We cut a slit somewhat longer than the zipper, turn down and press a ¼ in. fold and tack this on the right side to the zipper, strengthening it with additional stitches.

IX. BUTTONHOLES AND LOOPS

Buttonhole (369-374)

We mark with chalk or tack along the parts to be cut. These must fall in with the line of the thread (369). Then we make a long slit with buttonhole scissors. If we use ordinary scissors, we simply fold the material exactly halfway along the slit and cut the doubled material. We unfold it and work along each side (370).

For buttonholes in shirts, etc. (372), we make bars at the ends also. We take two or three threads of our cloth, using blanket stitch along the bar, or buttonhole stitch (371, 373). In shirts we find one end of the hole is rounded as in Fig. 374, while the other is transverse.

Fig. 374 shows a tailor's buttonhole with a strengthening cord inlaid.

Loops (375)

We form a loop by several times spanning a space along the edge of our material, then filling it up with buttonhole stitches upon the threads.

369—375 Buttonholes and loop

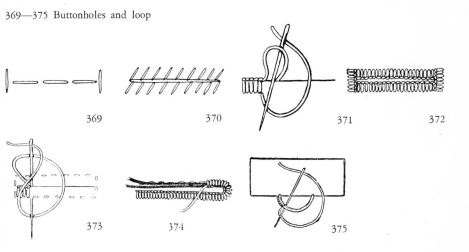

369   370   371   372

373   374   375

Simple but practical patterns for sewing

Coffee Cosy

We need a piece of foam rubber, 26 ins. x 15 ins., or a cheap bath mat. We stick together the two short sides with a rubber adhesive. In order to make it into the sugar loaf shape, we stitch obliquely from the top into little folds, thus producing eight fluted parts, and leave an opening about 2 ins. across.

Cover. We take an oblong piece of material, about 26 ins. x 36 ins., and make a double seam down its long edges, adding a broad hem for the draw thread (380).

The other end, which later forms the band of the ruff, can be finished by the selvedge or given a roll hem. When this sacklike cover is ready we insert the rubber as shown in Fig. 381. We pull the bottom of the material up through the central hole, then pull the string and tie a bow. The coffee cosy is now ready and its cover can easily be detached for washing.

A useful Pillow Case without Buttonholes

This pattern is for sofa cushions, but can also be used for pillow cases. It can easily be rolled and ironed, since there are no buttons. It is very quickly put on. It would do for foam rubber cushions also.

M a t e r i a l : We take about 1½ ins.- 2 ins. more than the width and about 8 ins. more than double the length of the case, and save work if both short sides have selvedges, since we can then use single instead of double seams.

F o l d i n g a n d S e w i n g : We turn down across one short end so that double the length of the case is left (384), and bring the other short end up to the fold (385). The edges are joined with a double seam (right side, then wrong). The case is then ready to have the cushion inserted behind the flap, so that it cannot slip

376 Coffee cosy

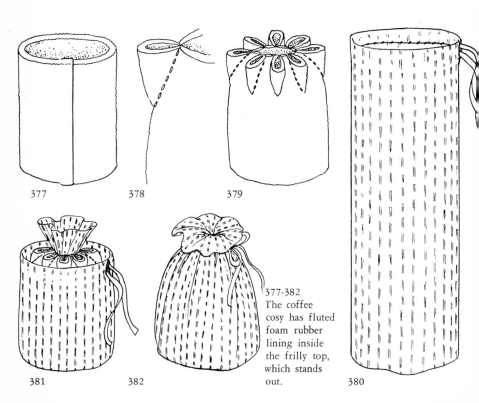

377

378

379

377-382
The coffee
cosy has fluted
foam rubber
lining inside
the frilly top,
which stands
out.

381

382

380

out. The case can, of course, be made transversely with side opening instead, when we must allow about 8 ins. more than the double width of the case and 2 ins. more than its height.

For a sofa cushion in stiffer material we can fit a band about ¾ in. - 1¼ ins. broad all round but must leave one end open. The material must then be somewhat larger.

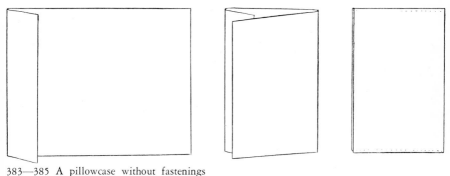

383—385 A pillowcase without fastenings

For travelling, camping and beach

Travelling Bags

The two little bags (386) serve many purposes, e.g. shoes, stockings and various oddments. They are made from cretonne or nylon.

Cutlery Holder (387)

It is best to make a paper pattern first so that we get the correct proportions and measurements. We take two oblong pieces of equal size of flannel and outer material, place them together, right sides facing, and stitch them along from join to join for the flap. We turn this inside out then fold back the pocket part and finally add the stitches for the channels.

A Shoe-Cleaning Outfit for the Handbag (388)

We make this from a strip of material about 4 ins. x 8 ins. and stitch to it a shorter strip of flannel like a pocket. It is given a button and loop after we have stitched it all up.

Coat-hanger Bag (389)

This is useful for gloves and other small things that often lie around in the wardrobe. A very simple bag is fixed on the bar across the hanger. It is best made from two strips, sewn together, and given an opening at the centre front. The hook can be covered in the same material.

Different Sleeping Bags (390-392)

Fig. 390. We sew the shape of an ordinary sack in a light woolly material. Long stitches may be used. Then we sew a wide hem at the upper edge. Next we make a

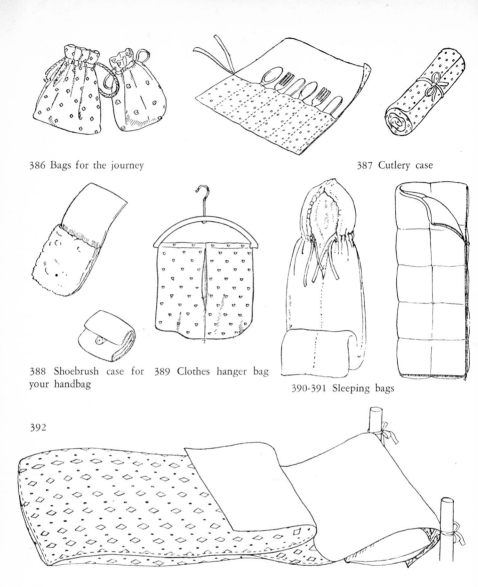

386 Bags for the journey

387 Cutlery case

388 Shoebrush case for your handbag

389 Clothes hanger bag

390-391 Sleeping bags

392

large hood from an oblong piece. It should be seamed, if possible, not along the centre back but along the top of the head. We then give a hem to the face opening, join the hood to the sack and fit an elastic band through the sack hem and a ribbon through the hood hem.

For another useful sleeping bag a blanket is folded like a sack and a zipper fitted down the side instead of sewing it. It thus has the advantage of being able to be used as a blanket if desired (391).

A Sleeping Bag in Washable material (392): intended for use in youth hostels or anywhere where blankets are also available.

A strip of material, 32 ins. x 80 ins. and 2½ times one's own length is sewn up like a sack to half way, leaving the ends of unequal length. The upper, shorter one is turned over like a sheet whilst the lower, longer one folds over the pillow. We can add little gussets at the sides as in Fig. 392.

Beach Bags (394)

This camping bag is both useful and attractive. It can be strapped up and carried as a plain bag with pockets on both sides to take newspapers, books, etc. We cut the material for the outer and inner parts to measure 17½ ins. x 24 ins.; for the pocket and lining 17½ ins x 30 ins. and for the handle 4¾ ins. x 20 ins. We also need a handsome button and two strips of foam rubber as lining.

393 Pattern for the beach case

The pocket pieces are joined to the main piece, facing right sides together, then turned out and faced to the opposite edge. Fig. 393 shows stitching in the shape of a cross for the compartments of the pockets, and a handle strap is sewn to one end ready to button upon the opposite end. The lining is caught in the middle and the lining cover is laid inside and sewn to the case.

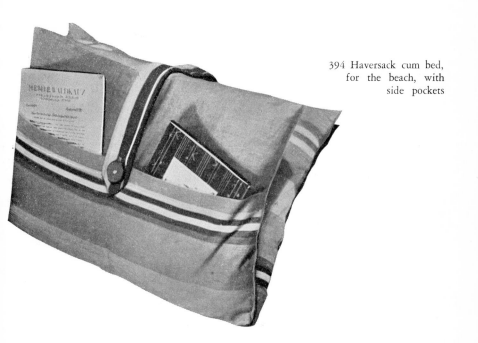

394 Haversack cum bed, for the beach, with side pockets

How to sew slippers

Simple Slippers, made without a last

When we have cut out the pieces, we should try the big shaped piece on to the foot. The cut must be generous, especially if the shoes are to be given a warm lining to make them really comfortable.

All the shoes illustrated here are made on the same principle. We need inner sole, padding, upper sole and binding for the welt, also lining.

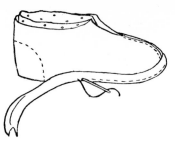

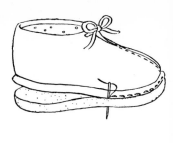

395 Inner sole 396 Fixing on the welt 397 Uniting upper and sole

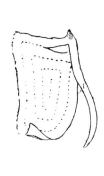

398 The cardboard sole is bound round with material

399 Cutting binding from small waste pieces of material

400 Plaiting the strips

401 Taking the plait as the outer sole

402 Finished sole

Inner Sole. This is cut from flexible cardboard and padded with cotton wool or a soft foam rubber material. We cover this with the lining. Then we bind the edges with a ¾ in. strip which we sew with running stitches and catch from side to side (395).

Outer Sole. This we cut ⅜ in. larger all round than the inner sole. It is easiest to use felt which is firm and strong and needs no further addition. But we can also make the outer sole from oddments. In that case, we would use cardboard, covered as before, then we would stitch on pieces of some hard-wearing material. This is done as follows:

a) Sew up plaited material as in Figs. 399-402. These plaits are quite strong and help to use up scraps. We cut strips as in Fig. 399, plait them and build the sole as in Figs. 401 and 402. The plait is sewn to the bound edge of the sole, beginning from the outside.

b) Sew bits of leather or old felt hats, to a sole cut from carpet scraps, and tidy up carpet edges with bias strips.

c) Sew on a rush or straw sole. See page 138.

Upper part

We cut four parts in the outer material and four in the lining, allowing enough to turn in and join and press the front and back seams. We unite the outer material

84

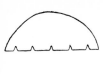

a / b

LEATHER STRIP

FELT SOLE

403 Heel support
404 Felt sole with welt. a. Sewing on leather strip. b. Sewing to the rest
405 Warm slippers with fur lining

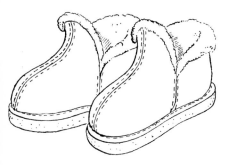

406 Baby's coloured shoes

with the lining, facing finally wrong side to wrong side. Then we cut out a heel shape from cardboard and again stitch near the front and back seams.

Adding the Welt

Now we add a leather welt or one of bias-cut material (396) to the lower edge of the upper part, the lining and the outside material fitted together. We double it lengthwise so that the fold fits to the shoe edge, and stretches around heel and toe parts. The outer sole is then pinned to its open edges. We must see that the shape of the shoe stands out well, and we must sew very firmly (397). If we want to cover the edge of the outer sole all round, we do as in Figs. 404a and b., i.e. we sew a broad strip of leather or felt along the lower edge, turn it down and stitch firmly, passing from top to bottom. The ball of the foot has thus a second sole of felt or leather.

The Upper Edge

The edge is strengthened with binding, which has an additional stitching outside, to prevent stretching. If the edge is to be piped in fur, we first stitch the lining then the outer material to the fur.

Baby's Shoes (406)

We can work these little shoes in leather or coloured felt. The centre front has a zipper. We join the lining to the outer material. If we use cloth, we can bind the edges with a crossway strip and draw through a little ribbon. The outer sole is made of soft leather, so that this little slipper can be used out of doors.

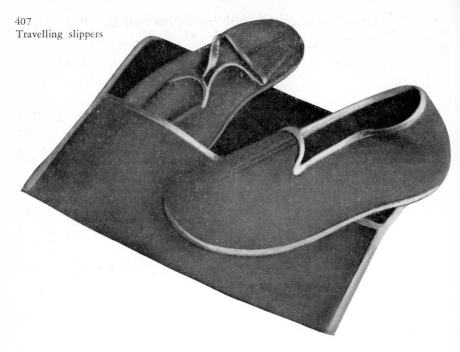

House Boots (405)

Here the portions for the heels overlap the uppers and are sewn over them. We can connect both portions at the top with a narrow elastic band. These shoes look particularly well if the outer material is chamois leather, and the lining white fur or fur fabric. We can add a zipper or strap.

Slippers (407)

These have little heel support and especially light soles. We therefore sew a thick felt sole to the outer sole and bind with a crossway strip.

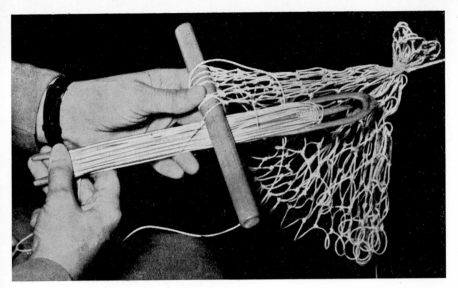

408 Knots of fisherman's netting, with mesh

409 Netted cloth in different effects, made in the Werkkunstschule Offenbach
This cloth was awarded the gold medal in Mailand in the 1954 Triennial Exhibition

NETTING, KNOTTING

Knotting and netting are extremely old crafts and are practised all over the world. Familiarity with the many different knots used on board ship belongs to the heritage of seafaring. Still, as of old, the fisherman knots his net for fishing. Since fishermen's nets were also fashioned in a fine material, decorative netting in cotton soon followed. In this way, we were introduced to the so-called "filet network".

Filet network

1. The Knots of the Mesh

As equipment we need a small mesh gauge and a netting needle together with strong thread (410). For the shoulder net (409) or a shopping bag, we shall use a linen thread, a fine bookbinder's thread or a thick coloured cotton yarn.

To start off, we make a firm loop and attach it to a hook or bolster and we then knot to it the thread that is wound round the netting needle. Next we begin knotting. Figs. 410-413 show the four movements involved.

1st Movement (410)

We hold the thread as a loop round the ring- and middle fingers of the left hand and mesh gauge, and keep it in position with the thumb.

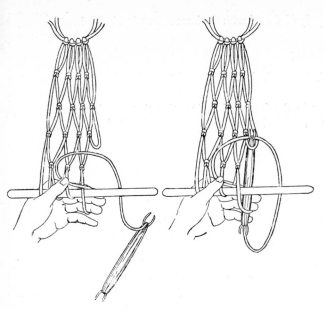

410/411 Start and loop taking

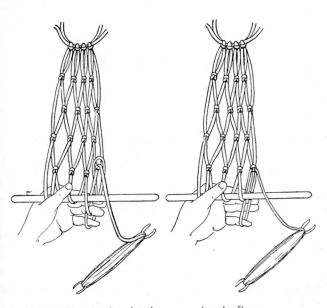

412/413 Holding the thread and manoeuvring the finger

414 Joining the threads. Making a slip knot. Pass the other thread end through the slip knot loop, then tighten it

a

b

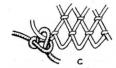
c

2nd Movement

We push the needle behind the mesh gauge first through the starting loop, (in subsequent rows this will mean the loop just above Fig. 411). Thus we make a second loop (not over the mesh gauge here) and hold it with the little finger.

3rd Movement

We now pull aside the needle whilst releasing first the left thumb and the ring- and middle fingers (412).

4th Movement

As we pull the yarn further out we hold the loop over the little finger very firmly in order to regulate the set of the knot at the connection, to make it fall into position just at the edge of the mesh gauge. The left index finger assists to a certain extent. The loop round the little finger vanishes as we tighten up the thread (413). Successive stitches are knotted in the same manner, till the end of the row, when we pull out the mesh gauge, reverse our work and knot the next row, travelling always from left to right.

We connect a new supply of thread with the knot shown in Fig. 414.

2. Stretching and Stitching

The finished network is stretched. It is pinned to a firm background such as a sofa, bolster, etc. or on to a frame such as can be bought at any handwork shop (416). We leave the net in the frame while inserting the threads to prevent them from pulling. Figs. 417 and 420 show a variety of suitable stitches.

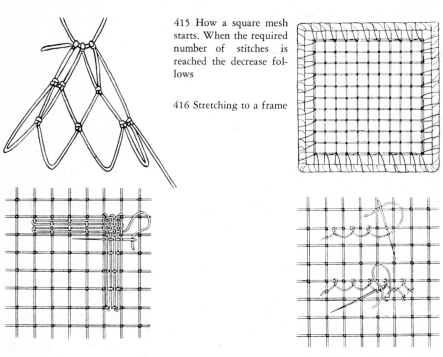

415 How a square mesh starts. When the required number of stitches is reached the decrease follows

416 Stretching to a frame

417 Decoration in darning

418 Filling in with loopstitches

419 Connected loops

420 Spiderweb

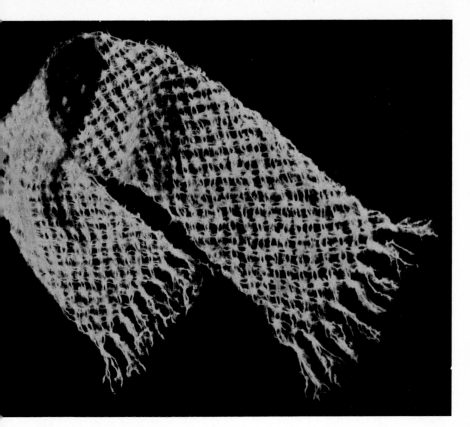

421 Knotted shawl from Mohair, with fringe

422 Flat knot work in fine French Mohair

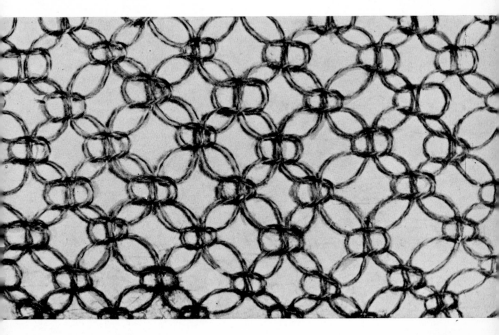

Macramée

The technique known as Macramée came originally from the Middle East. The term Macramée is Arabic and means trellis work. The name is very apt, for in Macramée work we entwine the yarn as in a trellis.

We can use the most varied materials for Macramée according to our purpose. In general, a strong thick linen thread is needed. The elegant Italian handbags and old hunting bags were made of a thick cord-like thread. The illustrations show how the first threads are knotted and also give the other basic knots used in Macramée.

423—425 Fastening the auxiliary loop to a chair back. Hanging on the doubled round threads, and making the first round of knots

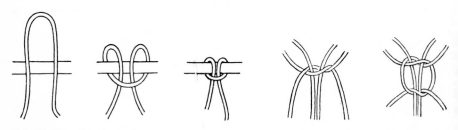

426-428 How threads are hung

429—430 Formation of the flat knots. Movements 1 and 2

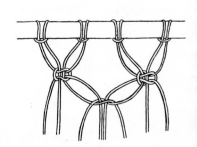

431 Interchange of strings

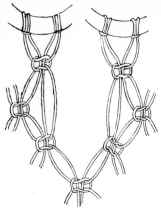

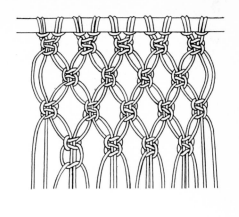

432 Gap in the work

433 Flat knot with treble formation

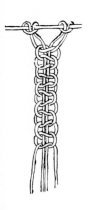

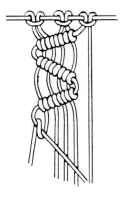

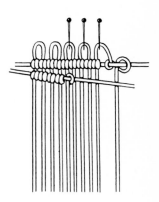

434 Four-corded
band

435 Alternating
knotting

436 Ribbed
knots, diagonal

437 Ribbed
knots, straight

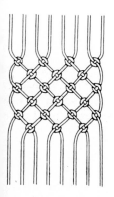

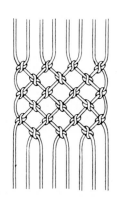

438—440 Trellis knots. Left: Front view. Middle: Back view. Right: Path of cords. The
diagram on the left shows single instead of double threads, but the work is done with double
threads

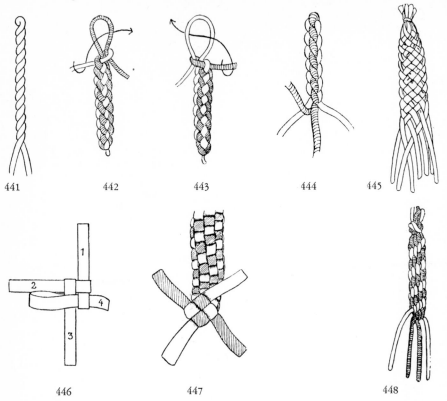

441   442   443   444   445

446   447   448

Twisted Rope (441)

A piece of thread forming a loop is attached to a hook. The other end is twisted in the same direction until both threads form a strong cord. The threads will stay in position when we join the two ends. We can afterwards smooth out small uneven bits.

Looped Rope (435)

We knot the left thread round the right one, then vice versa.

Loop Lacing (442, 443)

We knot two threads of different colours together, and, close up to the knot, we make a small loop with the thread on the left. This we hold up. Then we make a loop with the thread on the right and slip this through the first loop which we now tighten. Then we make a further loop with our first thread and so proceed alternately.

Crossed Threads (444)

We first cross a red and a blue thread half way, and then cross alternately the two red and the two blue ends until we have obtained a cord of the required length.

Plaits of Several Strands (445, see page 134)

Corded Rope (448, see below)

Plaited Rope (447)

Intended for leather or coarser thread. Follow the method shown in Fig. 446.

Cording

This is a very old form of plaiting. It can be done with four strands or even more. We knot the ends, attach them to a table or a hook and plait the threads as shown in Figs. 449 to 454. We can cord in coarse or a finer yarn and we can also use narrow strips of leather. In the case of long threads the ends are wrapped round the cording pegs. These can be made from small pieces of wood (455-457).

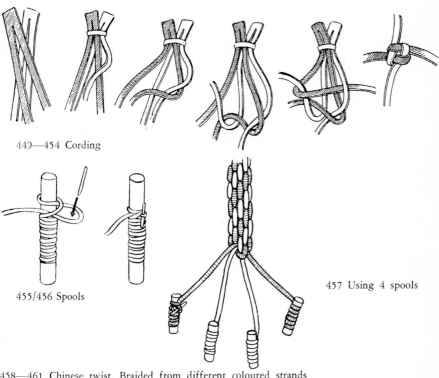

449—454 Cording

455/456 Spools

457 Using 4 spools

458—461 Chinese twist. Braided from different coloured strands

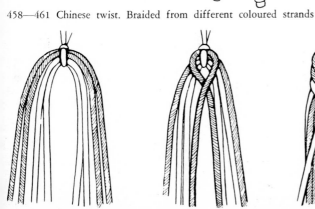

95

Chinese plait

The so-called Chinese plait also looks very nice in two colours and consists of only two strands of between four and six threads each. We begin plaiting with the thread on the extreme left which is brought to the right, across the others in the middle. We now repeat this with the thread on the extreme right (458-461), bring it to the left and continue in the same manner.

Accessories, knots and fringes

Tassels (462-464)

We first wind our yarn round a ruler or similar object. Then we bind it in one place, remove it from the ruler and again bind it at the same place. Finally, we push the end of the thread through the loop and pull the latter out at the top. The end of the ends will thus become invisible.

Woollen Bobbles (465-468)

We cut out two cardboard rings of the same size, place one on top of the other and sew wool through them and across the centre until the latter is completely filled. Then we snip the wool at the edges and bind wool between the two discs, tie this firmly at the waist, remove the disc and set the bobble. The finished bobble is trimmed evenly.

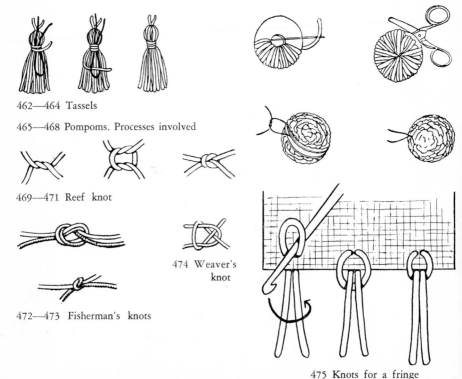

462—464 Tassels

465—468 Pompoms. Processes involved

469—471 Reef knot

472—473 Fisherman's knots

474 Weaver's knot

475 Knots for a fringe

Beadwork

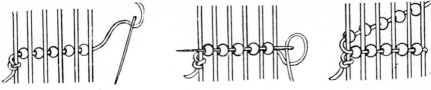

476—478 Bead weaving

We first of all span the longitudinal threads. We next tie on our transverse thread to the left outer thread. We pick up enough beads to set in the spaces, passing behind the upright threads, (476), then return through the beads again at the front of the uprights (477, 478).

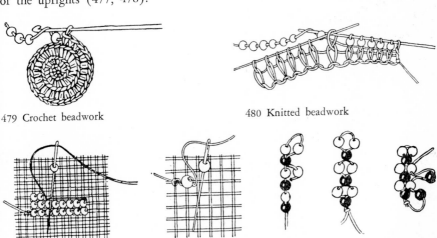

479 Crochet beadwork

480 Knitted beadwork

481—482 Sewing beadwork

483—485 Single beads threaded and single beads linked between alternate ones

Making a loom

We thread seven beads, go through no. 5 (483), add no. 8, go through no. 3, add no. 9, and knot the thread. We always add a fresh bead, then add the adjacent existing one (485).

Circular Bead Chain (486-489)

We thread eight beads, alternately white and black. We pass through them a second time (486). We take a white one, then no. 1 of the round, take a black one, then no. 2 of the round, and so on (488). We work two or three rounds, pulling to tubular shape as we continue.

486—489 Circular bead work

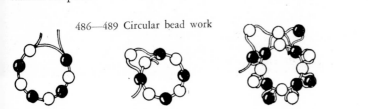

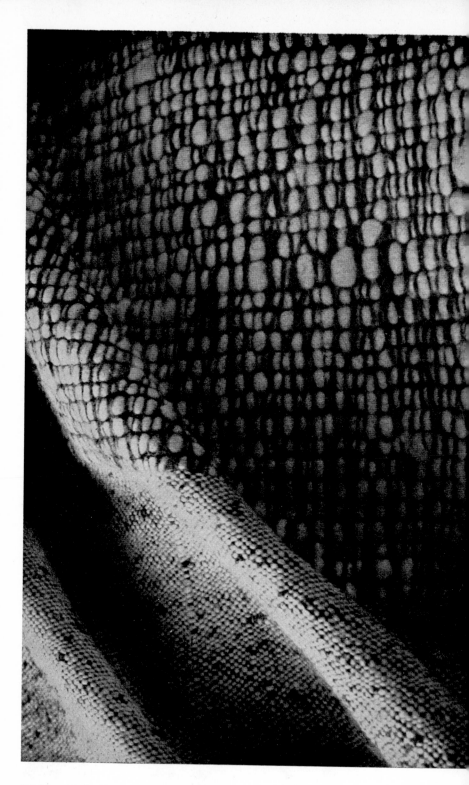

490 Material from raw sheep's wool

491 One of the earliest European illustrations of a horizontal loom, c. 1300. From the so-called "Weberfresken" (Weavers' Frescoes) in the "Haus zur Kunke", Constance

WEAVING

The Art of Weaving is ancient and its origins stretch back into the very beginnings of Prehistoric Times. In tales of mythology both spinning and weaving played important roles: for example, the Goddesses of Fate spin the threads of Destiny; "Rose-Red" in German Fairy Tales pricks her finger on a spindle and in other Folk-tales of Europe there is mention of spinning and weaving. Many figures of speech are also derived from the arts of spinning and weaving - among them, for example, "to lose the thread of" (conversation).

Weaving probably developed from braiding. Early man thrust twigs and branches into the earth and bound them together with vines and rushes in order to form the walls of simple huts, known as "wattle-work", (and made as we make fences now of slender vertical sticks bound together closely with wire). In such ways we may imagine the earliest weaving had its origins. There are no complete looms remaining from prehistoric times, but from discoveries of old textiles and simple

492 Old Egyptian Upright Loom

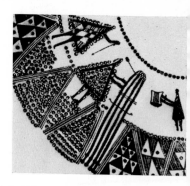

493 Earliest European Record of Weaving on an Urn of the Hallstatt Period (8th to 5th cent. B.C.)

weaving implements, we can reconstruct these oldest looms; for example, we may be sure that two wooden posts were stuck into the ground and were connected with a cross-bar at the upper end. To this cross-bar the warp threads were tied, and, since the warp threads were actually tied to the cross-bar, their length could be only as long as the height of the loom. In order to keep them spaced and at firm tension they were weighted with small stones, balls of hardened clay or the like. The oldest illustration of European weaving which has been preserved, was found engraved on a "Hallstatt" Urn, (493) dated about the fifth century before Christ. This very old type of loom was later improved with the addition of Cloth-beam and Warp-beam, but kept its original form of an upright loom for a long time still.

In the original, vertical looms the warp threads were tied to the warp-beam so that they were necessarily short. But when a warp-beam was added, the warp threads could be attached to such a beam, which could revolve, thus winding up any desired length of warp threads. Since longer lengths of cloth could be woven, the new cloth beam also revolved when the cloth was wound on it, as it was woven. This was a very important advance in loom construction. The horizontal loom made its appearance in Europe sometime in the Middle Ages and even to-day the basic principles of the loom remain unchanged (491).

It is commonly believed that the oldest material used in weaving was wool derived from sheep. The preparation of plant fibres, such as flax and hemp, is comparatively difficult, so that most experts consider that their use was developed later.

EXPLANATION OF WEAVING TERMS

Each textile is formed of two sets of threads which cross each other - of warp and weft. The threads of the warp run lengthwise through the fabric, while the weft threads are at right angles to them - or run horizontally.

One can picture the structure of a textile if one thinks of darning - of the lengthwise threads put in first and then of the horizontal threads passing alternately over and under the vertical threads.

The drawing in of the weft threads (or horizontal or "harness" ones) is made easier by an apparatus on a modern loom, the so-called "heddle" or "harness". It lifts alternating threads, or groups of threads, of the warp, so that the shuttle with the weft can pass easily between them. The space between the upper and lower warp threads is called the "shed".

When the shuttle with the weft thread has been passed through the shed, the weft thread is then pressed closely against the previous weft thread by means of the "beater" or "batten". The new shed is then made, and the next weft thread may be put through the shed. The edge formed by changing the direction of the weft thread is called the "selvedge".

To weave a long piece of material, the warp is stretched on large looms or frames in a special manner. Experts speak of "warping". It is wound round a roller called the "warp-beam". The finished material passes over the breast-beam (which is stationary) and on to the cloth-beam below it.

TYPES OF FABRIC

The structure of the fabric, i.e., the relation of warp and weft, depends on the yarn and its arrangement. Some of the most common fabrics are plain cloth or tabby, twill and satin weaves. Only the first two are really suitable for our simple looms.

Plain Cloth

Warp and weft are as a rule equal in size or "grist". The pass over and under each other alternately, as in darning.

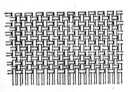

494 Plain Cloth   495 Repp with Weft showing   496 Repp with Warp showing

Types of Repp

We distinguish between two kinds of repp - warp face repp and weft face repp. In warp-face repp, the warp is set very close so that, in weaving, the weft is covered. In the case of weft-face repp, the warp is set much farther apart, and in the weaving the weft covers the warp. As a rule in weaving weft-face repp, the weft is somewhat heavier than the warp.

CARDLOOM WEAVING

No special equipment is needed for weaving smaller pieces of material. Some squared or graph paper is put over a piece of cardboard, the intended size of the

fabric is marked and the cardboard is pierced to take the threads of the warp
The finished material is afterwards cut from its frame.

We must be careful not to pull the weft too tightly with our needle - which here
acts as a shuttle - or the edges will be crooked. To avoid this, we can fix the first and
last thread of the warp to the card with a stitch. Better still, we might weave a knitting
needle - to be removed afterwards - into the selvedge.

If the loom is to be used again, the warp should not be set up directly on the cardboard, but on some thread that has been passed through the holes with a running
stitch. When the fabric is completed, the stitches are opened and the loom can be
used again.

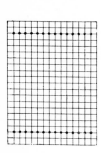 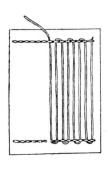 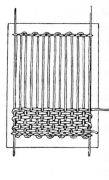

497—499 Small Children can use
a Cardboard Loom for Weaving
with Raffia

500 and 501 Weaving Shapes

Shaped Looms

We have described weaving certain shapes - as, for example, for raffia table mats -
on page 153.

Needle weaving is also suitable for the uppers of children's shoes, handbags and
many other things. A drawing is first made of the outline and then traced with
running stitches for setting up the warp.

A small raffia bag can be woven in one piece. The shape is outlined on a piece of
cardboard and holes are pierced along the bigger curve at equal distances. The rings
are sewn to each side of the cardboard on the smaller curve: the raffia is fastened to
one ring, taken round the cardboard, drawn through the other ring and brought
back to the first until the warp is set up. Fig. 501 shows how the bag is woven. To
get an even texture all round, the longer threads in the middle will have to be gone
over separately more often than the others.

Finally, the rings are detached from the cardboard and finished with button-hole
stitches. Cords or straps are fastened to them to form the handles. (For making
cords, see page 95).

WEAVING WITH A HEDDLE REED

The heddle reed has been used in simple weaving since antiquity all over the world. It is still employed in Scandinavian countries, especially in Sweden, Finland and Norway. These heddle reeds were beautifully decorated in the past. Young men would carve them elaborately for the girls of their choice. Heddle reeds are mostly used for making ribbons and narrow strips such as braces (suspenders), ties and belts. But we can also make wider fabrics in tabby or twill (510).

A heddle reed consists of a small board with alternate holes and spaces (slots) (505). The thread or yarn is pulled alternately through the hole and the space or slot. If the threads are stretched and the board lowered, the threads drawn through the spaces will go up and down, while the others will remain in position. A shed for the weft is thus formed.

Making a Heddle Reed

1. From hardwoods. We can cut out a simple heddle reed by taking a piece of hardwood and marking on it about sixteen strips, each about 4¼ in. in length and ¼ in. wide. These are pierced in the centre with a hot knitting needle or with a punch. The board is then cut into strips and the cut-out strips are glued at equal, narrow distances between two thin pieces of wood (502). A good glue should be used, and end clamps employed to hold the pieces until the glue is perfectly dry.

2. Wood. Anyone handy with a fretsaw, keyhole saw or jigsaw can make a heddle reed from a thin piece of hardwood (not ply-wood) by cutting into it at equal distances (504). A thin piece of hardwood is afterwards glued to the open ends. The holes can be made with a red-hot knitting needle or with a small drill.

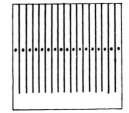

502 Home-made Heddle Reed from Hard-board

503 Cardboard Shuttle

504 A Wooden Reed

Setting-Up the Loom

We must remember that the warp determines the pattern when weaving narrow bands. The weft is only seen at the selvedge at regular, short distances. For a start, it is best to set up the loom simply with colours that go well together, without any special pattern in mind. The threads should be of equal length - about a third longer than the length of the band - and are drawn alternately through holes and spaces. A crochet hook will be of great help. The warp ends are then tied up at both sides and fixed to a hook, or door knob at one end, and to the waist at the other. The weft is wound round a shuttle. We can make the shuttle ourselves from stiff cardboard (503).

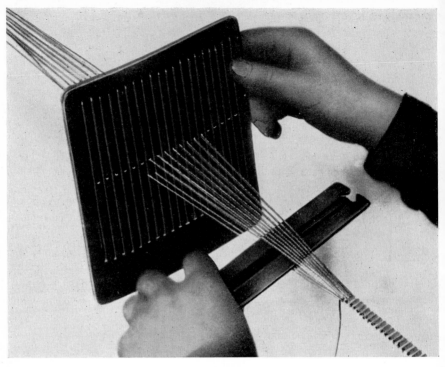

505

Weaving

We press the board downwards. A shed is thus formed for the weft, which we throw across. We then pull the board up, thus forming a new shed (505), go through it with the shuttle from the other side and repeat this process.

To make a firm cloth one must have the proper warp set and use the proper beat. Pulling of the weft thread is certain to make a poor edge, or selvedge, and is likely to cause threads in the warp to break near the selvedge.

Patterns

The patterns in weaving strips are determined by the way the warp is set up. The bands (506-508) show three basic patterns suitable for simple weaving.

Horizontal stripes (506) are made by pulling threads of different colour through holes and spaces.

Vertical stripes (507) result from using thread of the same colour for two or more neighbouring holes and spaces.

A pattern of vertical and horizontal stripes is shown in Fig. 508: the warp threads in holes and spaces on the right are of the same colour, those on the left of different colours.

A great variety of designs can be produced from these basic patterns.

Fig. 509 shows a further possibility. Bundles of wool have been woven into the fabric, and have been allowed to extend slightly at the sides, which may be cut open at the ends later, thus introducing variety. This example also shows that the

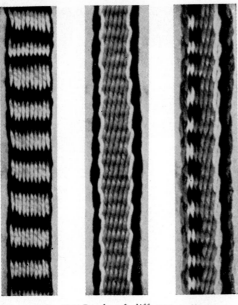

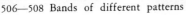

506—508 Bands of different patterns

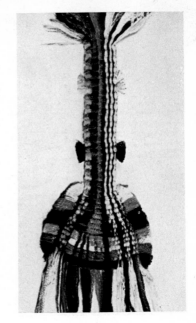

509 Changing the Width and Weaving in Coloured Wools

width can be changed in the course of the work. We only have to pull the weft thread a little less tightly to cause the warp threads to spread out. This type of weave is occasionally used for ties, small bags, purses or collars, as in our illustration.

How to Weave Wider Fabrics on a Heddle Reed

Fabrics up to the width of the heddle reed can be made as well as narrow ribbons (510). Handbags, berets and scarves could be made in this way. The heddle reed is particularly suitable for weaving in raffia. Warp and weft would both be visible in this case, or the warp might even be covered completely.

Weaving wider fabrics is slightly different from the technique described above.

1. The ends of the warp threads are not tied into one knot, but into several groups and fastened to a small stick so as to be widely spaced from the very beginning (510).

2. The weft thread is not drawn tightly - as in the weaving of bands - but as loosely as possible.

3. The heddle reed is beaten against the fabric after each change of shed as if we were using a standard reed. The fabric must be kept as wide as the distance between the first and the last warp thread.

Building a Heddle Reed into a Frame

It will be necessary to build the heddle reed into a frame for wider fabrics, as described on page 112 and in Figs. 544-560. This allows the threads to be stretched tightly and evenly.

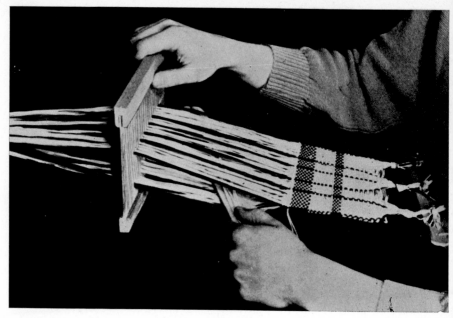

510 Making a wide Raffia Band on the Heddle Reed

TABLET OR CARD WEAVING

Tablet or card weaving is a very old technique. Small pieces of wood or cardboard - in earlier times also horn and parchment - are used instead of a loom. The craft still survives in Scandinavia, Russia, Japan, China and many other countries.

How the Fabric is Made

If we turn a threaded card forwards or backwards (512), the threads will be twisted into a small rope. If we turn several of these cards, all placed next to each other, a number of ropes will form (515, 517). These can be connected with a weft thread after each twist and woven into a firm band (516, 518). The shed lies between the upper and the lower layer of threads (530).

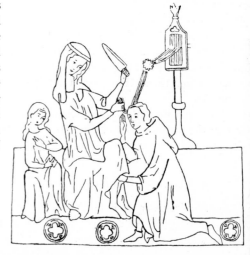

511 One of the earliest illustrations of Tablet Weaving in Europe

106

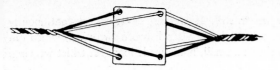

Tablet weaving is more difficult than using a heddle reed, but it offers far greater possibilities in the use of patterns, and also produces a really firm fabric.

The Cards or Tablets

The cards (531) are best made of hardboard or board. They should be about 2 in. square. The corners are rounded by tracing with a coin and trimmed with scissors; the holes are made with an ordinary gimlet (awl) (787) or an office punch. They should be about ¼ in. in diameter and slightly under half an inch from the edges. It is advisable to number the cards.

The First Trial Band

We should start weaving straight away. The band in Fig. 525 will make a good beginning. We need two colours, such as red and white. The material should be strong, and could be twine or a thick crochet yarn. The tablets are threaded as follows:

We need ten cards (tablets) each with four holes, and forty pieces of thread, each piece to be 60 in. long; twenty-four will be red and sixteen white. We will also need some red yarn for the weft thread and a small ruler as a beater.

Cards 1, 2, 5, 6, 9 and 10 are now threaded red, 3, 4, 7 and 8 white. Each hole must be threaded. The ends of the threads are then tied up. One end is fastened to a hook, doorhandle, etc., the other to the waist.

Arrangement: The tablets must be in the right position, before we can start weaving. They are arranged in pairs for our particular band, i.e., tablets 1, 3, 5, 7 and 9 must be placed as shown in Fig. 513 and tablets 2, 4, 6, 8 and 10 as shown in Fig. 514 so that there are always two tablets facing each other as if in a mirror. As a result, the ropes form a kind of herringbone pattern (515, 516).

Weaving itself is not difficult (530): we turn the entire set of cards forward at an angle of 90 degrees. Then we put the ruler or folder in the shed, knock against the crossing threads and carry the weft thread through. The cards are again turned at an angle of ninety degrees and the process is repeated.

Having woven like this for some time, we must change direction by twisting the cards towards us, instead of away from us. This change is necessary to unroll the ropes forming at the other end of the threads and gives this type of band its characteristic pattern.

The cards should be tied together with a ribbon, if we have to interrupt weaving for some reason. We can also push a knitting needle through one of the series of

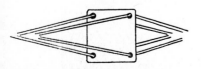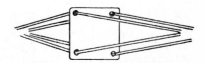

513 and 514 Differently arranged Tablets

holes. A rubber band would be better still. If we can never weave continuously for very long, it will be advisable to stretch the warp between two vices, which can be fastened to the table. Fig. 536 shows a small, home-made loom for tablet weaving.

Patterns

A great variety of patterns is possible in tablet weaving. Here are a few suggestions:

Horizontal Stripes (525) are already known to us.

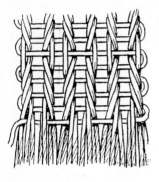

515 and 516 Tablets arranged in pairs produce 'knitted' patterns (cords not running parallel)

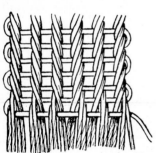

517 and 518 This effect is produced if the cords run parallel

519—524 Different Arrangements of the Cords. The numbers indicate the tablets, the letters holes

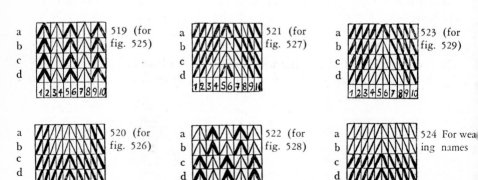

519 (for fig. 525)

520 (for fig. 526)

521 (for fig. 527)

522 (for fig. 528)

523 (for fig. 529)

524 For weaving names

The band with vertical stripes (526) was woven on ten cards, like all the other examples on this page. The four outer cords (Nos. 1, 2, 9 and 10) were threaded with red through all four holes. The inner cards were threaded red through one pair of adjoining holes and white through the other.

The cards are not arranged in pairs this time, but run parallel (517, 518). Cards 1 - 5 are arranged as in Fig. 513, cards 6 - 10 as in Fig. 514. The cards threaded in two colours must have the side with the red wool upwards to obtain the vertical stripes.

The cards for diagonal stripes (527) are threaded as for vertical stripes, but their position is different. Instead of the side threaded in one colour facing upwards, the cards are given a quarter turn.

We can start with diagonal stripes on our experimental band. It only needs a slight re-arrangement of the cards. We give the two innermost cards a quarter turn to the left and turn cards 3 and 7 similarly to the right. When we continue weaving, we will find that the red threads now follow each other differently in the top layer of threads and produce a simple pattern of vertical stripes.

The cards for the chequered pattern (528) are threaded as before. They have been arranged in pairs, the red threads in one pair facing upwards and in the next downwards.

The cards for the tufted pattern (529) must be threaded differently: the two innermost cards - Nos. 5 and 6 - have three white threads and one red thread each. The adjoining cards (4 and 7) have each two white and two red threads and the next cards (3 and 8) have three red threads and one white thread.

525—529 Basic Patterns for Tablet Weaving

525   526   527   528   529

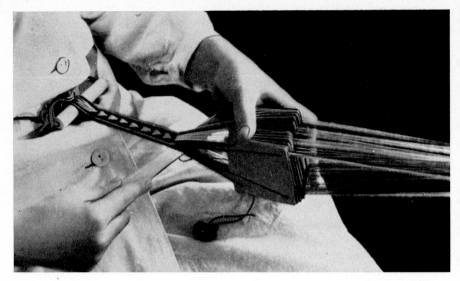

Button Holes

Woven button holes, as we need them for belts, braces, etc., are made with two weft threads. We simply weave separately: first we make the right portion of the band, then the left. When the opening is long enough, the fabric is again woven as before in one width.

Loops

Loops at the side of the fabric are made by carrying the weft round a thick knitting needle or a piece of cardboard, which is pulled out when the loop is finished. These loops are very convenient for adding further pieces of crocheting, knitting or weaving. The door curtain (539) has been woven in this way.

Tubes

If we arrange the cards pointing towards us (537), we obtain two sheds, one above and one below. If we now give them alternately a quarter turn to the right and one to the left and take the weft thread through the upper shed after each change of shed and back again through the lower, we obtain a tubular fabric of plain cloth pattern.

Double Bands

In the same way as we have just described, two bands can be woven simultaneously. We need two weft threads. One of them will run only through the upper shed, the other only through the lower.

Weaving-in Ropes

If we want to make the bands thicker and more durable or are using silk and yet want firm fabric, we can incorporate thin ropes. Each tablet will have to be pierced in the middle (532) to take thick cotton or yarn, which has to be tied up with the other threads. The coloured threads will wind round these ropes during weaving and will cover them completely.

Weaving with Five or Six-Hole Tablets

Five, or even six-hole tablets can be used in place of the square tablets with four holes. Although threading is more difficult, the possibilities are far greater. Fig. 538 shows a band woven on a five-hole tablet.

Simplified Threading

Threading can be simplified as follows, if several tablets have to be threaded in the same manner (535):

All the tablets requiring the same threading are put on top of each other, so that all the holes are in one line. We now take four balls of wool or yarn of the required colours and take each yarn through one series of successive holes. The ends are tied up and attached to a hook. Now the tablets have to be arranged. The first is left hanging close to the hook, the others are brought with the threads to another hook or chair, or wherever the other end of the warp is to be fastened. We then take them back to the first hook, leave the second tablet there, and continue in the same way with the other tablets.

Patterns for Tablet or Card Weaving

When we have mastered the fundamentals of tablet weaving, we can make our own patterns or discover how some old patterns were woven.

—534 Four Hole Tablet, Tablet with Centre Hole, Five Hole and Six Hole Tablets

535 A simpler Method of Threading the Tablets

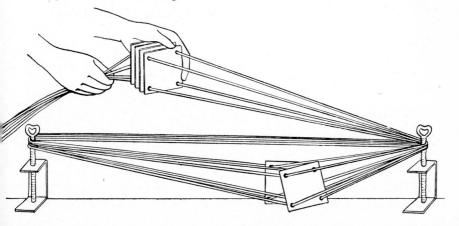

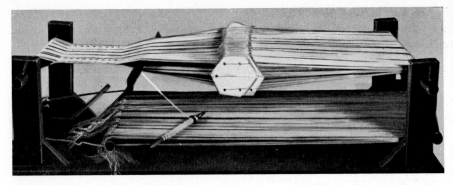

536 Reconstruction of an Old Egyptian Tablet Loom

To discover the structure of a pattern, it is best to make a drawing (see Figs. 519-524). Such drawings can give us some idea of the necessary threading of the tablets. The Arabic numerals give the number of tablets, the letters the respective hole and the diagonal strokes the run of the warp threads when the tablets are turned forward.

Key to the Patterns

Designs with figures should first be planned on paper to give us an idea how - if at all - they can be carried out.

Names were often woven into bands in the past (540). Two holes are threaded in a light colour, the other two dark. The tablets have to be turned during weaving: the required colour has always to be uppermost.

The door curtain in Fig. 539 has been woven in a plain cloth pattern on a home-made loom (560). The two wide bands give it a good finish. They were woven directly into the curtain on six-hole tablets. The weft was threaded on a needle and taken through the curtain while weaving the bands.

Tablet weaving is not easy and requires more time than weaving on a heddle reed. But its possibilities will thrill anyone who has really attempted it seriously.

WEAVING ON A LOOM AND MAKING OUR OWN LOOM

It is best to acquire a proper loom for weaving larger pieces.

MAKING A LOOM

The frame can either be made with hoops (544) or with wing screws.

A Frame with Hoops

We shall need:

a) Two wooden rods - a broomstick will do - for the warp beam and the cloth beam.

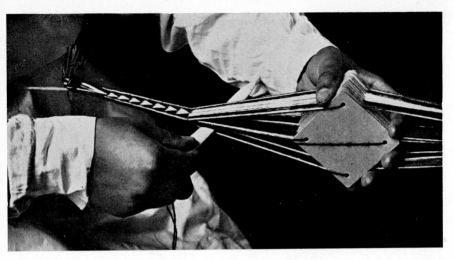

537 Tablet Weaving with Double Shed

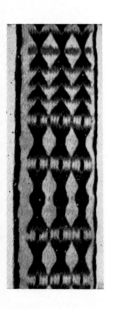

538 (left) A Wide Band, woven on Tablets

539 (right) Part of a Door Curtain (Tablet Weaving combined with Cloth Weaving)

540 Woven Names

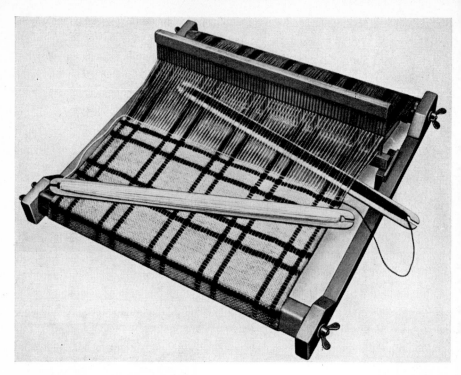

541 A Simple Loom for Use in Schools. The beams can be rotated and therefore make the setting up and beaming of the cloth much easier.

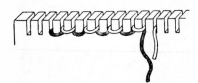

541a A method of making the ends fast

Each rod should be 26 ins. long, although it can be varied according to requirements.

b) **Two** battens (each 3 ft. long and with a cross section of 1 x ¾ in.) for the sides.

c) **Four** hoop irons (546, 547) to take the rods.

d) **Eight** wing screws for the hoop irons (545).

The rods are fastened to the ends of the battens with the hoops. The battens should be first drilled with a twist drill (1066, 1068) for the screws.

Frame with Wing Screws

We need:

a) **Two** wooden rods (see page 112).

b) **Two** battens, about 1 in. x 2 ins. across and three feet in length for the frame. Four smaller battens 1 in. x 2 ins. across and about 5 ins. long. They are bevelled at one end and are glued to the ends of the frame (550).

c) **Four** wing screws, which must be threaded like a wood screw at one end, so that they can be screwed into the rods (549). The wing screws (548) are screwed firmly into the rods, the latter having first been drilled as necessary. A pair of

542 Table Loom

543 Loom with Trestle

flat-nosed pliers will prove useful for putting in the screws. The height of the sides of the frame is raised by gluing on the four short battens at the ends. These four pieces should first have holes drilled of a size sufficient to allow the wing screws to turn easily.

MOUNTING THE WARP

This simple method involves hardly any expense: a piece of hessian, or denim, is nailed to warp beam and cloth beam respectively (551). The sides can be hemmed (not seamed); the loose ends, however, are strengthened with a firmly sewn seam. The threads are attached as follows: we spread the threads immediately behind the seam with a crochet hook and insert with the latter a bundle of between four and eight threads. We can now either put a long knitting needle through the holes, or we can cut open the threads and tie them with a reef knot (553).

We can also attach a strip of calico with eyelets to the canvas. In this case there would be no need to make the holes with a crochet needle.

HEDDLE AND HEDDLE HOLDER

Figs. 555-559 show two heddle holders. That shown in Fig. 559 consists of a piece of wood with a dowel rod, that in Fig. 555 of an iron angle, a piece of wood, a wing nut and two ordinary nuts. The loom in Fig. 560 was constructed on similar lines.

Making a reed is not easy. It is best to buy it from a handicraft shop.

544 Frame with Iron
Hoops

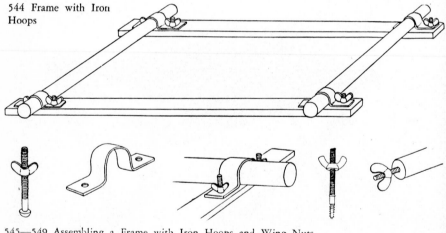

545—549 Assembling a Frame with Iron Hoops and Wing Nuts
550 Frame with Wing Nuts

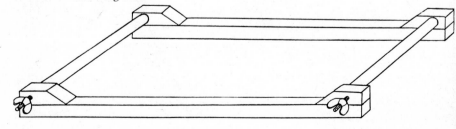

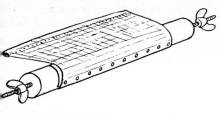

551 Attaching the Calico

552 Looping the Warp Thread

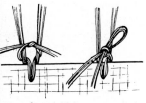

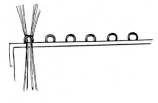

553 and 554 Tying up and threading the eyelets

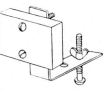
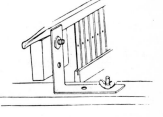

555—558 A Heddle Holder made from Angle Iron

559 A wooden Heddle Holder

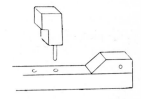

560 The Home-made Loom completed

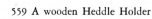
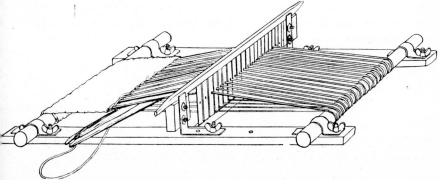

We can also use shed sticks in place of a heddle and tie the warp threads to them with loops. These are tied up with flat knots (see Figs. 429-430). The shed sticks, of course, are only used for changing the shed, and not for beating, which can be done with an ordinary fork.

The warp threads

The length of the warp threads will depend on the fabric. We add 10% plus between 16 and 20 ins. The stretch of the material must also be considered.

The number of warp threads will depend on the reed. It is best to multiply the number of inches in the required width by the number of threads per inch in the reed. We also add between five and ten per cent. for weaving in, and two threads for each selvedge. Since we shall want the selvedge to be really firm, the warp threads will be threaded double at the sides.

Mounting a short warp (between 60 and 80 ins.)

1. Shortening the Threads

A strand of yarn or wool is first re-wound between two chairs as far apart as we want the length of the warp threads. The strand is then cut at the ends.

2. Threading the Reed and attaching the Threads to the Warp Beam or Chain Roller

We put the frame on the table, place the reed into its holders and stand it upright between two books (563). We now pull the threads through the dents with a crochet hook and attach the ends to the kerfs, or hooks, in the warp beam (561) or to the piece of canvas in the case of a home-made frame (552, 553). The warp threads must run exactly parallel to the sides of the frame. If the kerfs or hooks are not exactly opposite the dents, we may have to use two threads for some of the kerfs (hooks).

3. Beaming the Warp

We shall need the help of a friend, who will hold the warp threads in front of the reed so that the tension is even on all threads. We then cover the kerfs or hooks in the batten with a strip of paper so that nothing can get tangled, and beam the warp, i.e., we turn the warp beam, so that the warp threads are wound onto it firmly and evenly.

4. Stretching the Warp Threads
(Attaching the ends of the chain to the cloth beam)

The chain having been beamed, so that the ends of the threads are about twenty inches from the reed, the warp beam is fixed in position and the ends of the threads are attached to the kerfs (or the piece of calico in a home-made loom) of the cloth beam (551-554). Now we start weaving, as described on p. 122.

118

61 Mounting the Warp

Mounting a long warp

Lengths of up to several yards can be woven on looms with rotating warp beams: we shall, however, need a set of warping posts (Fig. 562).

Our set of warping posts or warping bars will consist of three posts and three G-clamps, or, in U.S.A., C-clamps. Two chairs could be used instead (565). Two of the clamps are fastened to one table (562), the third is attached to another table some distance away. The ball of wool or yarn for the warp is then rewound by taking it round the posts, starting at point 1 and continuing as shown in Fig. 564 until we have the required number of warp threads. The threads should be tied into bundles of twenty, thirty or forty with coloured yarn to show immediately the number we have obtained. Finally, the threads are tied together loosely at each side of the cross between posts 2 and 3 (564). They are then taken from the posts and hung up by loops formed by the cross.

If we used two chairs, the length of the warp threads will be measured as if the chair legs were warping posts.

The reed has to be tied to the reed holders, before it can be threaded. We then take the warp with the cross in the left hand, pull the loop with a crochet hook through the gaps - but not the holes - of the reed and attach each loop to the warp beam, winding it first round the kerf or hook. In the case of a home-made loom we would pull two or three loops at a time through the metal eyelets or through the calico.

If the reed is not to be used in its entire length, we must take care to leave an equal number of gaps empty at each side, so that the warp should be exactly in the middle. Again, the warp threads at the sides will be taken double for the selvedge.

562 Threads crossing between Warping Posts

563 Reed in position for Threading

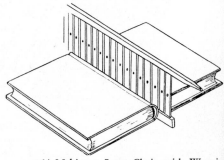

564 Making a Long Chain with Warping Posts

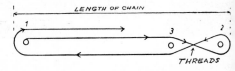

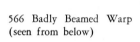

565 Chairs may be used instead of Warping Posts

566 Badly Beamed Warp (seen from below)

567 Well Beamed Warp (Seen from below)

568 Individual loose Warp Threads can be tightened with bits of paper (seen from above)

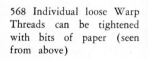

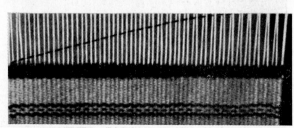

569 The Weft must be inserted loosely for a neat Selvedge

Having attached all the loops of the warp threads, we cover the kerfs, or hooks, of the warp beam with a strip of paper and wind up the warp on the warp beam, as described on page 118.

When most of the warp - except for about 20 ins. - has been beamed, we cut the strand open at the end, pull one thread out of each slot and insert it through the neighbouring hole. Finally, the threads are attached to the cloth beam (553 in the case of a home-made frame, otherwise as in 561 or 541a), taking care to stretch them equally taut.

WEAVING

The weft thread is wound round the shuttle. Now we take up the frame, place it on our lap and rest it with the back against the table. Then we press the reed down to form a shed, through which the shuttle goes from the right to the left. Then push the weft thread towards the cloth beam with the reed. Then we change the shed by raising the reed, take the shuttle through the shed from the left, press against it with the reed and continue as before.

We must put in the weft thread fairly loosely to prevent a "waist" (569). Since the weft runs through the warp in waves, and not in a straight line, the fabric would not have a straight selvedge if the thread were pulled too tightly.

The beginning and end of the warp should be woven in tabby, or plain weave, for about 1½ ins. - on the selvedge edge rather than in the centre of the textile.

If a warp thread breaks, it will have to be repaired immediately, or many others might follow. Since the ends will be too short for tying up, we shall have to tie in a new thread with a weaver's knot (414 or 474). This new thread will be fastened to the fabric with a pin, which will be removed after we have woven over the new thread a few times.

Loosening warp threads have to be tightened. Attach a suitable weight to the thread, and let it hang down behind the warp beam, and adjust it as the warp is used up in the weaving.

If we find that the shed is no longer wide enough, as a result of weaving a fairly

570 Portion of a Rag Rug

571 Mohair Shawl

572 Cushion of White Wool with interwoven tufts in raw wool

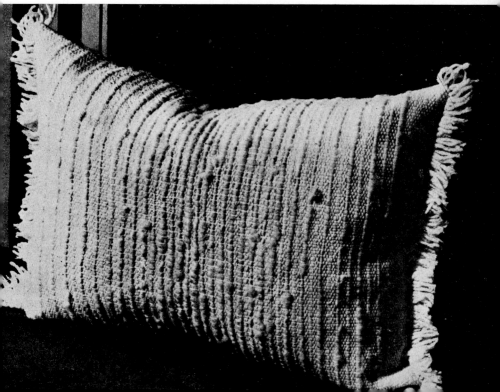

long piece of material, we loosen the warp beam slightly and wind the finished cloth round the cloth beam. It is best to insert a strip of paper between cloth beam and cloth to prevent the material from being pressed against the kerfs or hooks.

The cloth having been wound up, we can tighten the warp and continue.

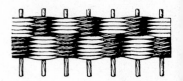

573 Two differently threaded needles produce checks

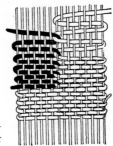 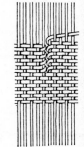

574 Tapestry weave for joining areas of different colour

575 Khelim Weave

576, 577 Different Gobelin techniques

578 Sennah knot used in Pomeranian Fishermen's rugs and Persian rugs.

579 Ghiordes knot used in Persian and Finnish rugs

 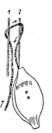

582 Weaver's Knot

583 Reef Knot

580, 581 Tying the Smyrna Knot

MATERIAL AND PATTERNS

We generally take a strong and fairly thin yarn for the warp.

Anything can be used for the weft: coloured wool, loosely spun cotton, yarn, candle-wick, wool, silk, or even - as in rag rugs - narrow strips of carpet rags.

A fine, yellow mohair was used for warp and weft for the scarf in Fig. 571. It was woven in plain cloth (tabby weave).

Fig. 490 shows a material in raw wool, drawn to a thick thread by hand and inserted in the shed. The warp is of linen thread.

The cushion (572) has a warp and weft of white wool, the ribbing in the weft was obtained by adding raw wool.

If we use two shuttles with different warp threads, we obtain a chess-board or checker board pattern: we might throw a black thread through the shed, change shed, follow with white, continue with black, and so on.

For plaids, warp and weft would be of the same material, but of different colours.

There are several ways of weaving figures or ornaments into the fabric. These are the most important.

1. Tapestry Weave, as used in Gobelins. Areas of different colours are joined (574) and the threads are usually interwoven as in Figs. 576 and 577.
2. Khelim Weave. In most - but by no means all - Khelim types of weave, the areas of different colours are not connected, but divided by narrow gaps (575). Khelim is an Arab term for a flat weave.
3. The Ghiordes Knot. The wool, wound on spindle, is tied into the warp (580, 581) and is afterwards woven into the fabric by crossing it twice with the weft.
4. The Sennah Knot (578, 579). This technique was also used for so-called Ostsee Fischer Teppiche, i.e., rugs made by the fishermen of the Baltic coast. Indeed weaving - now so often considered a craft primarily for girls - was at one time practised almost exclusively by men, as were knitting and many kinds of needle work.

All the techniques described above came originally from Persia and the Near East.

Further Possibilities

When we have become properly acquainted with weaving techniques and have made some really lovely things, we may want to possess a large loom for weaving bed spreads or rugs. Few things can be more rewarding.

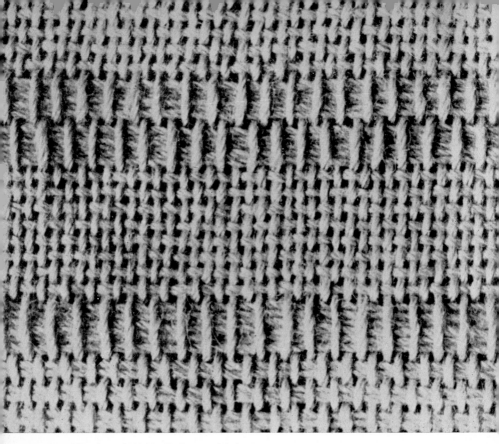

584 Portion of the Scarf illustrated below

585 Woollen Scarf, made on the Loom shown in 541

586 Rug in the manner of the Pomeranian Fishermen's Rugs

587 A Study in Texture

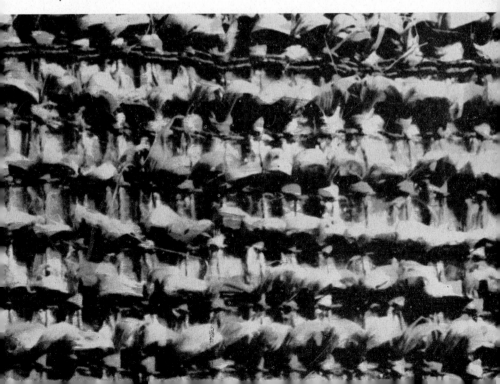

588 Basket in Broom and Raffia

589 A Useful Work Basket

Plaiting in RAFFIA, RUSHES and STRAW

When men were still living close to Nature, they made almost everything from the plants around them. Baskets, shoes, etc., were all made from rushes, reeds, cane, roots, bark or twigs. The willow provided the material for bow and arrow or wattle for fences and walls. Plaiting with raffia or cane belongs to the earliest forms of human activity. We can find many examples in museums and can draw a lot of inspiration from them. The work of the Red Indians is particularly beautiful: each tribe has its own designs.

Materials and their preliminary treatment

Raffia

Our native bast (the soft, fibrous layer between bark and wood) was formerly taken almost exclusively from willows and limes. It was short, of poor quality and scarcely used. The more beautiful raffia bast came with the development of overseas trade. It is made of the ribs of the leaves of the raffia palm, which grows in Madagascar. Raffia is soft, supple and very tough. There are two kinds. The superior white raffia is made in wide, firm strands, about 70 ins. in length; the cheaper, yellowish kind is not quite so supple and does not wear so well. Raffia is generally used in a dry state. We might damp the hand slightly to make it look better. But we must realise that the raffia shrinks when it dries and that the nice appearance would therefore not last long. Raffia can be bought in its natural colour - as used in the garden - or dyed. Dyeing is not difficult, but not worth while unless we do it for large quantities.

Maize Leaves and Maize Straw or Corn

Maize leaves are strong and durable and look well. We use the yellowish-white leaves close to the cob. The innermost ones are the best. They are removed during the harvest and must be dried properly, or they will get musty. Some of the leaves will be left on the cob, so that it can be hung up for drying. These will dry out evenly and can be used without any further treatment. The others are spread out in the sun to dry as quickly as possible. They will then retain their pleasant colour and will last indefinitely, if we keep them in a dry place where the air can get at them.

The individual leaves are between eight and twelve inches long. Sometimes they are used in their entire width, but generally they are split into three or four narrow strips, as shown in Fig. 592. They should be slightly damped before use and wrapped in a cloth to make them soft and supple.

Such strips can be made into long plaits, which can be used for bags, table mats and rather hard-wearing and goodlooking shoes. Maize leaves can also be knotted, as shown on page 147. Mats, bread baskets, fruit baskets and rope soles can be made in this manner.

Straw

After once using straw, we shall always want to use it again. The blades must have any remaining leaves stripped off and should be soaked in cold water for eight to twenty hours or in hot water for ten to twenty minutes.

Straw is ideal for making quite a lot of things, such as the basket shown in Fig. 643, with its thick coils of straw, held together with raffia. We can also make dolls, windmills or animals from straw. It can even be used for inlaid work in the manner of marquetry.

Ordinary, unthreshed straw can be used for braiding; threshed straw will be taken for coarser work and for stiffening. If we want to make slippers, mats, etc., we will first plait thick braids of three strands. These are afterwards sewn together. For fairly thin table mats, we shall use plaits made of several strands. These are flatter and therefore more suitable for this purpose.

Italian straw hats are made from a special wheat straw. It is grown for no other purpose and is harvested before it ripens.

Rushes or Cat O'Nine Tails

We find rushes near ditches, rivers and marshes. They are soft and supple and therefore suitable for plaiting. Since they will float on water, they can be made into all kinds of floating toys, such as ducks, divers, swans, rafts or boats. The baskets, used by German children for gathering all kinds of berries in the woods, are also made of rushes. They can even be plaited into skipping ropes.

The best kind of rush grows to a height of between four and ten feet. It has little brown flowers near the top. The shorter kinds can also be used, although not to the same extent.

Rushes are usually cut in July, when they have grown sufficiently tall, but not yet woody. But we can still use them, if cut later. We shall merely have to sort out those that have become too tough.

Although rushes can be used immediately after cutting, it is not advisable since they shrink considerably. They should be dried in the sun and stored where the air can get at them. To make them soft and pliable for use, they should be soaked for ten minutes and left under a cloth for about twenty-four hours to allow the water to penetrate. Although we must not use them too dry, we must also not use them entirely wet, as they would shrink too much.

Chip and Palm Fibre

Thin strips of wood, as used for baskets, are called chip. Chip mostly comes from the trembling poplar, but also from the conifer and the lime. We can also make it ourselves by planing the slightly damp wood along the grain. The chips should be kept between damp rags to remain supple. Palm fibre (672) is very hard-

590 Weaving a Raffia Mat in Africa

wearing and has many uses. It can be plaited like chip or wound with raffia. It does generally not have to be soaked.

Willows

Although willows exist in great variety, both as shrubs and trees, only one species called osiers *(Salix viminalis)* is grown for basket making. It is cultivated in special beds along rivers. The willows are planted as cuttings. Once established, the shoots are cut annually between the end of October and February, when the sap is at its lowest. The twigs are dried but they are soaked immediately before use.

The shoots are used as follows:

1. Brown, unpeeled, as for fruit and fish baskets (770).
2. Peeled, for bread baskets, laundry baskets, etc.
3. Split and peeled for more intricate work.

Willows do not need soaking, if they are used immediately after cutting. Otherwise, green twigs are soaked for about a fortnight, peeled twigs from three to four days. They are best left to soak in a rain water butt or in a ditch. In smaller quantities we can wrap them in some damp sacking like rushes. They should be slightly damped from time to time.

Bullrushes, Birch Twigs, Broom

We can use all kinds of other plants not yet mentioned. Birch twigs will plait very well, especially in spring. Small bowls and baskets (588) can be made from broom: hazel twigs used as stakes and wound with rushes will also make attractive baskets. Split into strips, they can be used for the most intricate plaiting. Even roots, especially those of conifers, can be made into baskets. Bullrushes (cat o'nine tails) too, have their uses. Thus we can see some possibility in every natural material.

131

PLAITING

591 Plaiting in Raffia

Since raffia, rushes and straw are very soft and supple, they can easily be plaited. Such plait can be made into mats for the table, walls or floor, small baskets, shoes, cushions or toy animals.

There are two kinds of plait: three-plait, made as we would plait hair, and plait made of any number of strands. The first is thick and almost round, the second rather flat, like braid.

Each material requires different treatment before it can be worked. The exact methods are given on pages 129 to 131 and must be strictly observed.

We first tie the strands or rushes to a hook or door handle. This leaves the hands free to tug at the strands with equal strength. We can also start as shown in Figs. 593a/b or 611. The result is a neat plait that does not have to be sewn, although this largely depends on material and purpose.

The strands for plaiting should not be of the same length, so that the joins do not occur in the same places. To make a plait of sufficient length and thickness, pieces have to be added as soon as it shows signs of getting thinner. The new material is always added at the thickest point and the new pieces should be distributed as evenly as possible. The ends are left sticking out (593c) and are trimmed when the material has dried.

SIMPLE THREE-PLAIT

Plaiting with Strips of Maize (called sweet corn or Indian corn)

Having damped and wrapped them in a cloth as described on page 130, we take the broad, white maize leaves, cut off their hard wooden ends and split each leaf

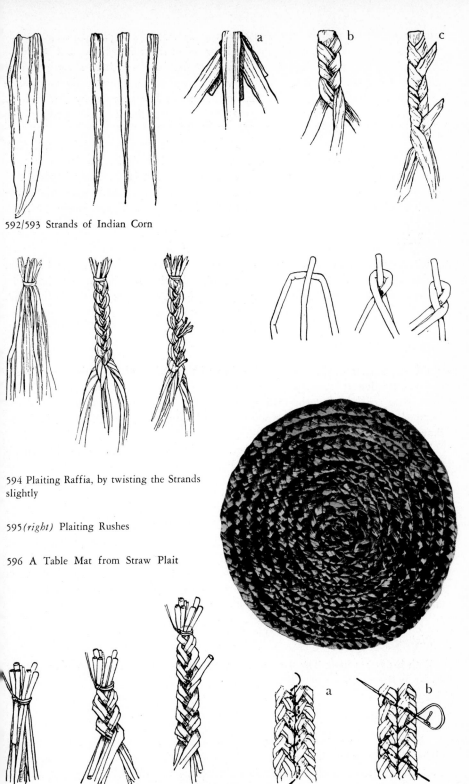

592/593 Strands of Indian Corn

594 Plaiting Raffia, by twisting the Strands slightly

595 *(right)* Plaiting Rushes

596 A Table Mat from Straw Plait

597 and 598 Plaiting Straw and sewing Straw Plait

into three or four narrow strips, as shown in Fig. 592. The plait is usually made from three strips, although we can double or treble this number. To start, the ends are bundled, or - as in Fig. 593a - slightly turned under to have everything neat and tidy from the very beginning. New strips are added as regularly as possible and always at the thick end. The plait can be made like an ordinary hair plait. It will look better, and will also be stronger, if we turn the strands slightly during plaiting, as shown in Fig. 594.

Raffia is smooth and supple, even when dry. It is therefore best left untreated, since damping will merely make it curl. If it should really be too dry, it is quite enough to touch it during plaiting with damp hands. It is extremely important to add at the thick part, or the individual strands will split and cause an uneven plait. Again, we get a better result if we twist the strands, as shown in Fig. 594.

Rushes

We begin as shown in Fig. 595. The plait is made as round, as thick and as tight as possible. Very thick rushes can be slit with the thumb nail. The air should be squeezed out. It is best to work with the right hand, while the left holds the plait, with the thumb pressed hard against the uppermost strand.

Straw

The straw is bundled together and tied to a hook. While plaiting, the straw should be creased where it is turned inwards, to give a clean edge for easy sewing (597). New straw is inserted at the thick end, is left to project for nearly an inch and is trimmed after drying. Suitable straw can also be plaited into all kinds of braid, as shown on pages 135 to 136.

There are many ways of sewing plait. Usually, the thread is drawn through alternating strands of each plait (598a). Fig. 598b shows a different method, where the thread goes through the entire plait.

Plait of several strands

A flat type of plait of many strands can be made of raffia, rushes, coloured yarn, etc. It can be used for making bags, hats, belts, shoes, tea cosies or various kinds of mats. Such plait will go round any shape, in contrast to braid. It is always sewn along the edges. Plait of this kind can be made in different ways. Strands can be taken right across or merely as far as the middle.

Plaiting towards the Centre

Both hands are used. The two outer strands are used in turn, but are only brought as far as the middle, where they cross (599).

Diagonal Plaiting

The strand on the extreme right is taken across to the left. Only the right hand plaits, the left holds the previous strand, so that the entire fabric can be clearly seen. When one strand has been brought across, the left hand bends it sharply round the next, and holds this in turn (600).

134

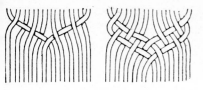

599 Plaiting towards the Centre

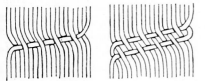

600 Plaiting across

601 A plait with several strands

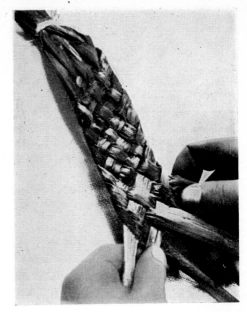

Joining

As described under "Plaiting with Raffia" above.

A plait of several strands can also be finished as in Fig. 603, i.e., the ends can simply be pushed back.

STRAW PLAIT

Only the best pieces of unthreshed straw are used for plait. Again, we do not use an entire straw, but only the *smooth part* between two knots (generally the section below the last knot). Having cut out the suitable portions of the straws, we remove all traces of leaf and sort our straws according to size. Sorting is very necessary, since the straws for really good and even plait must be of the same thickness.

The straws must be soaked in cold water between six and eight hours or in hot water for ten minutes before plaiting. They are then soft and supple.

602 and 603 Adding and Pushing the Ends in

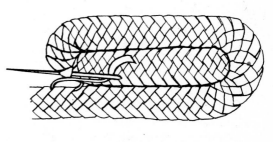

604 Sewing up a plait of several strands

605 Types of Straw Plait

We always plait straw *away* from us, in contrast to raffia, since bending the straws carefully at a right angle and pressing them hard against each other is easier that way and matters more than pulling them tightly.

We first flatten the straws and then crease them immediately as required (611, 613), so that our work should be neat from the very start. The ends should not be of the same length, so that new straws will not all be added in the same place.

The most important things about straw plait are care and accuracy. Edges must be neat, the straw must always be creased at the same angle and the plait must be made as tightly as possible, because the straws shrink after drying and thus cause the fabric to loosen.

Adding new straws: the thick end of the new straw is added to the thin end of the old. It should cover the latter and project by about ¾ in. Now we plait three times with both straws, before continuing with the new straw only. The ends are trimmed after drying. It is important to have the points where new straws are added fairly evenly distributed.

For sewing straw plait together see Fig. 604, for plaiting round a corner Figs. 606-610, for joining plait with jagged edges Fig. 612.

Straw can be bought in most handcraft shops.

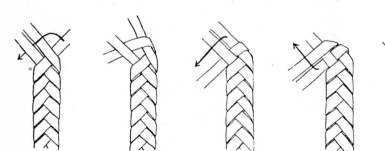

606-610 Three-Plait, forming a Corner

136

611 Flat Seven-Plait

612 Joining Plait with Jagged Edges

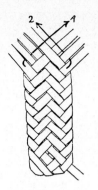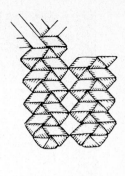

613—617 Four-Plait

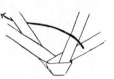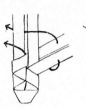

SHOES FROM RAFFIA

The soles for the light sandals (618) were made of plait, the toe straps and the heels were woven in raffia, the ends of the straps with the button holes were plaited (624).

We first draw a pattern for the soles, sew the sole for each shoe (619) and make in addition a smaller sole and a separate heel for each shoe. The plait is sewn flat, except for the heel. Before the extra portions for heel and sole can be fixed, we must weave the uppers. These were made on a heddle reed in the case of our sandals, but can also be made on a frame. The part round the heel will be woven as a short and comparatively wide strip. The end with the button can be hemmed or sewn up (624). The ends of the side where the strap is to be are partly sewn up and partly plaited to from the strap. To make such a plait of several strands is described in the previous chapter. If the strap is long enough, we can plait in the button hole (625). The plait has to be split into two smaller plaits for this purpose. Their ends are tied up and the projecting threads are cut off.

The portions with the strap and the band for the toes - having been woven earlier on - are now sewn to the outside of the long sole with raffia (623); we then sew on the separate sections of the soles and the heels.

SHOES FROM MAIZE STRAW

Shoes from maize straw are comfortable and look well (632). They are supple, cool and hard-wearing. If the soles wear out, we simply sew on another pair. Apart from maize leaves, we shall need material for lining, a strong yarn (preferably hemp

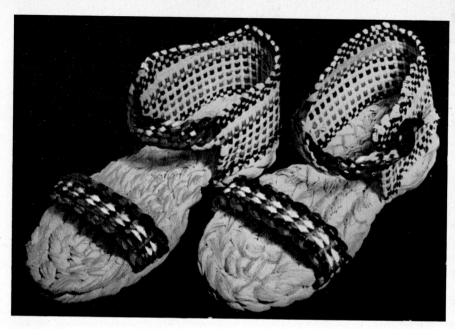

618 Raffia Sandals

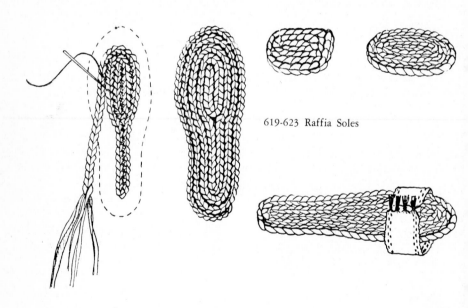

619-623 Raffia Soles

624—625 Portion for the Heel and Strap

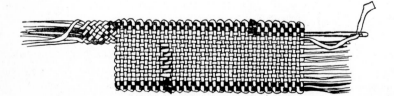

thread or some other strong thread), a pair of wooden heels, "Copytex", "Uhu" or similar adhesive for sticking on the heels, a curved cobbler's needle and some wooden lasts. Old solid wooden shoe trees can sometimes be bought from the cobbler and will be quite adequate for our purpose.

First we make a long plait from strips of maize leaves, as described on page 132. It is best made as three-plait, each leaf having been split into three. We shall need between 6½ and 8½ yds. per shoe. Having made the plait, the lining is stretched on the last. We simply place the last on the material (the warp must run diagonally

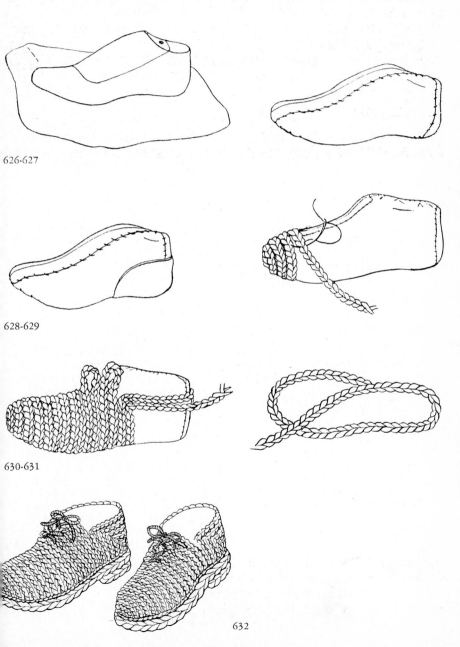

626-627

628-629

630-631

632

139

to the foot), mould this round the last and start sewing. The fabric must lie quite flat where the seams are to be. We then sew the edges of the fabric together very lightly (627). The heel can be reinforced with cardboard (628). Then we sew on the plait. This can be done in different ways.

The most common method is shown in Fig. 629. We begin sewing slightly below the tip, taking the plait round all the time. The rounds must be carefully sewn to each other and to the lining at the same time. The stitches - provided they are regular and we are using a natural-coloured yarn - need not be invisible.

When we come to the instep, we no longer take the plait round, but turn it down so as to form loops, which will later take shoe laces. Fig. 630 gives some indication of the way it is done. In reality the plait is proportionately thinner than in the drawing so that we shall have to make four loops on each side instead of two (632). Fig. 630 shows how the plait is brought across the heel. The lining is turned in at the top before starting the heel to have a clean edge from the start.

Attaching the Sole

We sew on a piece of three-plait while the shoe is still on the last, thus forming a narrow, visible edge (632). The shoe is then joined to the running sole by this edge, like any welt-sewn leather shoe. The running sole itself is made as shown in so that we shall have to make four loops on each side instead of two (632). Fig. 630 shows how the plait is brought across the heel. The lining is turned in at stitches along the middle.

WINDING WITH RAFFIA

This technique consists in rolling up strands of raffia, rushes, straw or cane and in tying these up with thread, raffia, split cane, hazel twigs, etc.

We must know how to use different materials. Raffia or dried rushes normally require no further treatment. But if rushes have become too dry, we damp them slightly, and leave them covered with a wet rag for the night. Newly cut rushes - always fairly damp - must be squeezed tightly before use and sewn very firmly. Straw should be soaked a little in hot water to make it more supple. Cane must also be soaked very thoroughly.

USING A SOFT BASE, i.e., RAFFIA, RUSHES, BROOM OR STRAW

Fruit Basket, Bread Basket and Waste Paper Basket

We take three or four rushes (or a bundle of straw, raffia, etc.) and wrap some thread or raffia - threaded previously on a strong needle - round it (634). The wrapped part is bent and sewn together like a button or a snail (635). We continue sewing, always twisting the rushes, straw, etc., slightly as we go.

Although the coil can thicken a little immediately after starting, it must not get any thinner and we must add to it whenever there are the slightest signs of this happening.

633 Flat Basket (for sewing see 637)

We can sew in different ways. Fig. 637 shows how the fruit basket (633) was made. We must always go through the same hole twice, exactly above the stitch underneath. Then we leave an interval of slightly under half an inch and continue sewing. Additional stitches will have to be inserted after some time, since the gaps would otherwise become larger as the basket takes shape. These new stitches should be made after every second or third double stitch.

We can also simply take the thread round the coil after each stitch for about half an inch and omit the extra stitches. It will be quicker that way, but we must be careful, or the basket will be no credit to us. The waste paper basket in Fig. 643 was made like that over a straw coil.

Another stitch was used for the basket made over a coil of broom (588). Here we have to go three times through the same hole. The third thread from one stitch always crosses the first of the next, thus keeping to the characteristic diagonal position (640).

The same stitch is generally used throughout. A fruit basket will be sewn from the inside, a waste paper basket - since we are more likely to look at it that way - from the outside.

Finally, we allow the coil to get gradually thinner towards the end so that the last two layers can be joined almost invisibly (638).

In the case of straw, we sometimes work through a leather ring (639) to obtain an even thickness. The straw should also be damped with hot water to make it more supple.

We can also make a rope from straw to avoid adding while working. This rope consists of straws, held together by thread. It must, of course, be of even thickness. Split cane or willow, etc., can be used to hold the coils in position in place of raffia or thread. They would have to be soaked a little, except for the point, which must be sharpened. The cane, etc., is alternately taken round the coil and through the previous layer. The hole should be marked with a bradawl to make piercing easier. In other respects we work as we would with raffia or thread.

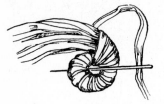

634—636 Wrapping over a soft base

637 Sewing (see also 633)

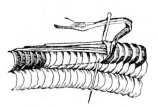

638 The Last Coil

639 Using a Leather Ring

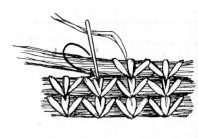

640 Another Type of Stitch (see also 588)

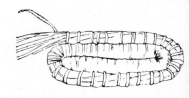

641—642 The first Stitches in an oval Mat

142

Doll's Pram

The doll's pram (644) has been made with natural raffia over straw. Figs. 641 and 642 show how such an oval shape is obtained. Two small pieces of wood were fitted to the inside to take the axles. If these are attached with raffia or thread - instead of screws - we shall have to cut grooves into the wood.

A Shopping Basket from Straw

This basket is extremely handy. It is made rather like the doll's pram and the waste

643 A Waste Paper Basket

paper basket, i.e. the straw rope is only closely wound with raffia on the first and on the last coil. We generally let the straw show in between. Raffia of several

644 A Doll's Pram from Straw and Raffia

645 Shopping - or Knitting - Basket

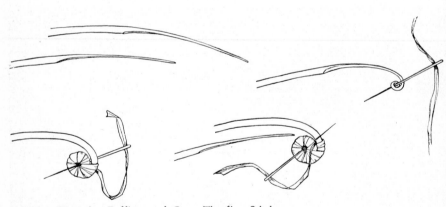

646—650 Wrapping Raffia round Cane. The first Stitches

651 (*right*) Another type of Stitch

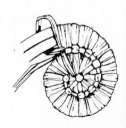

652 Raffia on Cane: Flat Baskets

colours has been used. Figs. 641 and 642 show how to start. The handle consists of thick raffia plait and is fitted to the sides very firmly.

RAFFIA WINDING ON A HARD BASE SUCH AS CANE

We can work over one or over two canes.

The ends of the cane - or canes - are first trimmed diagonally for about 2 inches and then softened for a few minutes in warm water. We then continue as shown in Figs. 647 and 648, leaving a small hole in the centre, add the second cane (649) and start sewing (650). The thread is guided as if we were drawing a figure eight round the first two coils of cane. Having made two stitches in this manner, we can wind the thread round the cane two or three times before we continue sewing. This pattern is repeated throughout: first two stitches, then winding, more stitches, etc. Otherwise we work as we would in the case of raffia or straw.

Patterns can be introduced by changing the colour of the thread or the type of stitch. We can even work with several differently coloured threads at the same time. Each is threaded separately; one is used for sewing, the others are taken along with it. Fig. 651 shows another stitch suitable for cane.

KNOTTING WITH MAIZE LEAVES

(CORN LEAVES)

Since maize leaves are very short, we cannot use them for wrapping like raffia, rushes or straw. But they can be knotted or tied into mats, baskets or soles without any sewing.

A mat or basket (662) is made as follows. The leaves are prepared and damped as described on page 129. Then we take one leaf, make it into a loop (653) and hook five or six strips of maize into it (654). Now we begin to knot, as shown in Figs. 655 to 660. After the first round, we insert more leaves, which are now knotted in (661). Since the round will be bigger, we have to increase. This means that we usually shall have to put two strips into each hole. Then we continue knotting all the way round. The hole for inserting the leaf can first be marked with a matchstick. It is also advisable only to put in a few leaves at first for the bigger rounds and to knot these together immediately.

The sides are made as in wrapping, i.e. the strips are not taken round the outside any longer, but are tightened a little and placed diagonally on the last layer.

Finally, we decrease gradually and cut out as many leaves as necessary to make the last layer level with the edge.

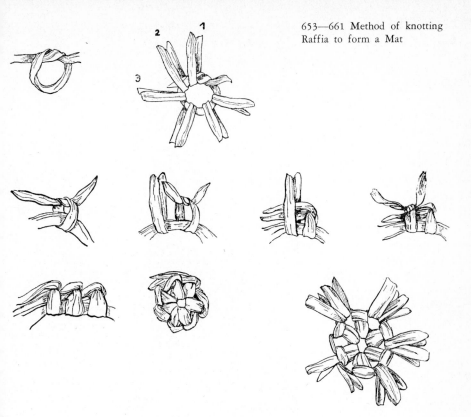

662
Basket made of
Indian Corn leaves

147

NETTING
WITH
RAFFIA

663 Knotted Raffia Net

The plant holder for the wall (664) is useful and beautiful because it does not push itself forward. It merely serves flower and flower pot. It can be made as follows:

Four - in the case of larger flower pots we would take eight - strands of raffia are arranged crossways and knotted together. The knot is then pinned through the centre to a cushion or a table and the threads are tied as shown in Fig. 667. The distance from the centre knot is roughly 2¾ ins. (smaller, if we use more raffia). We now take the ends and tie them for a second time. This process is repeated a third time. Finally, we put first the saucer and then the flower pot on the net, and knot the threads together closely above the pot. The loop is formed by the ends.

A Raffia Net

A raffia net is easy to make and useful for keeping coloured yarn, or rags, etc., since we can see the colours at once.

We first knot the ends of the raffia so as to obtain a loop between eight and twelve inches long. This is fastened to a chair with a second loop (423). Now we pull between ten and twenty threads of raffia halfway through this loop (424). The raffia threads are then simply looped in twos with the knot shown in Fig.

664 A Plant Holder

425. The knots should be between one and one and a half inches apart. The threads are tied together with a strand of raffia when the net is long enough. It is advisable to tie up two or three strands to keep the net in position. The thread at the top is then pulled out (423) and replaced with a firm raffia rope, which can be twisted or plaited.

RAFFIA WEAVING AND RAFFIA FABRIC

Raffia is very suitable for weaving. We can find many examples of raffia weaving in museums. The craft is highly developed in Africa and in the South Sea Islands. The only difficulty in raffia weaving is the length of the threads. They are at the

665—668

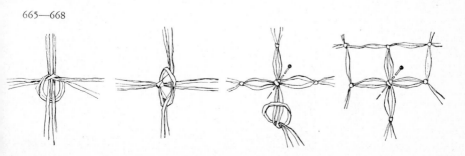

most only between 70 and 80 ins. long and therefore limit the size of any fabric.

Raffia fabric is a good looking material and can be bought ready made. There are two grades, coarse and fine. Table mats are usually made of the finer kind, the coarser type can be bought by the yard in many widths.

We should allow quite a bit for the seam when cutting raffia fabric. Between $\frac{1}{2}$ and $\frac{3}{4}$ in. should be added for the seam, which should be oversewn to about $\frac{1}{4}$ in. The projecting thread is cut off at the end. A paper pattern should be used before cutting out.

A Work Basket

The basket and lining should be cut (669, 589) to allow for the seam. The edges are turned back and tacked on immediately, the inside pockets are sewn on in the same material as the lining - the material for the pocket is taken in double thickness - raffia fabric and lining are sewn together, and the four sides of the bag are reinforced with cardboard. The inner cardboard lining will have been cut out according to the pattern and is simply pushed in. Now all we have to do is to attach the two narrow panels (B) with over-sewing stitches (the two flaps are not reinforced) to connect the two large panels at the top with a strip of fabric, and to sew on the handles, which are also made of raffia fabric.

A Bag for Newspapers

For pattern see Figs. 670-671. We shall need:

a) Raffia Fabric: one piece 21 ins. x 30 ins. (as cover for A), two pieces 13 x 9 ins. (for the side panels).

b) Cardboard: one piece 16 x 26 ins. (for the bottom and the two side panels), one piece 16 x 8 ins. (for the partition).

c) Wax Cloth (oil cloth) one piece 17 x 17¾ ins. (for the partition), two pieces 15 x 18 ins. (for the lining, the sides and the bottom), two pieces 11¼ x 7¼ (for the end panels).

The cardboard (A) is first marked with a knife along the dotted line and bent. It is then covered with raffia fabric, which is turned round the edges and stuck on with Uhu, Polywog, etc. The cardboard must be folded into its final shape before we can cover it, or the piece of raffia fabric would stretch too much. The two pieces of wax cloth or oil-cloth are turned in at the edges and are sewn on with cross stitches.

The pieces of wax cloth are then lightly glued to the sides of the partition. We only now line the latter. The wax cloth is glued on as shown in Fig. 670. The smaller panels are made separately - i.e. lined neatly, etc. - and are only then attached with cross stitches to the main portion. The handle consists of a thick raffia plait.

669 A and B Pattern for Work Basket   670 Section through a Reading Case
671 A - C Pattern for the Reading Case

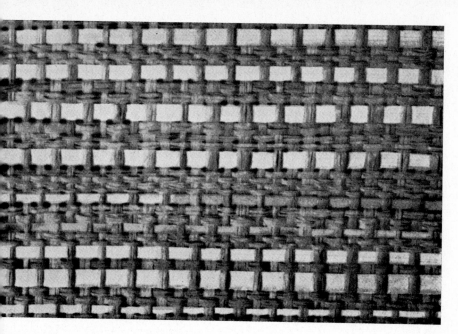

572 Natural Raffia used with Palm Fibre

673 Bag for Newspapers

674 Raffia mats

675 Book Covers

676 Round Raffia Mats

Book Jackets

Both book jackets (675) have one pocket for the front cover. The book jacket on the right has a lined pocket, the back cover is held in position with a loop of raffia fabric.

The other jacket is unlined and therefore very light and flat. The fabric is simply turned round the back cover. The edges have been closely oversewn with natural raffia.

Round Raffia Mats

We first draw a circle, about an inch more in diameter than the mat, and pierce it at the sides at intervals of ⅜ to ¾ in. The cardboard disc is then cut out along the holes. These can now be enlarged slightly (unnecessary if we have used a punch) as shown in Fig. 678. Now we set up a raffia "warp" (677). The raffia used for this

	678	679	680
ting the Warp	Starting to Weave	Sewing up the ends	Weaving with a Wooden Ring

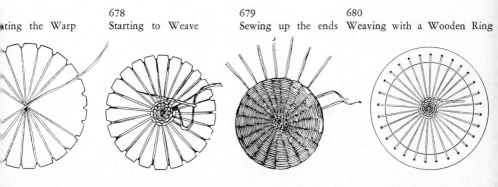

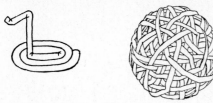

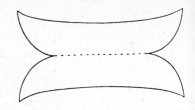

681—682 A Duck and a Ball from Rushes

683 Pattern for the Bark Canoe

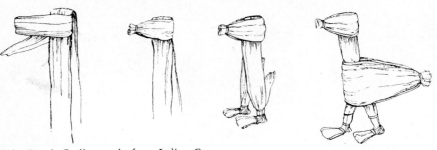

684—687 A Gosling made from Indian Corn

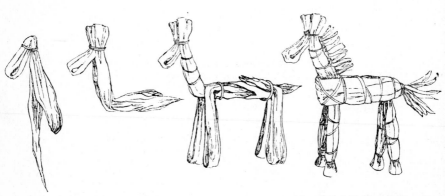

688—691 A Horse of Indian Corn

692—694 A Doll of Indian Corn

purpose should not be too wide. We start at the back, leaving the thread hanging from the centre, bring it to the front and continue until the entire loom is set up.

When the warp is ready, we can start weaving. We bring the thread to the middle and work as we would when darning. The needle moves along a spiral, going alternately above and below the warp threads. Finally, the warp is cut off at the back of the disc and the ends are cleaned up (679) by pushing each thread into the adjoining section with a darning needle.

Patterns can be obtained by changing the colours or - in case of an even number of warp threads - by using two differently threaded needles.

Two raffia mats can be made into a handkerchief case. They can be given a pattern as described above.

SIMPLE TOYS

A Duck Family and a Ball

These ducks can really swim! A duck is quickly made. Fig. 681 shows how it is done: we bend a rush for the beak and crease it again as shown. The end is simply tucked in or pinned together with a little twig. Ships or rafts can be made similarly.

A ball from rushes (682) is strong and bouncy and can also float. We merely roll some rushes into a ball and tuck the ends in.

A Horse from Maize Straw

We fold a maize leaf as shown in Fig. 688 and tie off the head. Then we add a folded maize leaf for the ears (the loop must project at the top) and tie it off again (689). The thread (raffia or darning cotton) is then taken round the neck (not too tightly), and used for tying the legs into position (690). Now we wrap one or two thick maize leaves tightly round the body, tie off the tail and knot a few pieces of thread into the neck for the mane.

A Doll

We arrange a large and a small maize leaf as shown in Fig. 692. Then we tie off head, chest, arms and legs, as shown in Fig. 693 - if the doll is meant to be a girl - and add a skirt of maize leaves and a hat from maize plait.

A Little Goat from Raffia

We make this little goat (700) from a few bundles of raffia thread. It is not much different from the horse shown in Figs. 688 to 690. We wrap raffia round the basic form and attach the loops for horns and tail and sew on nose and eyes. Finally we give the goat a few dark spots by tying in some wisps of dark raffia.

A Gosling

Two maize leaves, one large and one small, are arranged as shown in Fig. 684. We then tie off the beak (685) and feet (686). Then we tie a maize leaf between neck and legs for the body, cover it with another, very wide leaf, and tie off the tail (687).

A Horse from Raffia

These horses were made as shown in Fig. 698. We need three short raffia plaits and three pieces of wire of the necessary length. Wire and plaits are then wound tightly with ordinary raffia. The individual parts are bent and sewn together. Fig. 699 shows how the coloured manes were made.

American Indian Canoes from Bark

These canoes from the bark of the birch are copies of old American Indian boats. They can swim beautifully and are still popular toys amongst Indian children. The joins are held together with resin in the case of real canoes.

696 Canoes from Bark

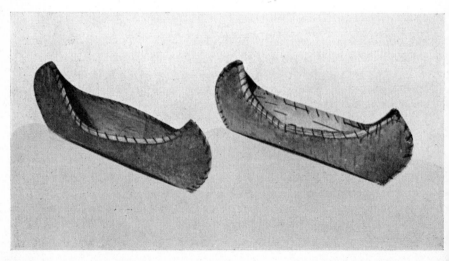

697 Raffia Horses

Our small boats were cut out from bark. They are lightly glued together and sewn with large stitches in thin raffia. The edges are reinforced with strips of wood, twigs, roots, etc., of about ¼ in. in width. These pieces of wood - also attached with large stitches - follow the curve of the boats on the outside but are straight on the inside. A very thin piece of wood is sewn in at the same time to form the seat. It will also stretch the side a little and thus give the boat more shape.

698 How to make a raffia horse
699 The mane

700 A little Goat

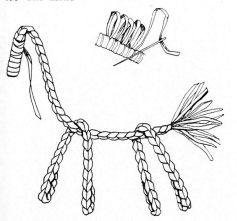

701 A simple Bread-or Fruit-Basket with a two-rod three-stroke Plaited Border

703 (*opposite page*) Making a Cane Base

702 A Basket with an Open Border

BASKETRY

CANE AND REEDS

TOOLS AND MATERIALS

Cane is the core of the cane or rattan palm *(Calamus rotang)*. The rattan palm is not a tree, but a climbing plant, whose shoots can grow up to a length of 600 feet. It grows mainly in the Indian Archipelago. After the leaves and thorns have been peeled off, a glossy surface remains. This is in turn removed by machine and used for chair seats. The pulp, or centre cane, is cut to different thicknesses by cylindrical machines. The waste is used for matting, ropes, and stuffing for furniture.

Cane, or reed, is sold in various diameters. They are numbered up to size twelve and are then described according to diameter (see Fig. 704).

We shall need a strong knitting needle, or, better still, a bodkin or awl and a sharp knife. A pair of pruning shears is desirable, but not essential. A pair of ordinary pincers might be enough.

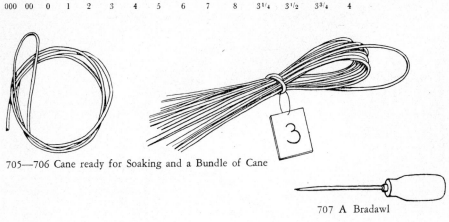

704
Size of Cane

000 00 0 1 2 3 4 5 6 7 8 3¼ 3½ 3¾ 4

705—706 Cane ready for Soaking and a Bundle of Cane

707 A Bradawl

PREPARING THE CANE

We must keep cane bundled according to thickness so that the pieces of cane form a loop at the top (706). A label with the appropriate number should be attached to each bundle. Each piece of cane is simply pulled out from the looped end.

We always take two different thicknesses for plaiting, a thick cane for the frame or stakes, a thinner kind for the sides. Thin cane merely has to be damped, thick cane has to be left soaking for between ten and twenty minutes. Long soaking spoils the cane and makes it grey and brittle.

The pieces used for staking are not soaked at first, because they should make a firm structure. They are only soaked for raising or when they are plaited into the border.

Staining

Small quantities are best bought already stained. Larger quantities can be stained with any of the numerous stains sold either liquid or in powder form. We must make quite sure which stains we use, since some of them are not waterproof. The cane should be soaked in warm water before staining.

THE FIRST STEPS

Base and Table Mat

It is best to start with a simple table mat. It is made like the base of a basket and instructions for both will therefore be found on the following pages.

We take eight and a half pieces of No. 5 cane about 12 ins. long for the table mat, (and for the basket between ½ in. and ¾ in. longer than its diameter). Four of the canes are slit with a sharp knife in the middle of the length and the other four and a half canes are pushed through the slits. The half cane is necessary, because we need an odd number of stakes. The canes will now form a cross (710).

708 Mats with Open Border

A well-soaked piece of No. 2 cane is now inserted (711), and plaited from right to left over four stakes, under four, over four and again under four; this progress is repeated once more. We then turn the base over (713) and divide the stakes into groups of two by weaving over two stakes at a time (715). The half stake is done separately (716).

We continue like this for from twelve to sixteen rounds, until the gaps are large enough to plait round each stake separately.

Great care must be taken to keep the gaps equal. We can use a knitting needle or an awl for this purpose.

The rows must be pressed together closely with the fingers of the left hand after each round (703).

When adding more cane, the old and the new piece are made to cross behind a stake (722). The ends are not trimmed until the work is completed and has dried.

If the mat has a diameter of between five and six inches, the ends are tucked in close to the next stake.

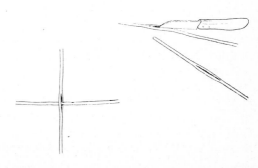

709 Slitting the Cane

710 Forming a Cross for the Base

We have now made our first step in basketry. Our next piece will be the bread basket shown on page 158. We can miss the next pages and turn to page 168, where all the basic processes for making a basket are explained. We shall now deal with the different techniques of making borders and bases.

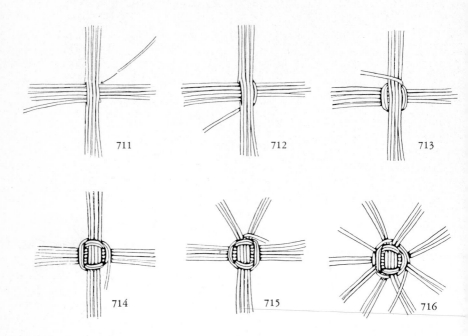

711—716 Starting to weave

TECHNIQUES

Fig. 717 Randing or Making Strips

The simplest method, generally used for weaving with a single cane on an odd number of stakes. The cane is taken alternately over and under the stakes. For randing using an even number of stakes, we use two canes, one for the first and one for the second row; use the first cane for the third row and the second cane for the fourth row (718).

Fig. 719 Slewing

This is merely another form of randing, using two or more canes simultaneously. We need again an odd number of stakes.

Fig. 720 Pairing is possible on odd or even numbers of stakes. The first piece of cane is taken behind stake 1, the second behind stake 2. We now weave with the first piece over stake 1 and go under stake 2. Cane 1 will point towards us. Now we weave with cane 2 over stake 2 and under stake 3. Cane 1 is then used again, going over stake 3, behind stake 4, and so on (720).

162

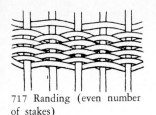

717 Randing (even number of stakes)

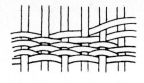

718 Randing (odd number of stakes)

719 Slewing

720 Pairing

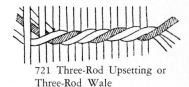

721 Three-Rod Upsetting or Three-Rod Wale

722 *(left)* Adding a New Length of Cane in Randing

723 *(right)* A Single Row of Upsetting immediately at the Base

Fig. 721 Three-Rod Raising or Three-Rod Waling

This method is used whenever we want to make something particularly strong, i.e., near borders, at the base, etc. When this method is used above the base it is called waling. Three canes are placed between the stakes in three consecutive spaces. Each cane is now taken in turn over two stakes, behind a third stake and brought out again. This is continued until the starting point of the row is reached, i.e., when the last used cane comes out to the left of the first stake.

When raising with four reeds, each cane goes over three and under one stake.

Fig. 723 shows the finish of a single raised row, where the ends of successive canes meet (used for finishing a base, etc.).

Figs. 760 and 761 show different patterns for the sides.

THE BASE

When we do randing or make strips (718, 720), the base can be formed by an even number of stakes. The stakes are made to cross as described on page 160, i.e. they are slit open along the middle and the other stakes are pushed through. Very thin canes can also be tied together.

The number of the canes depends on their thickness and on the diameter of the base. Two sets of stakes are sufficient for small baskets, larger baskets will need between two sets of four and two of eight.

Fig. 724

This cross is formed by two sets of six stakes. The piece of cane used for weaving must be well soaked and is bent to form two pieces. It is not however, bent exactly in the middle, since we do not want to add two new pieces exactly above each other. The cane is looped round one of the bundles of stakes (724) and woven according to the method shown in Fig. 720. We go four times over each group of six, then divide the stakes into pairs, and finally weave round individual stakes until the base has reached the required size.

Fig. 725

Two sets of six stakes each are arranged as before, except that we leave a small gap in the centre of each lot, thus further dividing them into four groups of three. It might be advisable to make smaller slits instead of one large slit through one set of the canes. We again use pairing (720). The loop is formed in one of the gaps. We weave alternately over and under six stakes for altogether four rounds, then we weave round groups of three for a while (725), finally round single stakes.

Oval base (726)

Since an oval base easily pulls out of shape, it is best to use peeled willow rods for the stakes. We cut five stakes of the length, and nine, eleven or thirteen of the width of the base. The latter are slit along the middle and have the other five inserted as illustrated. Since we cannot use a half stake for an oval base, we weave as described in Fig. 718. When we have woven four rounds, the long stakes are split into groups of two, one and two, and are woven with the two canes, until we can weave round each stake separately.

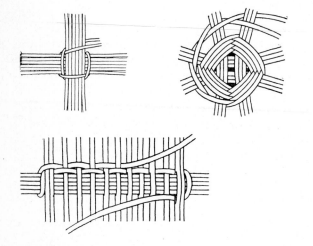

724—725 Starting the Base with an even Number of Canes

726 Making an Oval Base

RAISING AND THE SIDES

We start the sides for the bread basket (page 158), by thoroughly soaking the finished base - with the stakes for the sides inserted in the holes. Having become supple, the stakes are then bent upwards close to the edge. This should be done very firmly, but nevertheless carefully. If one of the stakes should break off, it is cut off close to the base and another stake is inserted as close to it as possible.

The stakes of baskets intended to have curved sides must not be bent sharply, but should merely be curved to the desired shape.

The sides usually begin with one or two rows of three-rod raising (721), and can be completed in any of the methods shown.

164

727 Side of a Basket. Above Pairing, below
Waling, with a row of Waling in thicker
cane in the middle

728 A Three-Rod Plain Border

Giving the basket its shape needs some experience. If we want it to curve outwards, we must press with thumb and index finger of the left hand slightly against the inside during weaving, while pulling the cane gently.

If the basket is to narrow again towards the top, we simply bend the stakes toward the centre and weave a little more tightly.

BORDERS

The ends of the stakes must be very supple for the borders. They are therefore all cut to the same length and soaked for five to ten minutes in lukewarm water.

Fig. 729 *Simple Scallop Border*. Extremely easy to make.

Fig. 730. *Scallop Border*. Each end of a stake is inserted by the side of the next stake. If necessary, the gimlet or awl can be used to help push in the stakes.

Fig. 731. *Track Border*. Each end is placed behind the next, in front of the next but one and again behind the next but two. Although the stakes are trimmed fairly short when they are dry, we must take care not to cut off so much that the ends will slip from the border.

Figs. 732 and 733. *Simple Plaited Border*. This border is made in two stages. First each stake is taken round the next from the back and brought forward (732). The ends are now woven in by being pushed *under* the one stake, *over* the next, and under again (733). They are left to dry and are trimmed afterwards.

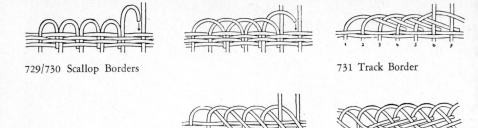

729/730 Scallop Borders   731 Track Border

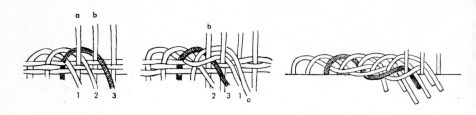

732-733 Simple Plaited Border, first and second stage

734/736 Three-Rod Plain Borders

Figs. 734-736. *Three-Rod Plain Border.* One of the most usual borders is a three-rod plain border: each stake is passed behind the two adjoining and then brought forward (734).

Then we take the projecting end. No. 1, past 2 and upright stake "b" and push it behind the stake next to "b", so that it comes to lie immediately next to the end marked "a" in Fig. 735. We do the same with 2, and tuck in "b"; "a" has already been disposed of in Fig. 735 by having been taken past "b" and the next stake.

We continue, taking the fifth stake - counting from right to left - in front of the next upright, behind the next but one and out in front again. The next upright stake is then bent and treated as "a". We must always have three pairs of ends in front and only use the right of each pair for weaving.

Finally, the beginning and the end of a border will meet. To learn how to finish properly, we must study the drawings carefully, and note how to plait the stakes.

All projecting ends are trimmed flush.

Plaited Border

A plaited border is not easy to make, but looks extremely well.

Fig. 737. Stake 1 and 2 are bent forward.

Fig. 738. Stake 1 is bent upwards and inserted between 2 and 4, towards the inside.

Fig. 739. Stake 3 is bent down over stake 1, towards the outside.

Fig. 740. Stake 2 is inserted between 4 and 5, crossing 3, towards the inside.

Fig. 741. Stake 1 is turned outwards between 4 and 5, crossing over 2.

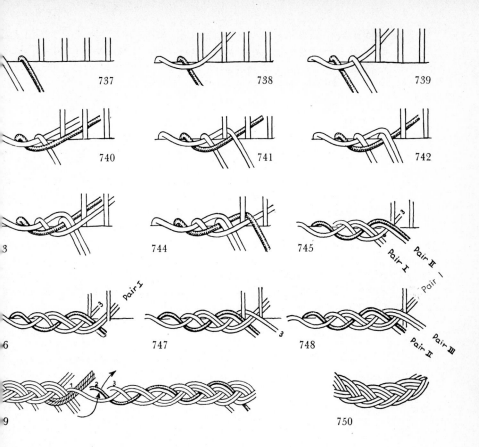

Fig. 742. Stake 4 is pressed down, resting next to 1 on outside.

Fig. 743. Stake 3 is inserted between the next two upright stakes, to point towards the inside.

Fig. 744. Stake 2 is bent round the next upright, to point towards the outside.

Fig. 745. The next stake (5) is bent down to form a pair with 2.

Fig. 746. The first pair, crossing the second, is inserted between the next two upright stakes.

Fig. 747. Stake 3 is bent round the first pair towards the outside.

Fig. 748. The next upright stake (6) is bent to join 3, thus forming a third pair.

Now we continue weaving with three pairs of stakes as if they were single stakes. We have groups of three canes, of which the shortest stake (first 1, then 2, etc.) is always left hanging on the outside (749, *right*). The plait consists of three canes on the outside and two on the inside. This must also be remembered when finishing (750). The ends are cut off when the basket has completely dried.

An Open Border

This is a combination of the scallop border and the double stake track border. The border in our case also forms the sides.

Each pair of stakes is taken back to the base in a wide arch, crossing behind the next pair, then in front and finally behind again, (751, 752). When all the ends have been woven in, our border is finished with a simple plaited edge (753, 754). For description of plaited border see page 166.

Handle and Ring

With a knife, we sharpen a very thick piece of cane - or three or four thinner pieces - and insert it with the help of a bradawl. Then we attach a very long piece of cane at the edge of the basket (755), and wind it round the thick piece until we reach the other side (756), where we push both ends through the side of the basket. Then we repeat this process, until the handle is entirely covered (see also the handle of a willow basket, pages 175 and 176). Finally, the ends are plaited, one end upwards and one downwards.

The ring can be made from one piece of cane (757, 758). Its ends are plaited into the side of the basket. We can also make it as follows: a long piece of cane is wound round the edge of the finished lid a number of times at the same point in such a way that it forms a loop. We thus obtain a ring that only needs to have some thin cane or raffia wrapped round it.

Bread Basket with Plaited Border (701)

Our second piece can be a bread basket. The base is plaited as before (see page 160), except that we use shorter stakes (6 ins. each). When the base has reached a diameter of 5 ins., we cut the upright stakes from No. 3 cane (twice the number of

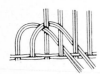

751 An Open Border, First step

755-756 Attaching the Handle

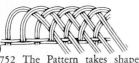

752 The Pattern takes shape

757—759 How to Join Lid and Ring

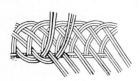

753 and 754 Foot-border, first and second stage

760-761 The Side can be made in Open Work for Smaller Baskets. The Randing or Slewing across Open Work is called Fitching

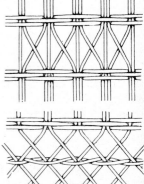

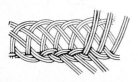

762 Oval Base and Two - rod, Three - stroke. Plaited Border

the projecting ends of the stakes of the base). The upright stakes should be 16 ins. long. This is the length required for the border, plus the height of the basket plus half the diameter of the base.

Now we cut off the projecting ends of the base and insert an upright stake to the right and left of each end. To insert the upright stakes as deeply as possible, we shall have to prise open the cane with an awl or gimlet or a thick knitting needle.

When all the stakes have been inserted, we weave a row of reed with three pieces of No. 5 or No. 7 cane (721, 723). This row is really a finish for the base and should always be woven from left to right, i.e., the canes should run in an opposite direction from those of the base.

We then soak the basket and three No. 1 canes in a pail of warm water for several minutes. The sides of our basket are worked until entirely waled, (721). This method uses a little more cane, but gives the basket a good shape.

Before starting on the sides, we must carefully bend the well-soaked stakes, so that they will point upwards. Now we can hold the basket lightly on our knees and we continue plaiting from left to right, the ends always pointing towards the outside of the basket. We shape the basket gently at the same time. The first four rows are woven over double stakes, then we take each stake singly.

When the basket has reached the desired height, (21 rows in the case of our example), we make the border. Ours is a plaited border (see page 166 and Fig. 762).

A Basket with a Handle

Dimensions: base 4¾ ins. diameter, height 3¼ ins.

Materials: eight and a half pieces of No. 5 cane, 6 ins. each for the base,

36 pieces of No. 5 cane, 10 ins. each for the upright stakes, No. 2 cane for weaving, 3 pieces of No. 7 cane, 28 ins. each, for two rows of raising round the middle and for the last row of the sides.

We shall also need a piece of willow or bamboo - about 22 ins. long - for the handle. It will be inserted in the usual manner, i.e., the ends will be placed into the sides opposite each other, and will have two or three pieces of No. 2 cane wrapped round.

W e a v i n g : we make a base as described on page 160, with a row of raising in No. 7 cane. Having inserted the stakes, we weave seven rows of waling with No. 2 cane, then one row of (718), and finally another row of waling. We use a three-rod plain border (734-736). The handle is made as for the willow basket (772-777).

An Open Work Basket (764)

D i m e n s i o n s : 5½ ins. diameter at the base, 6¼ ins. at the top.

M a t e r i a l s : 8 ½ pieces of No. 7 cane, 7 ins. each for the base, 36 pieces of No. 5 cane, 20 ins. each for the upright stakes, No. 3 cane for weaving, 3 pieces of No. 7 cane, 28 ins. each for the raising near the base.

W e a v i n g : we make a base as described on pages 160 and 161. After the

764

first raised row - having also inserted the upright stakes - we weave the entire basket in waling and finish with a three-rod plain border (see page 166). As before, we shape the basket while weaving.

A Basket with an Open Border (702)

D i m e n s i o n s : 4¾ ins. diameter at the base, 8 ins. at the top.

M a t e r i a l s : 8½ pieces of No. 5 cane, 6¾ ins. each for the base, 51 pieces of No. 5 cane, 18 ins. each for the upright stakes, No. 3 cane for weaving.

W e a v i n g : the base is made as described on pages 160 and 161. When it has reached a diameter of about 4¾ ins., we insert the stakes and start making the open border. It consists of two parts. First we weave two rows of raising with No. 3 cane. Then we make the actual border, which also forms the sides. The plaited edge at the base also serves as a base rim and is made last. A more detailed description of the border is on pages 167 and 168.

BASKETS WITH A WOODEN BASE

It is sometimes advisable to weave the sides only and to have a base of wood (for a tray, waste paper basket, doll's pram, etc.).

We cut the base from plywood with a fret saw. Then we drill holes into it about ⅛ in. from the edge and between ⅜ and ½ in. apart (the exact distance will depend on the thickness of the canes). The holes - of exactly the same diameter as the upright stakes - can be made with a bradawl and a small hand drill. However, ready-made bases, complete with holes, can be bought in almost any shape and may often serve our purpose quite well.

The stakes are inserted as shown in Fig. 766. We damp them at first only at one end, then we push them through the holes with the dry ends. The damp ends are left to project and are plaited into a small rim (766, 767). They can also be plaited in the manner of a three-rod plain border. When the rim is complete, we stand up our work. The dry ends now point upwards. The sides are worked in pairing if the number of stakes is even, or randing (in strips), if it is odd (768).

When the basket is high enough, the ends of the stakes are soaked and plaited into a border.

Under no circumstances must the base be soaked, since, being of plywood, it would warp badly.

A Small Mat

The base has a diameter of 6¾ ins. and has been cut out with a fret saw. The stakes, 45 in number, are No. 3 cane and are 10½ ins. long. The sides were worked in pairing in No. 1 cane, and were finished with a three-rod plain border (748-750).

A round Tray

The base has a diameter of 14 ins. and is again cut out with the fretsaw from plywood. The stakes are No. 5 cane, 47 in number and 13¾ ins. long. Again, we use a three-rod plain border for the base rim and for the top (748-750). The side is worked in pairing in No. 3 cane.

A Waste Paper Basket

The plywood base is 9¼ ins. in diameter, the stakes - 51 in number - are No. 7 cane. We use white No. 5 cane and brown No. 3 cane for weaving. We can either buy the cane already coloured or we can use a ready-made inert stain.

We pierce the base as described on the previous page and insert the stakes. The base rim is made as shown in Figs. 766 to 768. Then we weave the side as follows: 14 rows of three rod raising (white), 14 rows of randing in dark cane, 4 rows of waling in white, another 14 rows of randing with dark cane, 8 rows of waling in white, five more rows of randing with dark cane, two rows of waling in white and finally a white three-rod plain border (734-736).

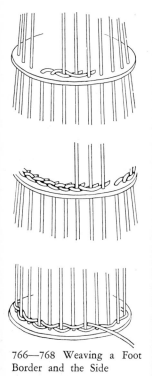

766—768 Weaving a Foot Border and the Side

769 Waste Paper Basket

173

BASKETS FROM BROWN WILLOW RODS

The two baskets (770) were made from fresh, unpeeled osiers (willow). We have previously dealt with the preparation of the material.

Though working with willow or osiers is similar to working with cane, there are certain differences in the method of plaiting, due to the nature of the material. Here we can see again how the material influences the shape. While cane is of even thickness and comparatively long, osiers are thick at one end, thin at the other and much shorter than cane. Since they are less supple, they have to be soaked longer and are harder to plait. It is sometimes even necessary to tap down the weaving with a special tool - the so-called rapping iron - to get a really firm structure.

We begin as for cane (see pages 160 to 161). The thick or butt ends of the osiers are used for staking. We take eight and a half stakes for this purpose, i.e. eight stakes eight inches in length, and one stake five inches. Four are slit open in the middle for about ¼ in., the other four and a half stakes, are inserted through them. We proceed as described on pages 160 to 161, insert the thin end in the slit, plait twice over stake four, then under four, turn, plait again twice over four, under four and then start to divide: over two, under two, etc., until the stakes can be separated. The ninth, i.e. the half stake, is only plaited over once.

When joining a new piece, we always place a thick end against a thin end. In the case of a thin end, we simply plait over three or four stakes with both rods; for a thick end we cross the rods behind the stake. The rods are not trimmed until everything is finished and completely dry. When the base has reached a diameter of about 5½ ins., we turn it round and make a border on the other side (721). We always join a *thik* end to a *thin* one for a border. Fig. 732 shows how a border is finished.

Now we cut off all the projecting stakes one by one and put in fresh stakes for the sides. They are pushed into the foot border as deeply as possible to the right and left of the old stakes. In *one place* we only put in a new stake on one side. This is done to keep the number of stakes uneven. The stakes for the sides must be between 20 and 24 inches long. They are pointed at the thick end to make them easier to insert.

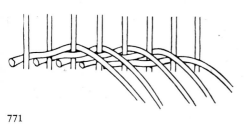

771

When the stakes have all been inserted - having been thoroughly soaked - they are raised for the sides. It has to be done very carefully, or the basket will not have a good shape. Practice is needed here. We press the knife against the stakes from the inside and bend them without raising the border. Now we can plait the sides, working from right to left. (Larger baskets are nailed to a special board for this purpose. Sometimes they are merely attached to the board with an awl. The board is kept on the knees and the basket is turned round the awl.).

We plait again two rows of waling. Then we continue in the manner characteristic for willow baskets (771), i.e. we place a rod behind each stake, bring it in front of the next, and again round the following stake from the back. When we have finished one round - i.e., when all 33 rods have been plaited - we plait a second round in the same manner and continue until we get to the top of the basket. The rapping iron has to be used after each round to make the basket really firm. When the basket has reached the required height, we plait two more rows of waling and then make the border. All the ends of the stakes will have to be plaited in. The stakes - which must be damp - are bent over the knife. If any stakes should break, they have to be replaced. Our baskets have a three-rod plain border (734-736). It is very widely used, can be varied and is very firm. It is used for most laundry baskets, fruit baskets, etc.

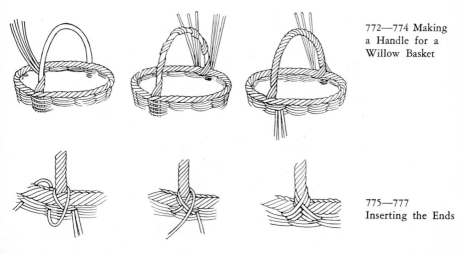

772—774 Making a Handle for a Willow Basket

775—777 Inserting the Ends

Handles

We first insert a strong piece of willow into the sides of the basket down to the bottom. We then take six thin pieces and insert three on each side of the handle. Having wrapped them round the latter, they are pushed through the basket from the inside, and left to project on the outside. Now the other three pieces are wound over the handle, thus filling the gaps shown on Fig. 773. The ends are again pushed through.

Figs. 775-777 show how the ends are attached. The piece projecting on the extreme left is wound round the handle (775) and plaited into the border. The second and third pieces are treated similarly.

SHOPPING BASKETS

Shopping baskets (778) can be woven from rushes and only need a few willow rods for the stakes. They are also made from splints (split willow). But undoubtedly, they will look better if they are made entirely from willow rods. The method is always the same.

We need two strong rods for the basket shown in Fig. 778. These are trimmed aslant at the ends, joined to a circle and tied with raffia through two small kerfs. If they are joined with small wire pins instead, there will be no need for the kerfs. It is best to bend the rods round a tree trunk to get a really good shape.

778

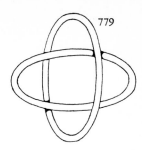

779

780

779 The Two Rings for the Frame

780/781 The Frame. Starting to Weave

781

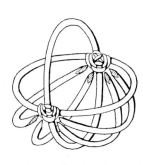

782 Frame of a Shopping Basket

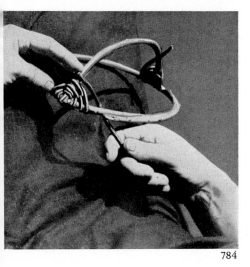

784

783 Round Basket without a Handle

784 Starting to weave a Basket without a Handle

The basket in our illustration is plaited with rushes, but a few thin pieces of willow have been woven in to give it strength. We shall also need a few stout pieces of willow or hazel for the stakes.

One ring is now pushed through the other (779). We start plaiting where the two rings cross (780). If we use willow rods, we shall begin with the thin end and continue for the length of the rod. To get a fairly even shape, we do not add when a piece of willow is used up, but start plaiting from the other side. The rod must be given a slight turn at the side before it is looped firmly round the frame. The material used for plaiting, whether cane, rushes, cat o'nine tails, osiers, or splints, is at first only taken round the frame once, although it usually has to be taken double later to give a firm edge and to prevent ugly loops.

But first we have to insert the stakes. This must be done very carefully to give the basket a good shape. Figs. 781 and 782 show the required length. The basket will not be entirely round, since the stakes should project slightly beyond the ring forming the handle to make it stand properly.

Having inserted the four stakes, we continue plaiting with a piece of rush - for three or four rounds - until we can insert a further stake on each side. Now we go on until both sides meet. The rushes can be taken round the central stake twice, if necessary, as we did at the edges. Again, it is better to insert an occasional piece of willow as a reinforcement.

The handle can be left as it is or wound with rushes.

An oval basket without a handle can be made similarly. Figs. 783 and 784 show the frame. We take a rather longer stake in place of the second ring, trim the ends at a slant, turn them round the ring and tie them with raffia. Otherwise we continue as for the shopping basket.

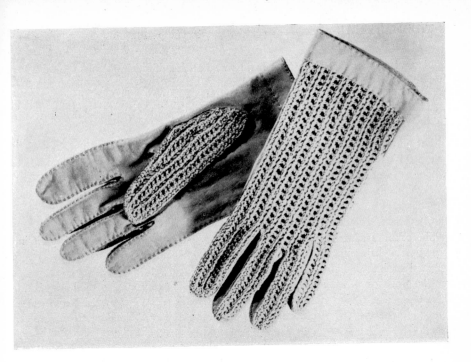

785

LEATHERWORK

Leather is one of the most handsome materials. Soft, supple and virtually indestructible, it can be made into a number of things.

Leather, like wood, or a beautiful piece of fabric, has its own individuality. We therefore must let it speak for itself and must use it in accordance with its nature.

The choice of a particular leather depends on the size and function of the object we want to make. It may also be influenced or even decided by the price. But we must avoid cheap, artificially dolled-up leather which aims to be more than it is: sheepskin may have been made to look as if it had come from the back of the ox, the lizard or even the crocodile. Sometimes, leather has been sprayed with paint and has thus lost its character. If we use old leather, we must first clean it with surgical spirit, cleaning fluid, or lighter fuel. (This must not, of course, be done near an open flame, or even in the kitchen or bathroom, where there might be an open flame from a geyser.) Dirty edges must be cut off. Occasionally, we may also have to damp the leather. It has to be stretched on a board and fastened to it with drawing pints afterwards. If the leather has become very hard, we add a little glycerine to the water and then treat the leather with this mixture.

THE MATERIAL

Natural calf is one of the most handsome leathers. It is supple and yet sufficient-ly strong to be used unlined for a handbag. This also applies to pigskin. But these leathers are not cheap. Pigskin is also available specially prepared and is then called peccary. It can be made into lasting and elegant washable gloves that will give pleasure and hard wear for many years.

For gloves we will generally use goatskin - mostly the natural smooth-grained kind - but also kid and chevreau. The finely grained morocco is used for wallets and articles where a tough, but comparatively thin, leather is required.

Cowhide is very strong, but rather hard. It is therefore suitable for brief cases, key cases, purses and other articles demanding a certain stiffness and solidity.

Chamois is comparatively cheap and very suitable for smaller articles.

Sheepskin is generally cheapest, but not very hardwearing. Sheepskin is split into the outer or hair side (skiver) and the under-side, chamois. Skiver is usually smooth-grained or has an entirely smooth surface.

The price of skins will depend on the animal, quality and method of tanning. Cheaper grades have more defects as a result of disease, injuries from barbed wire, insect bites, etc., and quite often are not really worth buying. It is more eco-nomical to plan the work in detail on paper first.

Pieces of leather are sewn together with thongs. These are narrow strips, $\frac{1}{8}$ in. and less in width, and can be bought either by the yard or by the piece. In the former case they will have been joined to almost any length; in the latter, they will be of the length of the skins from which they were cut. We should only use good quality thongs, since others, especially those made of inferior split skins, will soon wear out.

We can also make our own thongs. Undoubtedly, those we make ourselves from the same leather as the object we are working at will look better than any others. They can either be made with knife and iron ruler or cut out in the shape of a spiral from a round piece of leather to almost any length. But the first method is better and well worth the extra trouble, since the pieces will be really straight. Also, the joins will not show afterwards.

Cellophane is very useful for lining season-ticket holders, licence holders, etc., and also gives some additional strength. It is punched with the leather and laced in at three sides, so that the document can be inserted at the fourth. Old film strips can also be used for this purpose, but they must have everything washed off first in warm water. This must not, of course, be done near an open flame, or they will catch fire.

TOOLS

Leatherwork has one great advantage: we need no special tools apart from a knife, a hammer punch (787) and a plier punch (789). The plier punch most suitable for our purpose should have six exchangeable punches of different sizes. But a hammer punch will be sufficient, if we are only going to do leatherwork occasionally.

A trident thonging punch (788) will prove useful for making smaller pieces from chamois. It makes small slits. Single slits can be made with a bradawl.

Thonging is usually done without a needle. But if we have to sew through several layers or if the holes are very small, it is advisable to use a special thonging needle, which holds the thongs as a larding needle holds bacon.

Although an ordinary needle can be used for linen thread, buttonhole silk or cotton, a special gloving needle (786) is better, since it makes small slits in the leather and therefore makes sewing easier. These needles can be bought in varying thicknesses.

The holes for sewing with linen thread should first be marked with a stitch punch (792).

Leather can be cut with the knife and iron ruler used in bookbinding, etc., or even with an ordinary ruler and a *sharp* pocket knife. But if we do leatherwork often, it is best to acquire a special knife with a long and very thin blade.

A special set of press-stud tools is used for attaching press buttons. But press buttons should be used as little a possible. Although very practical, they seem somehow not in accordance with the character of a natural material like leather.

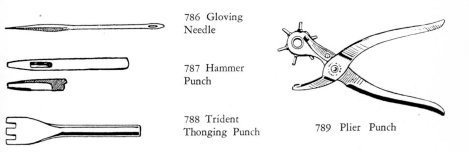

786 Gloving
Needle

787 Hammer
Punch

788 Trident
Thonging Punch

789 Plier Punch

CUTTING

A paper or cardboard pattern of the main portions and the flaps, etc., must always be made first. Having cut out the pattern, we put the parts together to see if they fit and then place them on a piece of leather. By experimenting that way, we shall soon discover the most economic way of cutting. We *only then* transfer the pattern to the leather and cut it out with a sharp knife and an iron ruler.

LINING

It is best to use leather that does not need lining. But this is not always possible and if the leather is too soft or rather thin, we must line it with a piece of thin skiver. A thin rubber solution is best for attaching the lining since it does not harden the leather.

The lining should be cut slightly larger than the leather and should project between 1/2 in. and 3/4 in. all round. Both pieces are then coated with the rubber solution on one side and left to dry for a minute or two, since the power of the adhesive will then be greatest. They are then joined and pressed between books for about half an hour.

790 Making a Gauge

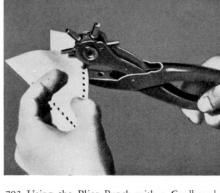

793 Using the Plier Punch with a Cardboard Base

791 Marking the Holes

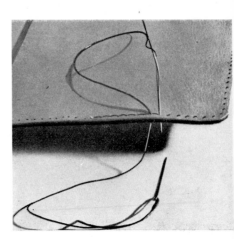

794 Using two Needles for the Saddle Stitch

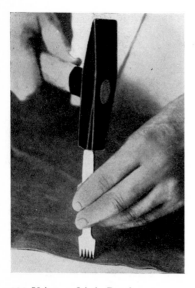

792 Using a Stitch Punch

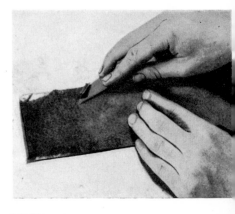

795 Trimming

JOINING

Leather can be joined in many ways. If thongs are to be used, we must first make small holes. These should be about ¼ in. from the edge and between ¼ in. and ⅜ in. apart, according to the size of the article.

Joining the different sections can be made easier by glueing them together very lightly. Adjoining parts can then be punched together. Consequently, the holes will then be exactly above each other and thonging will be very simple. It is best to make a gauge for marking the holes (790, 791). The gauge is placed on the leather (791) and the holes are marked in pencil.

We then make the holes with the hammer or plier punch. If we use the latter, a cardboard strip must be put under the leather, or our punch will wear out rapidly, because metal will hit metal (793).

Having made the holes along the edges, we can start thonging. One end of the thong should be given a slight point, twisted a little and coated with rubber solution to harden it. We can also use a thonging needle (see page 181). The thong can then be inserted anywhere along the edge. The end of the old thong and the beginning of the new should be left to project slightly more than ¾ in. When thonging is completed, the ends are trimmed back to ⅜ in. and flattened with the knife towards the outside. They are then glued together where they meet; if this is done carefully, joins will be barely noticeable.

Finally, we go over all the seams with a hammer - having first covered the work with a piece of paper or an old cloth - to flatten the thongs.

Making holes with a trident punch - only possible in the case of small articles - requires a strong cardboard base. The punch is then hammered into the leather. The resulting slits will have to be prised open with a knitting needle, to insert the thongs.

A cardboard base also has to be used with a hammer punch.

Quite often, we shall use linen thread and a gloving needle instead of thongs. The thread is drawn across some wax once or twice. The parts are then sewn together with running stitches. It is best to mark the holes first with a stitch punch (792).

We can also work with two needles at the same time - using the running stitch - and do double stitching to give extra strength.

BUTTONS AND FASTENINGS

A large flap often needs no special fastening. But we often want handbags to be made to close properly. The bag in Fig. 816 is closed by a firm, simple and good-looking device; the handle is merely pulled through a wooden ring. We can also lace some strips of leather into the sides and plait them across the bag, so that the flap is simply pushed through. Moroccan bags have a leather rope with a button laced in at the bottom of the flap. It is wound round the bag and held in position as shown in Fig. 802. The button is made as follows: we cut a wedge-shaped piece of leather (800a) and make two small insertions with a sharp knife or a razor blade, as shown on the drawing. The leather is then covered with a leather glue and rolled up firmly, starting from the base. The end is pushed through the slit (800b) and thus held in position. It must be long enough to be sewn to the leather rope (800c).

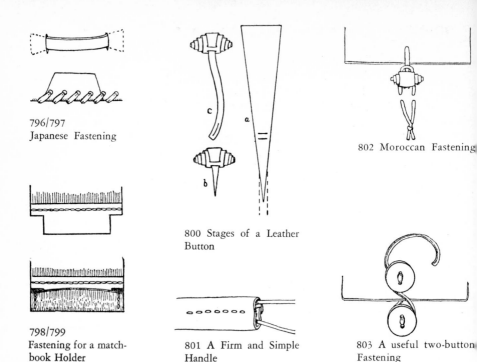

796/797
Japanese Fastening

800 Stages of a Leather
Button

802 Moroccan Fastening

798/799
Fastening for a match-
book Holder

801 A Firm and Simple
Handle

803 A useful two-button
Fastening

An invisible fastening can be made as follows: a piece of hard leather, horn, cellophane, etc., is attached with the lid, which will be just large enough to pass through a slit or a sling on the bag itself (796). The lining, which is not stuck to the lid, is best made from a strip of leather, inserted through two slits and glued to the inside of the bag.

A flap with a buttonhole, closed with a simple button of wood or leather, can also look very nice.

The handle for the bag can be plaited from three or four leather thongs (447).

SIMPLE ARTICLES

Season Ticket or Licence Holder

We first buy the ready-made cellophane pockets and then cut out the leather case accordingly. The folder consists of a long strip of leather. It is turned in on the right and left to form two pockets and is then punched along the upper and lower edge and laced up.

A Key Holder

Fig. 807 shows a simple pattern for a key holder. The pattern - having first been made in paper and folded to make sure that everything fits - is cut out twice and the pieces are then punched and laced together. A small opening is left at the top. We then cut a strip between 3¼ ins. and 4 ins. for the key ring. One end is cut to finish in a triangle (807), the other is given a small slit for the key ring and is inserted from the top before attaching keys and ring. We can add a press button as an extra fastening.

Wallets

a) The simplest type of wallet consists of a piece of leather 6½ ins. wide and 9¼ ins. long (809). It is folded in the middle and sewn together along the lower edge (810).

b) Another simple and useful wallet is shown in Figs. 811 to 813. It has one closed and one open pocket. Part 811 is folded and part 812 is put in the middle to form two pockets: the pocket in front is closed with the flap, the pocket at the back remains open. The sides are closed with running stitches.

c) The pigskin wallet in Fig. 806 has a large leather pocket on each side. There are two other pockets in addition, a small leather pocket on the right and a cellophane pocket on the left for a driving licence, season ticket, etc. The sections are cut out, punched and laced together (806).

Matchbook Holder

We buy a book of matches and cut a strip of leather of the necessary width (about 2¼ ins. x 4½ ins.). One end is folded to form a small pocket (799) and sewn with running stitches. A small strip of vellum is then sewn to the other end. We must trim this vellum strip sufficiently to fit into the pocket to act as a fastening (798, 799).

A Simple Folder in Calf (814)

We cut out the following pieces from calf: 1 piece 12 x 22 ins., one strip for the side pocket (805a) 12 x 5¼ ins., two side panels (805c) 5⅛ ins. x 2¼ ins., one strip 12 x 1 in. for holding the blotting paper (805b), two triangular pieces, (805e) the short sides to be 4⅜ ins. long, one strip for the flap (805d) 3⅝ ins. x 8 ins. and a piece for holding the flap down, 10 x 4⅜ ins.

We first attach the strip for holding the flap in position (796) and glue the parts together provisionally along the edges before punching. Then we make the holes and lace the parts together. Finally we insert two large pieces of blotting paper halfway into the inner pocket on the left so that they are held down in the middle by the long strip of leather and on the right by the triangular pieces.

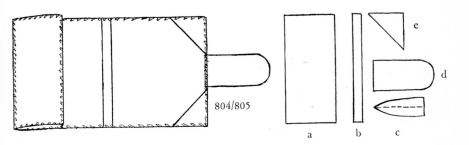

804/805

A Folder with Interchangeable Pad and Side Pocket (815)

This folder has a cellophane pocket for the writing pad on the right. The case is lined on the left with a large piece of leather, which goes beyond the middle and covers the cellophane along the edge to a width of nearly ½ in. Lining and cellophane are sewn to the case with back stitches. The stitches show on the outside.

806

Pigskin Wallet with Cellophane Pocket

807 A Key Holder

808 Matchbook Holder

809/810 The Simplest type of Wallet

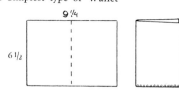

811-812-813 Wallet with Flap

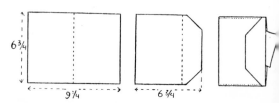

814 A Simple Folder

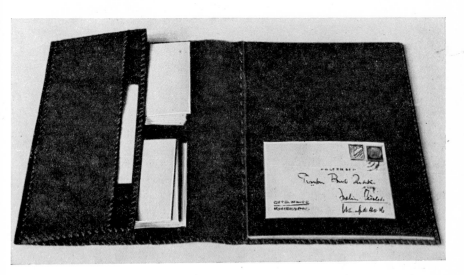

A Folder with Interchangeable Pad and Side Pocket (815)

The large double pocket on the left of the folder consists of a narrower and a wider strip, both lined with leather. They are laced together and are each joined to the folder by two triangular pieces (805c).

The dark strip along the fore edge of the folder is attached as shown in Fig. 817. The other edges were punched and thonged in the usual manner.

Handbag with Wooden Ring and Loop (816)

We first make a paper pattern (818). Apart from the large piece for the main portion, we also need two small side panels and a wide strap for the handle. We can cut out the ring ourselves with the fretsaw from a suitable type of wood. It can afterwards be treated with linseed oil and is then given a matt polish, or a coat of flat finish varnish, the following day.

There is no need for a lining, if we are using calf or cowhide. But a bag made

187

Handbag with Wooden Ring (816)

from a soft leather will have to be lined - including the strap - as described on page 181.

First we attach the handle, then we put in the side panels, using the saddle stitch (794) for sewing. If we want an inner pocket, we cut a piece of the required width from the same leather, a softer leather or even cellophane, and sew it either with the seams in front or with those at the back.

A Tool Bag (819)

First of all we have to assemble the tools that are meant to fit into the bag. Then we make a paper pattern. We need two oblong pieces of leather. The piece for the outside should be rather hard, the lining somewhat softer. The soft piece should project beyond the narrow sides by slightly under an inch for the edging and by about 3¾ ins. at top and bottom for the edging and the flaps. We also need a strap long enough to be drawn through the entire bag for fastening and to hold the tools down.

817 The Fore Edge of the Folder shown in 815

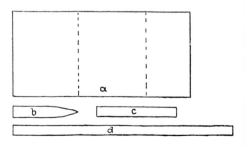

818 Pattern for the bag shown in 816

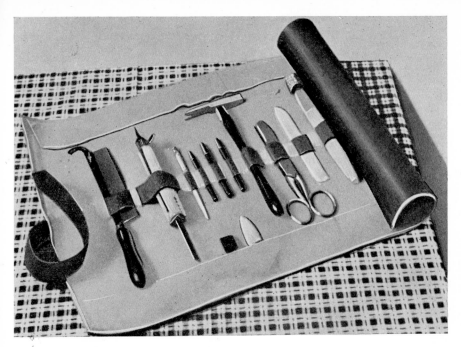

A Tool bag (819)

We first make slits in the lining for the tools We then turn in the edges of the lining, so that it only projects beyond the outside by ⅛ in. all round. Then we sew the two pieces together and finally we pull the strap through the slits.

SHOES AND GLOVES

White Fur Slippers

We are not so much concerned here about the patterns, as about techniques. Indeed, many things today may be technically perfect, but are completely without life. The instructions given for making these fur slippers can be applied to almost any simple pattern.

Fur is never cut with scissors, because the hairs might easily get damaged. We cut it from the inside with a sharp knife or a razor blade. The fur must be held very tightly and can even be pinned to a board. The slippers have been sewn with coloured yarn by going backward and forward with the needle so that the seam should form a zig-zag line. Strips of coloured cloth were inserted along the seams through small slits in the leather, made with a chisel, a pocket knife or a razor blade. A loop on one side and a wooden button on the other serve as fasteners.

Leather Gloves

Making gloves can give great joy. We need a fairly soft leather, button-hole silk or the finest linen thread, a gloving needle (786) and wax for smoothing the thread.

There are many basic patterns available, but we can also make our own. As always, a pattern is absolutely essential.

We first stretch the leather thoroughly in all directions. Then we place the pattern on the back of the leather twice, once from the right and once from the left, taking care that the leather will stretch *across* and not along the glove (822). Otherwise the fingers will grow longer, while the glove will be too tight. Then we mark the outline with a sharp pencil and cut out without allowing anything extra for the seams.

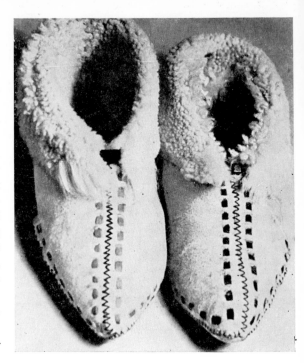

820 White Fur Slippers

Sewing

A thread of buttonhole silk is drawn once or twice through wax to keep it smooth and to make it firmer. We then thread the gloving needle (786) and sew with simple stab stitches. Right and left thumb can be distinguished easily: if the thumb is cut into on the left, it belongs to the left glove and vice versa (823).

We start by closing the thumb at the top (823). Then we push the little pointed tip into the thumb hole (824) and fit in the thumb corner by corner as shown in Figs. 825 and 826.

821 Hand-made Pigskin Gloves

190

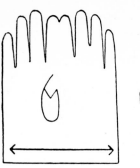

822 Basic Pattern and Thumb

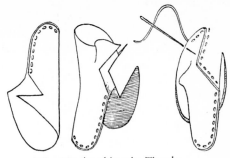

823—825 Attaching the Thumbs

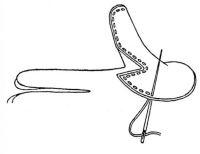

826 The Thumbhole is closed with Small Running Stitches

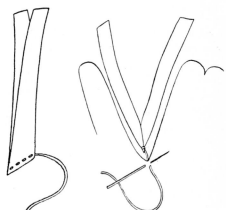

827—830 *(above* and *below)* Show how the fourchettes are fitted

831 The Points on the Back are made with running stitches

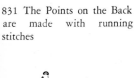

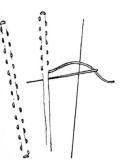

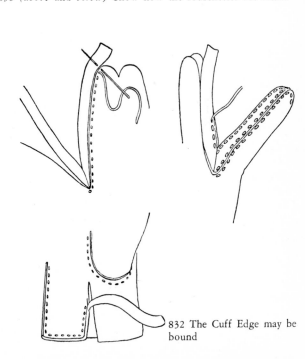

832 The Cuff Edge may be bound

Points on the back of the gloves can be made with running stitches (831) or with various kinds of thonging.

The wedges between the fingers - called fourchettes - are sewn in as follows (827-830): a right and a left fourchette are backstitched together, starting from the left at the longest point (827). We then sew the fourchette to the index finger with the same thread. The fourchettes are trimmed at the tip to follow the shape of the finger (830). Then we continue sewing on the other side of the index finger and insert the next pair of fourchettes between index and middle finger. When all the fourchettes have been sewn in, the gloves are sewn up at the sides.

The basic pattern can easily be varied. We can use more wedges, the gloves can be edged with leather of another colour (832), or lined with fabric. We can also build in a little pocket or purse. Linings can be bought ready made in leather shops

Gloves with Crocheted Backs

Here we only use leather for the palms, the thumbs and the fourchettes. The back is crocheted in strong double crochet yarn. We can use all kinds of yarns and patterns.

The backs of the gloves in Fig. 785 are crocheted from the right side to the wrong in alternating treble and single stitches (one treble, one single) and from the wrong side to the right in alternating plain and single stitches. Working from the right side we start as for the rose stitch (163), from the wrong as for ribbing. But we take the hook through the front portion of the loop, so that the ribbing should be raised. Starting along the back with a row of single stitches, we crochet to and fro, casting on and off for the fingers as necessary.

When both uppers are finished, they are sewn to the leather. We continue as for ordinary gloves.

833 a and b. These Lino cuts are the work of boys aged between 14 and 15.

The Theme, "Giant Cats in the Jungle" was given to the class after a visit to the Zoo.

The blocks were cut to make negative prints, as described on page 199. They were then used

on a light ground. They are also suitable for fabric printing and endpapers.

834

A fine old silhouette made about a hundred years ago by J. J. Hauswirth, a Swiss peasant. It shows the cattle being driven to their summer pastures

SILHOUETTES

The silhouette relies for its delightful effect on two things only: form and contrast. But these limitations allow a wide range of expression. Indeed, as in cross stitch, the very limitation is a challenge and an inspiration. It calls for clarity, strength and harmony, since the smallest mistake stands out clearly.

The art of the silhouette therefore demands clear and simple forms. *The outline is everything.*

We should all try our hand at the silhouette. It can be used for all sorts of greeting cards, and even for the figures of a little theatre. It is also an excellent practice for figure design in embroidery, appliqué, fabric printing and lino cutting.

We need gummed or ungummed black paper(silhouette paper). But we can also use white paper on a black ground.

A pair of small scissors or a razor blade in a holder will serve for cutting out. If we use a razor blade, we must, of course, cut on a firm base (not directly on the table).

We must know what we want to make before we start. Vague cutting about can only lead to meaningless, purely "decorative" forms. It is best to start with a simple folding cut, where the paper is folded and cut out double to give a symmetrical form. But the effect must not be one of dull repetition. The symmetry must appear justified by the nature of the object (835).

We choose a simple shape for a start, such as a tree or a flower. If we have never cut out a silhouette before, we might draw it in outline on ordinary paper. Then we look at the drawing critically, make perhaps a few improvements and draw it again on the back of a sheet of silhouette paper. But we must not trace it or copy mechanically. The drawing must be made again, as if we were drawing something fresh. It is best to indicate the basic form only, since the detail is much livelier if we cut it out in the course of the work, when we experience its association with the object we are making. Indeed, after some practice, we shall cut out without any preliminary drawing, but this is not necessary at the beginning. When the

835 A Tree. It has not been stuck down very firmly and therefore throws shadows that give it a charm of its own

first shape - a flower, etc. - has been a success, we can try a branch with blossoms and leaves, a letter heading and other things. We must advance step by step and not be too ambitious at first.

After a little practice, we can try to make a tree (835). We must imagine a tree with its winding trunk and with the wind blowing through its branches to make it really well. But we must not copy detail slavishly. It is a question of bringing out the tree's character and its basic form rather than of naturalistic copying. Stylization must also be avoided. The silhouette must remain two-dimensional; it is not in its nature to represent space. Figures should not overlap.

When we have some experience in making symmetrical shapes from folded paper, we can try to cut silhouettes freely from nature. Again, we must recapture the spirit and not copy slavishly.

In the case of smaller pieces, we paste the silhouette down as follows:

We take a sheet of paper, exactly the size of the sheet to which we are going to paste the silhouette. The silhouette is placed on this sheet the wrong way round, so that we look at it from the back, and is then coated lightly with paste. Now we take the other sheet and press it very lightly against the silhouette, taking care that it is exactly above the first sheet. The silhouette does not need to be stuck down evenly. It adds to its beauty if it throws an occasional shadow, as in Fig. 835.

Larger pieces, or scenes with a number of figures, are treated differently. We put the cut-out figures on the paper exactly where we want them to be. A few spots can be marked with pencil for guidance. Then we take the figures and keep them in position by weighing them down at the base with a book, a pane of glass, etc. The other portion is raised up slightly and coated with paste on the back (or damped, if it is gummed). The whole figure is thus stuck on bit by bit.

We can also use coloured tissue paper, or even pieces of wall-paper. Each will produce an entirely different effect.

LINO CUTTING
AND FABRIC PRINTING

LINO CUTTING

Linoleum is not an old invention. The art of lino cutting only dates from the beginning of this century. It has developed out of the wood-cut, an art that was at its height in the late Middle Ages.

Woodcuts are beyond most amateurs. Lino cutting is very much easier and can give great pleasure for making greetings cards and announcements.

TOOLS AND MATERIALS

We use a not-too-hard linoleum of one colour only. It should be about ⅛ in. thick. V-tools (838) U-shaped gouges and sharp knives are used for cutting. The paper must be fairly absorbent to take the colour properly (M. G. Poster Paper, Sugar Paper, Cambridge Paper and Oxford Paper are suitable kinds). For printing on paper we use printer's ink, for fabrics, fabric printing ink. Beginners can also use printing water colour for printing on paper. In addition, we need a sheet of glass and a rubber roller.

DESIGNS

We first try out the different knives on the linoleum to get some idea of the effects we can produce with them. Here, too, really good design will be determined by the technique.

We mark the outlines with a lino cutting knife (836) and cut away with the V-tool (838) and the U-shaped gouge. A narrow V-tool can remove very thin strips, a V-tool, called a V-Verner in U.S.A., with a rounded tip makes wide grooves of an interesting shape. It is advisable to make a print of the first experiments.

836/839 Lino cutting Tools

837

836

839

838

840 Houses on the Hillside (Work of a sixteen-year-old boy)

Having thus gained an introduction to the fundamentals of lino cutting and to the characteristics of the technique, we make our first design in black ink, since black and white effects are very similar to a lino-cut. Once we know our tools, we shall quite naturally aim at *broad generous lines*. Meticulous details come out very badly. We must also appreciate that we shall only get black and white without any intermediate tones, as we do in pencil drawing. The effect must be *two-dimensional* and perspective must be avoided. Black and white areas must be balanced properly.

"Houses on a Hill-side" (840) is an example of a lino-cut at its best. The areas are well-balanced, the motive is treated two-dimensionally. The block has been used as an all-over pattern. It is the work of a boy of sixteen.

MAKING THE BLOCK

Now we transfer the design to the linoleum, which can be given a light coat of flake white first. This will make the pencil or pen drawing stand out better. The black areas can also be filled in with printer's ink.

Then we start cutting. There are two possibilities: we can cut out the lines and the gaps in between to obtain a positive print (842, 844), or we can do the reverse and cut out the forms; this gives us a negative print (833a and b). We always begin with the outlines, whatever type of print we want to make.

The finished block is washed and is then ready for use.

TAKING A PRINT

We apply some colour or printer's ink to the sheet of glass with a knife or spatula. Then we go over it with a roller a few times and apply the colour to the block with the roller until it is distributed evenly.

Since the first print cannot be used, we can make it on a sheet of newspaper. The paper is damped lightly with a sponge and is pressed against the block with a bone folder or a second, clean roller. When it has been taken off carefully, we shall see if the block needs any further cutting. Then we can use the block as often as we want on good paper.

The finished print can be mounted on cardboard after drying. But only the upper edge must be pasted down (not too heavily) or the print will lose shape.

Block, roller and glass are cleaned afterwards with turpentine.

FABRIC PRINTING

We can find some of the most beautiful examples of fabric printing in our national museums. They include almost every subject, from simple animal or floral patterns to views of cities and scenes from history. Fig. 841 shows an old blue and white print with a view of Torgau (c. 1700). Fabric printing is only done very rarely in Europe to-day. But when it is done, the old blue and white technique is still used. This consists in covering the pattern with a special substance. The entire cloth is then dyed, but the treated areas do not take on any colour and thus remain as a pattern. In another process the pattern is removed from the dyed fabric with chemicals. Both methods are unsuitable for amateurs and are therefore not described in any further detail.

We shall find most good standard dyes very convenient. They are easy to handle and are to some extent fast.

MATERIALS AND EQUIPMENT

We first make a block from a fairly soft, monochrome linoleum. Here we use the same tools as for ordinary lino printing.

The colours are again applied with a small rubber roller, although an ordinary brush is adequate for a start.

The colours are sometimes mixed with turpentine or with a special thinning agent. However, a particular dye may not always be available. We should therefore find what thinning fluid is used for each dye.

We shall also need a sheet of glass, an old tray or a piece of hardboard, a few sheets of newspaper as a base for printing, some unsized paper, and a sponge or a clean rag for damping the material. Any kind of untreated linen - and sometimes also silk - can be used for printing. If a fabric seems rather stiff, it must be washed first, or the colour will not penetrate properly and may therefore not be fast.

THE DESIGN

Everything we said about the linocut applies here: no perspective, no landscape, no genre scene. But we do not merely want to have a lino print on fabric, instead of paper. The purely decorative effect is even more apparent on fabric. If we use human beings and animals, they must be part of a pattern and two-dimensional, (842) as they always are in peasant art (841).

842 Printed Hanging. Design, blocks and actual printing are the work of a
fifteen-year-old girl

Since the blocks will be used repeatedly over a piece of material, the joins should
be invisible. Details can be worked out after the trial proofs. To avoid gaps in the
pattern, the edges of the blocks should follow the pattern a little and should not be
entirely straight.

PRINTING

We put a few sheets of newspaper and one sheet of unsized paper on an old
table, drawing board, etc. Then we pin down the fabric with drawing pins and damp
it lightly with the sponge.

The colour is put on the sheet of glass and mixed with a few drops of turpentine until it forms a pliable mass that is neither too thick nor too thin.

We now make a trial print on an odd piece of fabric. The colour is applied to the raised lines with a brush in the case of small blocks, otherwise with the roller. The colour must be applied very thickly on rough fabrics, thinly on others. The block must be pressed down firmly and evenly. Larger blocks can be weighed down with a flat iron. We can also glue the stencil to a piece of wood, to which we have fitted a handle for better printing. The limits of the pattern should be marked on

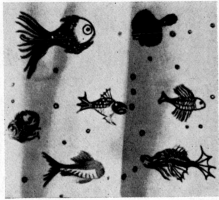

843 Printed Fabric (Negative Print) A square block has been used repetitively as a pattern

844 Printed Fabric (Positive Print). Various independent objects

the back of the stencil or the piece of wood. The colour must be re-applied each time after the stencil has been pressed down. Stencil, roller and glass are afterwards cleaned with turpentine.

The fabric should not be washed for at least a week, and then only with a good soap powder in lukewarm water. It must not be ironed very hot.

USES

Even a single stencil provides us with many opportunities. It can be used in horizontal or vertical rows to form coloured borders. It can also be printed with large gaps in between, if suitable, or it can be used as a close pattern, as in our illustrations.

Fabric printing has many possibilities. But we must not allow our enthusiasm to make us cover everything indiscriminately. Many fine materials are better left undecorated.

845 Hand-printed Fabrics. *Above:* Positive Print, *below:* Closely patterned Negative Print

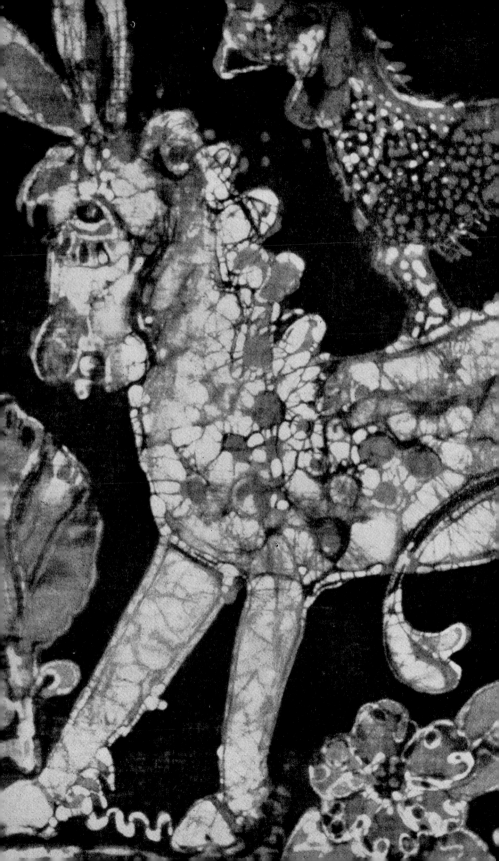

847 Silk Batik Scarf

846 *(on opp. page)* Portion of a Batik Curtain 'The Travelling Musicians'

BATIK

We can see many fine examples of batik from Japan, China, Russia and Turkestan - in fact from all parts of the Far East - in our museums. It is still practised in Java and on the island of Madura. The technique was for the first time described in Stamford Raffles' *History of Java* (London, 1817). A large collection of Javanese batik work was shown at the Colonial Exhibition in Amsterdam in 1883 and caused great interest everywhere.

The process is carried out as follows: the drawing is applied to a fabric in hot wax. The fabric is afterwards put into a bath of cold or lukewarm dye. The parts covered in wax are not affected by the colour and will stand out clearly when the wax has been removed.

If we are going to do batik work with a group of children or for the first time, we should first make some preliminary exercises. Batik paper and mottled paper (page 240) require a similar technique and are therefore very suitable as an introduction, as are pictures with outlines formed by threads of wool, or by ordinary cotton, held in a tracing pen.

The drawing for a piece of batik should be made in actual size on brown paper or tracing paper. There must not be too much petty detail. Once we have gained a little experience, we can "paint" directly with the wax on the fabric. We can also indicate the outlines first with a soft pencil.

TOOLS AND MATERIALS

We need a piece of fabric, wax, a tool for applying the wax (a tjanting or a brush), dyes, a double saucepan and flat iron, newsprint and preferably an appliance for holding the fabric in position.

1. T h e F a b r i c : raw silk, cotton, etc., or any fairly loosely woven material. Any traces of starch, etc., must be removed by washing or even boiling.

2. W a x : a mixture of beeswax and paraffin is best. The beeswax is melted before being used and heated until all traces of water have been removed in the form of bubbles. The wax is ready when it can be seen through a cloth. It must be reheated - but not overheated, since it then begins to smoke and deteriorates - before use.

The wax is made coarser by the addition of paraffin. It is then possible to produce different effects. Resin, on the other hand, makes the wax softer and is added to avoid any changes.

3. T o o l s : the *tjanting* - the word means ladle - is a small copper vessel the size of a thimble. A real *tjanting* is round and is the best tool for applying the wax. But there are other quite useful types of *tjanting* (848-850).

Tjantings are not easy to find. We can make them ourselves from discarded toothpaste or Seccotine tubes or from a small tin (849). The curtain in Fig. 853 was made with such *tjantings* - a young student teacher had made fourteen for her pupils - by fourteen-year-old girls.

Brushes. In the case of larger areas, the liquid wax is applied with a brush of hard bristles. We can also wrap a soft rag round a small stick and "paint" with it. But the outline must first be made with the *tjanting*.

4. There is great danger of wax catching fire. An electric ring is therefore preferable to an open flame. The two tins (951) are stood in a saucepan of water. The old wax is put into the larger tin, fresh wax into the smaller. A special spirit ring for glue is very useful for this purpose.

5. Stretching the fabric; we can simply put the fabric on some sheets of newspaper when we apply the wax. But it is better to stretch it properly. This can be done in several ways: the fabric can be stretched over a piece of cardboard and held in position with clothes pegs (only clothes pegs with wire springs can be used) (852). We can also use an old mirror frame or hang the material over a stick and hold

it in position with clothes pegs (851). The cloth is weighed down with keys attached to the pegs.

We can either cut kerfs into the stick, pull threads through them and hang it up, or we can screw little hooks in at each end and pull the thread through these. But we can also make a frame from battens or even a special batik stand.

6. D y e s : either cold-water fabric dyes or a special batik dye. Again, we must get an instruction leaflet with the dyes, since the same type of dye is not available everywhere. Instructions suitable for one dye might prove disastrous for another. We should always try to get dyes that need no special preparation. Any good handicraft shop will help.

We also need some jars - jam-jars, etc. - for the colours, sticks for stirring and rubber gloves. In the case of most colours, we pound an ounce of colour in a mortar,

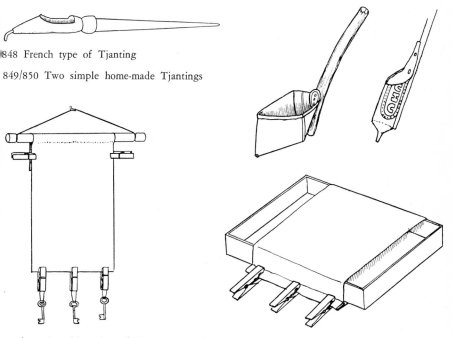

848 French type of Tjanting

849/850 Two simple home-made Tjantings

851/852 Stretching the Fabric over a Stick and round a flat Box

add a teaspoonful of salt, and then gradually stir the mixture into two pints of boiling water. The colour is then filtered through a cloth and kept in a well-closed bottle (salad-cream bottle, etc.). The colours go very far and are therefore comparatively cheap. Three tablespoonfuls of the bottled mixture, an equal quantity of vinegar and the required amount of boiling water (the fabric must be covered with the liquid completely) are enough for any fabric. Darker tones require more colour in the mixture. The prepared colours in their bottles last from between two and three weeks and can be used for any quantity of batik work.

7. F l a t I r o n for removing the wax.

8. U n s i z e d p a p e r (filter paper for very delicate work).

APPLYING THE WAX

Having marked the pattern lightly in pencil or charcoal on the stretched, washed and ironed material, we heat the wax or paraffin in a double saucepan and keep it liquid. We then take out a little wax with the *tjanting* very carefully. A little rag should be placed against the spout, so that no drops can fall on the fabric. The tip of the tube must be in contact with the fabric if we are to get outlines of an even width. The wax must remain fairly thin to penetrate the fabric (if necessary, we can wax it again from the back). Large areas are waxed with a brush. There must be no accidental drops of wax.

DYEING

We now crumple the wax-stiffened fabric in our hands, and put it first into cold water and then into the lukewarm dye mixture (if the mixture is too hot, i.e. above 95 deg. F., the wax dissolves too soon). The batik is now left in the bath until it has the required shade of colour. The colour will penetrate all the parts not covered by wax, including the creases made by crumpling the cloth. These accidental lines add great charm and are a characteristic feature.

How long the cloth remains in the solution depends on the desired intensity of colour. If it is to have only two colours, we rinse it thoroughly in a mixture of water and vinegar, dry it and iron out the wax with unsized paper until the last trace of it has gone. We must always start with the lightest colour. Thus if we have a white ground and want two shades of blue, we first cover the white areas with wax and then put the cloth into the colour mixture for a short time. Then we take it out, dry it, cover the light blue areas with wax and put it into the mixture for somewhat longer. We can also use several colours. We will have to remember in this case that not all colours mix well. Red and yellow produce orange, blue and yellow produce green, and many other colours merely produce unattractive shades of brown. The mixtures must therefore always be tested.

853 (on opp. page) Portions of a Batik Curtain

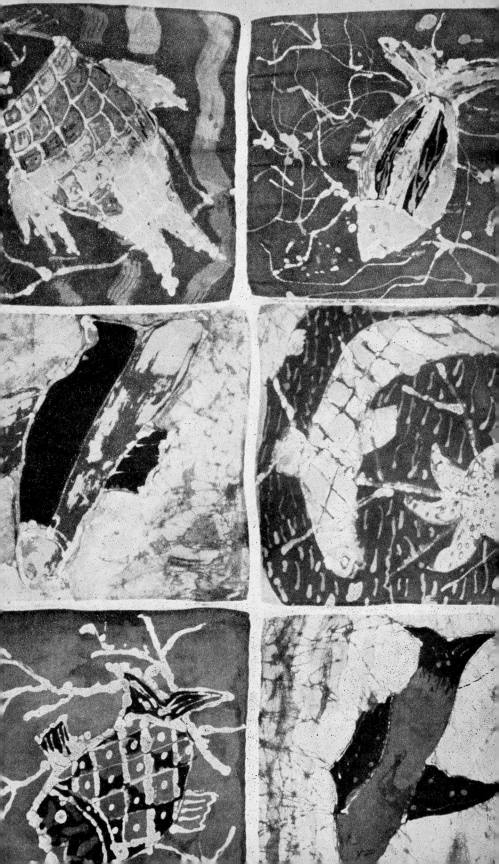

854 These vases were made from coils of clay

855

COILING

FIRST STEP IN POTTERY

Potsherds, i.e. fragments of fired clay vessels, belong to the earliest traces of human activity, and date from long before the invention of the potter's wheel. They are made of lumps of clay or built up from coils, a method we still use after thousands of years for making simple pots without a wheel.

TOOLS AND RAW MATERIAL

Clay

We differentiate between the sandy, and rather sticky clay, used for cementing fire-bricks, and the geologically older clay, used by the potter and in our own work. There are innumerable varieties of clay, according to chemical composition and places of origin. One type takes on form more easily, another less so. One kind fires red, another white, yet another yellow, one sort cannot be treated like another - indeed all clays have characteristics we must know and respect. In general, we distinguish between the fat, loamy and pliable clay and the sandy, less pliable kind.

Clay contains water in its physical and in its chemical structure. The first evaporates when the vessels are on the drying process, the second only during firing to about 1500° to 1600° Fahrenheit in the "bisque" fire. We then no longer speak of clay, but of "biscuit". The air-dried vessel is still very fragile and can be restored to its original, pliable state by merely adding water. But we could not do this to "biscuit", even if it were finely ground. The clay becomes so firm and hard, that it will last for thousands of years, like the prehistoric finds.

If we dig up clay ourselves, we cannot use it immediately. It must be cleaned, i.e. stones and impurities must be removed, and it must be mixed with water and thoroughly kneaded, until it is soft and pliable. We must also take care to eliminate air bubbles, because the pots would burst in these spots during firing.

We can look for small stones and lumps while we knead the clay and we can also mix the clay with water to make the stones sink to the bottom of the mixture. The softened clay and resultant liquid slurry is then put on thick Plaster of Paris slabs, called "batts" so that the surplus water is allowed to soak into the batt and evaporate into the air until the clay dries to a soft, malleable and "plastic" state. The clay which we refer to here is an "earthenware" type, fusing at a comparatively low temperature - 1650° F. to 1859° F. We must also remember that formed clay *shrinks* upon drying and firing. The drying shrinkage ranges from 3% to 6% overall and the firing shrinkage and additional 2% to 4%. Before the clay is worked, it must be kneaded thoroughly so that an even consistency results.

In some districts, clay contains little bits of chalk. These must be washed out very carefully. They are hardly noticed at first and do not harm, if the clay is merely used for modelling. But later, after firing, they are apt to destroy the finest work, because the burnt chalk absorbs humidity from the air, is turned into slaked lime, expands and causes the form to burst.

If we get our clay from a pottery, or pottery supplier, it will be already washed and ground. We merely knead it a little, as we would knead dough, and can start work.

The Tools

Tools are hardly necessary for coil pottery, if we have the vessels fired professionally. A smooth wooden board as a base, a spatula and a palette knife for smoothing are sufficient. The clay is kept in a bin with a lid and covered with damp rags. If a lump of clay is to be divided - as for example, in class - it is best done with a piece of wire, fixed between two small sticks, as shown in Fig. 856.

WORKING PROCESSES

The clay may be formed on a potter's wheel, or may be built up by hand. A potter's wheel is a manually or motor-driven horizontal disc mounted on a shaft which revolves in a counter-clockwise direction when the shaft is turned and propelled. The vessel formed on the wheel is made of one lump of clay, with walls that rise slowly from the base. In coil pottery it is built up in layers, as shown in Figs. 857 and 858. This is a basic hand method of forming clay.

The first step in coil-built pottery is first of all to flatten a piece of clay and cut out or stencil a round base as for making jam tarts. Then we roll out thin and even

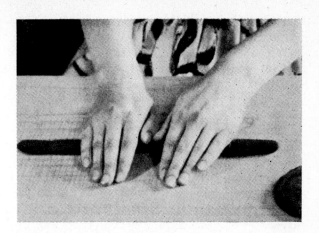

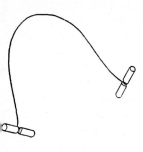

856 Wire used for cutting clay

857 Rolling the clay

858 Putting on the first coil

'sausages', about the thickness of our little finger. (857). Now the work proper can start. One of the sausages is put on the base and pressed hard into position (858), and one layer follows another, as shown in Fig. 855. We must take great care to join the ends of the coils properly, and to press the coils down hard to avoid air bubbles. A 'slip' made of clay and water is applied to each coil before the placing of the following coil.

If the vessel is to spread towards the top, we take a longer sausage or coil for each layer. If it is to narrow we take shorter coils. It means that one layer does not rest exactly on top of the other, but on its outer or inner edge.

To join the coils firmly, the gaps between them are usually filled in and smoothed with the spatula or modelling knife on both sides. It is best to do this in the course of the work, i.e. whenever a new coil is put on, a dampened sponge should be used to wipe the surface of the work. But sometimes we may only smooth the inside of the vessel to show the beauty of the structure, formed by the coils.

DRYING AND SURFACE TREATMENT

Now the vessels must be dried. They are put on a base of wood or plaster - in any case on an *absorbent base* - and not on metal or glass. Larger vessels should stand on a wooden base while we form them. We can turn the board around from time to time and look at the rising vessel from all sides.

Drying takes from four days to a fortnight - according to season - and should preferably be done in rooms of a cool, even temperature. The clay easily cracks in centrally heated rooms, because the vessel cannot dry evenly throughout. It should therefore be watched while it dries and turned round from time to time. Handles can be covered with damp rags, to stop them from drying faster than the body of the pot. Not all types of clay are equally delicate in drying. Greasy pliable clays crack more easily than the lean, sandy kind in the drying process.

We can continue treating the surface in a semi-dry state. It can be beaten with a flat piece of wood - a spoon for example - when it has reached a leathery texture. This strengthens the structure of the clay and the well-beaten vessel can be used unglazed after firing, especially if the clay is greasy and clean. The leathery form can also be polished and smoothed with a slightly damp rag or sponge.

If we use the clay dug by ourselves - and this usually contains a certain amount of sand - it is preferable to scrape the vessel with a knife. The rough surface has a beauty of its own.

FIRING

When the vessel is bone-dry, it must be fired in a kiln; that means it must be heated to a temperature of 1652° F. in a gradual manner so that the clay will harden because of the chemical and physical changes which take place in the process. The kiln is then shut off and allowed to cool to room temperature before being opened. It is very nice to have a small electric kiln of one's own and this is possible as they are now available at a low cost. Such kilns may be bought from potters' suppliers in England and the United States. However, if a kiln is not available, the decorated ware may be brought to a potter who will fire them with his own wares.

Vessels are usually fired twice. The first firing is called the 'bisque' fire and the second, the 'glaze' or 'glost' fire.

The firing time varies as to the type and size of the kiln used. The complete firing and cooling process takes from one to two days. The kiln temperature is raised slowly so that any impurities or moisture may leave the ware gradually and not cause any violent eruptions. Also, the chemical changes which occur to harden the clay must take place in a gradual manner to avoid warping, cracking or other defects which may occur in the 'fast' fire. For the same reason the cooling period must be gradual and the kiln opened only after it has cooled to at least 300° F. Earthenware clays may be fired to 'bisque' at a lower temperature than the subsequent 'glost' or second firing. The lower firing temperature is recommended so that the bisque fired pot will have an absorbent characteristic facilitating the glazing process which will take place later.

SLIP, GLAZES, MAJOLICA COLOURS

Decoration of pottery with coloured clays in liquid form, called slips or engobes, is a commonly used method. A slip is a creamy mixture of water, refined clays and metallic oxides, which are used as colourants. It is important that the slip is composed of clays similar to those used in the making of the pot. If dissimilar clays are used, the layer of slip used to cover or decorate the work may lift off and separate during the firing. Slips are mixed with water and stirred until a smooth even consistency results. Approximately one pint of water is added to one pound of coloured clay (slip). Colours or oxides used in the slips must be ground and mixed with clay in a mortar and pestle so that a complete dispersion is achieved. This provides an evenly coloured result after firing. Naturally coloured clay may be used as a slip colour. To obtain white, we would use a clay that burns white in firing. Additions of oxides to basic neutral coloured slips are generally made in the amounts of 1 to 3% by weight of the clay batch. Cobalt oxide will produce blues, copper oxide for greens, red iron oxide for reds, and iron, manganese and cobalt combinations for blacks. Slips are applied by brushing, dipping or spraying so that a thickness equal to five sheets of paper is developed on the unfired ware. A transparent or clear glaze is generally applied over the entire surface of a slip if a smooth glassy surface is desired.

Slip Ware

In slip ware, the damp, still leathery vessel is soaked or covered in a nearly liquid paste of coloured clay, the so-called slip. After the slip has soaked in, the still leathery vessel is covered with a transparent glaze mixed with water and fired at a temperature of 1970° F. to 2120° F. after it has first dried completely. This ware is fired only once and can be recognised by its shiny, transparent glaze.

To make the glaze more elastic - so that it can adjust itself to the fast shrinking vessel in drying instead of becoming detached - some dextrin powder should be added to the glaze (2-3 ozs. per 2 lbs. of glaze mixture). The professional potter also uses a flour-paste or ox-blood.

We can also let the slip-covered vessel dry, fire it, cover it with clear glaze and fire it for a second time. This method uses more fuel and is therefore not quite professional. But it is easier for beginners.

Majolica

Majolica or faience is always fired twice. A temperature of 1652° F. to 1714° F. is sufficient for the first firing of the unglazed, bone-dry vessel. During this first firing, the clay is transformed into biscuit, a porous (flower-pot), but dissoluble, mass. To make the vessel waterproof, it is covered with a majolica-glaze - a tin-glaze - sometimes painted with majolica-colours, and fired a second time. A temperature of 1859° F. - 2000° F. must be reached during this second firing to melt the glaze.

The name majolica takes its origin from the island Majorca, where the Moors introduced this type of ware in the ninth century. It was later taken up in Italy and named faience after the town of Faenza.

Majolica glaze is an opaque, matt, tin-glaze - in contrast to the shiny lead-glaze - and is made of so-called frit, or previously melted materials. Majolica colours consist of finely ground glass. They are mixed with water and can be painted on the biscuit with a brush. A small quantity of dextrin is added to the water to make the colours adhere better to the glazed biscuit. Vessels made in coil pottery are generally not painted, but covered with a monochrome glaze, which is made by adding majolica colours to the majolica glaze.

Glazes generally are mixtures of minerals, mineral oxides, metallic oxides and inorganic chemicals. The mixtures are combined according to definite formulae which have been predetermined by laboratory testing. The materials which make up a glaze are ground and mixed very thoroughly in a mill so that the particle sizes are very small. The prepared glaze is mixed with water and suitable binders to a creamy consistency. Approximately one pint of water is added to one pound of glaze for correct consistency. The glaze/water mixture is applied to the surface of the ware by means of brushing, dipping or spraying. A thickness equal to six sheets of paper must be applied to the surface of the pot. The application must be even and regular as an uneven application will cause objectionable shading and streaking which will be seen after the firing is complete. The prepared glazes often do not resemble the colour which they will show after firing, and a test pallette should be made on all glazes used so that the craftsman may determine the colour combinations which he wishes to use in his work. When the glaze mixture is fired, the glaze will fuse in the firing and form a coating of glass over the clay ware on which it has be applied. A glaze that has no colour added to it is called a "transparant" or "clear" glaze. Metallic oxides may be added to the transparent or clear glaze to produce glazes of varying colours. It is important that the glaze be applied in the prescribed thickness; otherwise, it will not form the correct thickness of glass necessary to show good gloss and good colour.

Another interesting method of decorating a vessel is with the use of underglaze colours. These colours are mixtures of oxides which have been roasted and finely ground so that they are very stable. Underglaze colours are used to produce a clearly defined design, such as flowers, figures, lettering and general painted designs where outlines must be sharply maintained. Underglaze colours are applied either to the unfired ware or the bisque ware by means of brushing or spraying. The dry colours are first mixed with water and a small amount of clay so that they may be easily applied.

Glazes and coloured glazes as indicated in the foregoing have a tendency to flow and move when they are fused in the kiln. Therefore, they cannot be depended upon to keep a sharp outline in any decorative process. Underglaze colours obviously, because of their characteristics, do not flow and move in the firing and, therefore, are generally used for decorative designs. A clear glaze is used as an over-all application over underglazed coloured work so that the glossy finish produced by the clear glaze will protect the design and sharpen and brighten the colour.

Stoneware

Stoneware is a type of clay ware which has a very hard, dense and almost impervious body. It is made of clays which are essentially of the earthenware type, with the exception of the fact that they contain larger quantities of refractory materials which fuse at the higher temperatures. Because of the fact that they contain quantities of iron and manganese, stoneware clays will not fire out to be very white but rather a buff, grey or brownish colour. When fired to their maturity, approximately 2,300° F. they present a very hard, almost glassy texture, and the oxides which are an inherent part of the clay begin to fuse with the clay and give the clay its colour. Many potters allow the natural colour of the clay to remain without glazing as the natural colour is very pleasing. However, glazes which fuse in the higher temperature range of 2,100° F. to 2,200° F. are often used on a stoneware body. Stoneware is used where great durability is required and frequently finds an application in products where an acid-resistant material is needed.

An interesting method of glazing stoneware has been carried on for many years in Germany where common salt is fused in the firing chamber of a kiln and the fumes developed from this salt rise in amongst the ware and form a glaze called "salt glaze". It is known that a kiln once used for "salt glaze" cannot be used for other glazes.

PAINTING ON PORCELAIN

HISTORY

Porcelain, brought to Europe by the Arabs in the ninth century, was invented by the Chinese, who guarded the secret of its manufacture jealously. Imported porcelain was at the time extremely expensive, like everything imported from the East. European attempts at imitation did not go beyond a feeble substitute - from a technical point of view - the so-called soft paste. Böttger, a German, rediscovered the secret in 1709. He was an alchemist in the service of Augustus the Strong. His unsuccesful attempts at making gold led him accidentally to porcelain.

The Meissen factory built by Augustus the Strong, was for a long time the only European centre of porcelain production. In Meissen, too, the secret was carefully guarded, until it reached Vienna and, later, Hochst and Furstenberg.

The Berlin Porcelain Factory was founded by Frederick the Great, who was so interested that he even gave technical instructions.

The earliest vessels, made by Böttger, were monochromes, at first red, later white. Colours suitable for painting porcelain were only discovered several years after Böttger's death. Ordinary colours would have been quite useless. The newly invented porcelain colours only unfolded their full beauty during firing. They stuck firmly to the glaze and were very brilliant.

The themes were at first borrowed from the Chinese, until an original style began to develop.

217

859 Children love a Tea Set of their own

PAINTING UNDER AND OVER THE GLAZE

We distinguish between painting under and over the glaze. In underglaze painting, the colours are applied directly to the biscuit on the fired, but not yet glazed, surface. The glaze comes later and fuses with the colours during firing. This type of porcelain painting is practised almost exclusively in the factories, and it is more difficult, since it makes corrections impossible.

In overglaze painting, the finished, twice-fired porcelain, is painted and fired once more at lower heat in the so-called muffle kiln. This is the method we are most likely to use.

TOOLS AND MATERIALS

Ready-made porcelain colours are best for our purpose. They are not easily obtainable and we therefore include a description of powdered paints.

We should limit ourselves to one shade. So-called Delft blue and Delft red are most suitable. They change colour very little in firing and are also suitable for using without other colours.

Apart from the colour, we also need some copal oil to fix the colour to the porcelain. Purified turpentine and oil of cloves is best for thinning the colours, ordinary turpentine will do for palette and brushes. High grade brushes should be cleaned with alcohol. An old plate can serve as palette.

Powdered Colours

If we use powdered colours and have to prepare them ourselves, we need a sheet of frosted glass, a glass pestle and two horn spatulae of different width.

To mix the colours, we put one to two teaspoons of the powder on the glass, add a few drops of turpentine and mix everything thoroughly with the glass pestle. The mass should always be moved towards the centre with the spatula. Then we add a little more turpentine and continue mixing, until we have a smooth syrup-like paste, that must not grind under the pestle. Finally, we add some copal oil and a few drops of lavender oil and mix it all thoroughly. The finished mass should have the consistency of oil paint. It is put into little jars or into the hollows of the palette and covered immediately, to stop it drying up or getting dusty.

Brushes

We can use good quality water colour brushes, but they must be very supple and have a good point. There are special brushes for different stages of porcelain painting, but they need not concern us in our first efforts.

It is absolutely essential to keep the brush clean and to rinse it thoroughly immediately after use. This can be done with turpentine or, better still, with alcohol or soap and warm water. If this should have been forgotten accidentally, we must put the brush in alcohol and wait until the colour dissolves.

PAINTING

Before painting, the porcelain is cleaned thoroughly with a piece of cloth soaked in alcohol or turpentine. Used porcelain, i.e. porcelain that has been used in the house and washed a lot, is not suitable for painting. It is apt to turn dark or spotted during firing. Before we draw the outlines with a sharp pencil, we rub the porcelain with an equal mixture of copal oil and oil of cloves. The thin film thus formed is a good base for our work. Now we can start painting.

We mix some copal oil with some oil of cloves in a jar, dip the brush into it and mix the colour with the oil, until it becomes smooth and easy to apply (this is already so in the case of the powdered paint you have prepared yourself). The colours must not be put on too thinly or too thickly. Thinly applied colours melt away in firing, those applied too thickly burst and get detached. We must also take care to make the individual brush strokes at one go instead of interrupting and starting again.

When colour is applied, too, we must fill in the outlines as vigorously as possible and not mottle with dainty touches.

Porcelain paints can be mixed, but it is better to use the colours pure, since they change in firing. It is difficult to judge how they will turn out, if we have not much experience.

Having finished painting, we carefully remove the outline and any marks with a rag soaked in turpentine. The work is now left to dry for about a day and then dusted carefully and taken to be fired. Only firing really brings out the colours. If some colours have burned away or were not applied sufficiently strongly, we can put them on again and have our piece re-fired.

METALWORK

Many craftsmen work in metal, from the blacksmith, who forges glowing metal on his anvil, to the smith in copper, silver or gold. But it is also the basic material used by the locksmith, the tool-maker and the machine builder. Any description must necessarily be very elementary. We only cover the following fields: hammered work, filigree and box work.

THE MATERIALS

The materials are found in the earth as ore, i.e. mixed with minerals, and receive their pure form through melting in furnaces. When we receive them for our work, they have been rolled into sheets, of varying thickness, or drawn into wire. We mostly use copper with its reddish glow, brass - an alloy of copper and zinc - sometimes bronze and the more precious silver. The ordinary white metal used for tins is good enough for our first efforts.

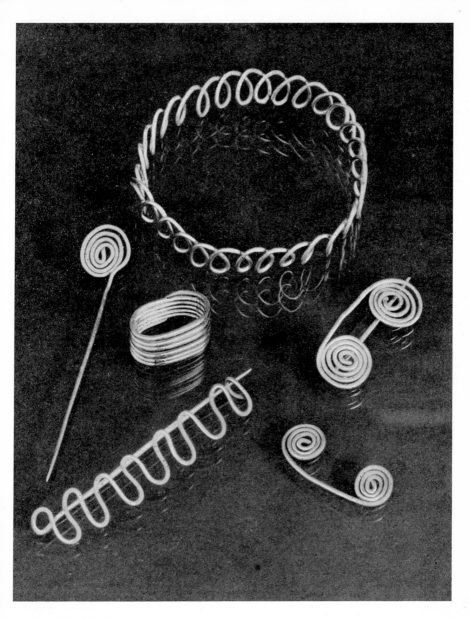

860 Bent Wire Work

Copper is soft and expands and therefore is very suitable for chased metalwork. The hardness of brass depends on its zinc content, but it is always harder than copper and therefore more suitable for pieces with a plain surface, which does not have to expand. Bronze is an alloy of copper and tin and therefore even harder and more brittle than copper. Silver, however, can be worked fairly easily. But since it is rather expensive, it should not be used until we have gained some experience in metalwork. We can use sheets of copper and brass in various sizes, of different gauge and of different degrees of hardness. We use sheets from 0.02 in. to 0.04 in.

thick according to the work. Only the softer kinds are suitable for our purpose.

Metal foil of aluminium, copper or brass, in thicknesses of 0.002 in. to 0.004 in. must not be confused with sheet metal.

FILIGREE TECHNIQUES

Anyone who holds a piece of wire in his hands is inclined to twist it into all kinds of shapes. Many little objects, suitable as presents, such as bracelets, tiepins or brooches, can be made of wire. Bending wires into shapes, or filigree, is an ancient craft. The Etruscans were making bracelets of skilfully entwined filigree in 800 B.C.

A strong piece of brass wire, about 0.04 in. to 0.06 in. (about Gauge 18) thick, is most suitable for our purpose. We can also use some coppered iron wire of the type employed in place of string for heavy parcels. Anyone who has acquired some skill can also use a silver alloy wire.

We need a pair of ordinary pincers or wire cutters to nip off the ends of the wire, a file to give it points, a pair of flat-nosed pliers (862) and a pair of round-nosed pliers (861) with very fine points.

HEATING AND HARDENING

If we want to soften hard wire, we use the same methods as in hammered work. The wire is heated over a gas burner until it is red, and is then put into a mixture of one part sulphuric acid and twenty parts of water (called 'pickle' in U.S.A.). This process is called annealing. Great care must be taken not to inhale any of the fumes and to avoid splashing. The wire is pulled out with a wire hook, thoroughly rinsed, and polished.

Hammering on an iron base will harden soft wire.

BENDING

To make a simple pin (863) we take the end of a piece of brass wire about 0.04 in. thick, (Gauge 18) with a pair of round-nosed pliers and make as small a coil as possible. While the left hand tugs slightly at the wire, the right continues to turn the pliers until the wire is rolled up like a snail. When the spiral is long enough, the wire is bent sharply and cut off. The end is then filed to a point and smoothed with emery cloth. If the point is too soft, it can be hardened as described above.

MAKING A BROOCH

A brooch (867) is made over a rack, consisting of a piece of wood with nails (866). The wire is bent round the nails, to get the desired wave-like shape. Such a rack can be used repeatedly. One end of the wire is bent, sharpened, and if necessary, hammered. The other end is shaped to take the point.

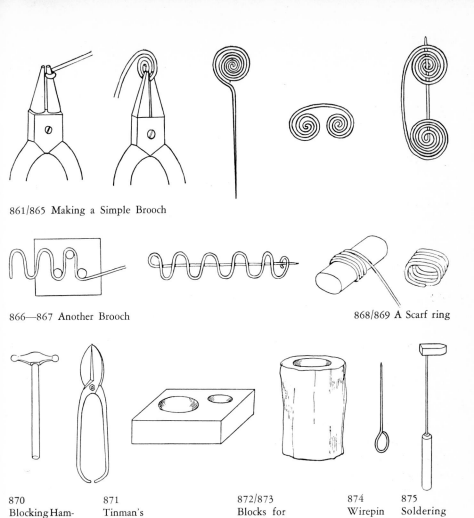

861/865 Making a Simple Brooch

866—867 Another Brooch

868/869 A Scarf ring

870
Blocking Hammer

871
Tinman's
Shears

872/873
Blocks for
hammering

874
Wirepin

875
Soldering
Iron

A Bracelet

The wire is bent round nails, as for a brooch.

A Scarf Ring

The wire is bent round a piece of wood, the ends are afterwards soldered to the ring (868, 869).

SURFACE TREATMENT

To give brass filigree a professional finish, it should be dipped in nitric acid with a pair of pincers and thoroughly rinsed afterwards, or polished with very fine grade steel wool and a little linseed oil. Having dried, it is polished with a soft cloth or chamois. (Take great care with nitric acid. It is dangerous.)

Colourless varnish may then be applied to the slightly warmed metal, but this method of protection is a difficult one for the amateur to employ satisfactorily.

HAMMERED WORK

TOOLS

Hammered work needs comparatively few tools. We need a blocking hammer (870), a pair of spring dividers (950), and a pair of tinman's shears (871) or a fret-saw with a blade for cutting metal. We also need various wooden blocks, preferably hardwood, with a slight hollow for making bowls (872 and 1140). A portion of a tree trunk, as employed for chopping wood, can also be used. This makes a table or a bench-top unnecessary. A wooden mallet for smoothing the metal is also necessary, but we can easily make this ourselves.

BLOCKING

It is best to start with a small bowl or ash-tray from sheet copper of about 0.03 ins. (about Gauge 21). We first draw a circle on the metal and cut out the disc with the tinman's shears or with a fret-saw with a metal-cutting blade. The edges are filed down smoothly. We then put the disc on the appropriate block, take the blocking hammer and start work. Beginning in the centre, we work towards the periphery in the pattern of a spiral, blow for blow. We must work out the form very *gradually*, as if we would feel our way along it. During blocking, the left hand continually turns the metal very slightly, To make the blows more gentle, the hammer can have leather wrapped round its head. When the edge of the bowl has been reached, we return to the middle and thus hollow out the shape more and more, until it is quite even.

ANNEALING

Continuous hammering hardens the metal. Its surface tension makes further beating impossible and may even cause cracks. We must therefore soften the metal by heating and plunging, especially when we are making bowls. Our piece is held by a pair of flat-nosed pliers over a gas-flame - we could also use a coal-fire - and is afterwards thrown into a bowl of cold water in the case of copper. Brass and iron are left to cool more slowly. The metal thus softens and work can be continued.

Blocking can also be done on a sandbag, without wooden blocks, if, for example, we should want to produce some asymmetric forms. But this requires considerable experience and practice.

If the bowl has a distinct base, as in Fig. 876, we use a round block for hammering the centre into shape.

FINISHING

The completed bowl is first polished with the finest emery cloth and afterwards

876

with metal polish, or with fine grade steel wool and linseed oil. The final polishing should be done with buffing powder and a chamois skin. Instead, the bowl can also be put into a solution of sulphuric acid and water (one part of sulphuric acid to ten parts of water) and rinsed in water and dried carefully afterwards. (Great care must be taken over anything containing sulphuric acid).

BOX WORK

Box work, i.e. work that is not blocked, but given sharp edges by bending or hammering - as, for example, a match-box holder - requires a small, but efficient vice with two smooth iron bars to grip the metal and to prevent it from getting damaged.

The metal is put into the vice, the projecting part is bent over and beaten with a wooden mallet to form a right angle at the point where sheet metal and iron bars meet. To give the surface a finish as in Fig. 876, we need a small metal punch.

A Match-box Holder

This match-box holder is made of a square piece of brass. If we don't know the exact dimensions, we can make a pattern of strong paper or cardboard.

A folding pattern should be made for any symmetric shape. Since the pencil does not mark the metal sufficiently, we need a sharp, strong pin (874). We can make such a pin ourselves from a sharpened piece of iron wire.

877 Children's Work

Often, as in the case of the frame for a lampshade or when fitting a shank to a button, soldering cannot be avoided. If we use some of the ready-made solders available from ironmongers, or a hardware store, it should not prove very difficult. It is best to use a non-oxidising solder. We need a small soldering iron, or at least a small blow-pipe. Anyone who does a lot of soldering would be well advised to buy a small electric soldering iron. Soldering is done as follows: the wire-shaped solder is held with its end to the spot to be soldered and is melted with the soldering iron, so that it unites the parts we want to join. We wait until the solder has turned solid and then quickly dip the piece into cold water. If we want to solder a shank to a button or a needle to a brooch, the needle or shank should be put into the liquid solder and plunged into cold water afterwards.

PAPERWORK

Paper is one of the basic materials of handwork. It was invented by the Chinese in all the forms known to us to-day, whether wall-paper, tissue paper or papier mâché. The actual inventor was Ta'ai Lun, who made his discovery in 105 A.D. The Arabs in Samarkand did not learn the secret until 757, when it was revealed to them by some of their Chinese prisoners-of-war.

Vegetable fibre, wood, rags, old paper, straw and bamboo can all be used for making different kinds of paper. These materials are torn up by machines, mixed with glue and turned into a paste, which eventually becomes paper.

Paper has enormous possibilities. It can be balled up, torn and shaped, cut, glued and folded. It can cover boxes and folders, it can be used for making transparencies and coloured or turned into lampshades, masks and papier mâché heads for dolls. Yet for all this, we hardly need any tools beyond knife and scissors.

TRANSPARENCIES (Folding cut)

Transparent paper is used, preferably white tracing paper. A razor-blade, with paper wrapped round it or in a holder, will do for cutting and a piece of cardboard will act as a base.

It is an essential feature of transparencies that patterns are cut out only halfway. The cut-out part is then folded back. Thus we obtain three different degrees of transparency, as becomes evident when we hold the paper against the light: the brightest section lets the light through completely undimmed, since it is really the

878 Transparencies made by children at school

hole left by the cut out pattern, the second shows the paper in its original state and the third is darkest, since the paper is folded double. We get this effect in reverse, if we put the paper on a dark ground. In addition, we have the play of light and shadows giving movement and life to the surface. It is best for the novice to cut out such patterns quite freely at first. That way, we can quickly discover new forms and gain a lot of experience. We should pay careful attention to the distribution of the planes.

PAPER SCULPTURE

Cutting, bending, folding and rolling over the scissors or the table edge can turn paper into the shapes of human figures, animals, trees, masks, lanterns, etc. Here, too, it is best to start quite playfully, without definite intentions, to discover the possibilities of the material. A piece of paper can be folded and cut into, as shown in Fig. 883. If both ends are stuck together, the folded edges will turn outwards and produce a lantern shape (882). (This lantern should be stuck to the top and bottom of a roll of lamp-shade paper, to give it support). If a piece of paper is cut into in a similar fashion (884) and every other strip is folded inwards, we obtain a shape like that shown in Fig. 885, which can be greatly varied. The paper can also be cut into with a knife without previous folding, rolled round the knife edge, stuck

228

879—881 Simple Transparencies, made by cutting and folding back

882 A lantern

886 A paper bird

887—888 Some of the Inhabitants of the Cut Paper World

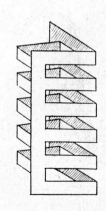

89—890 The Castle and the Forest

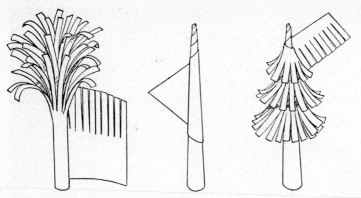

891—893 Paper trees have many shapes

894 Paper folded into visitors from Africa (plus cage and flora)

895 Basic patterns for 894

896—897 The Anatomy of Paper Animals

through the hole, etc. A great variety of things can be made that way: fishes, trees, animals that can stand up, little toy theatres and much else.

FOLDING PAPER

Every child has folded paper and has learned how many simple things can be made that way. Arrows, boats, aeroplanes and other paper objects go on inspiring new forms. Though many of these shapes are traditional, new ones seem to come to life all the time. Each generation passes on something to the next.

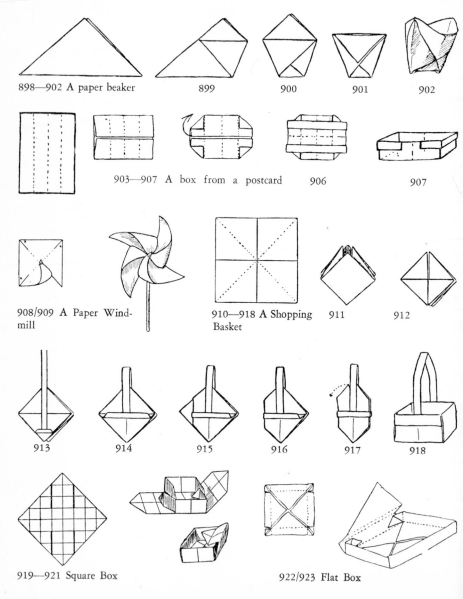

898—902 A paper beaker   899   900   901   902

903—907 A box from a postcard   906   907

908/909 A Paper Wind-mill

910—918 A Shopping Basket   911   912

913   914   915   916   917   918

919—921 Square Box   922/923 Flat Box

Watertight Beaker

Fold a square piece of paper diagonally. Turn one corner back to the opposite side, as shown in Fig. 899, and fold the other accordingly. If you turn down the remaining triangles, you have a beaker (902). A paper ball tied to it turns the beaker into a ball-game.

Postcard Box

The little box in Fig. 907 comes from an old chemist's shop or pharmacy. It was used for weighing different powders and can still do service as a container for beads, pins or nails. It is also folded in such a manner that it will hold water. A postcard or a piece of cardboard is folded lengthways, and unfolded again (903). It is then folded, so that the two narrow sides should meet in the middle and opened out again (904). The corners are turned inwards (905) and the inside strips of paper are turned back over the corners (906). Then we merely put our fingers into the two folds formed inside, raise the box into position and crease the corners sharply (907).

A Paper Windmill

Paper windmills are very old and very popular toys. The paper is folded and cut as shown in 908. The marked points are turned to the middle and fixed to a stick with a pin.

Shopping Basket

This basket can also be used by children for playing shop, at Christmas it can contain presents, and at Easter eggs.

We need a fairly large square piece of coloured paper - although wrapping paper could be used as a substitute - and a strip, at least as long as the edge of the paper for the handle. We work as follows: fold the paper first diagonally each way to form a cross on the coloured side, and parallel to the edges on the back to form another cross (910). If the diagonal creases are raised and the others appear like grooves, the work has been done correctly.

Take the four corners so that the diagonal creases touch inside and smooth the paper down (911).

Turn back the point of the uppermost section of the paper, turn the folded sheet round and do the same on the other side (912).

Fold the turned-back corners inwards three times, take the strip for the handle and fold it once, so that the ends can be tucked into the pockets formed by the turned-back corners (913).

The corners holding the handles should then be folded back with the latter until the central crease is reached (914).

Fold the corners on both sides back towards the centre; as the arrow in Fig. 917 shows, turn the point downwards, press the basket into shape from the inside and turn the two points inwards or glue them to the bottom of the basket.

A Square Box

Such a box can be a beautiful present for Mother's Day. We could even fold many such boxes to fit into each other. The innermost box might contain a very special surprise.

We fold as follows: the paper is creased diagonally and is folded in such a way, that, when opened out, it looks as shown in Fig. 919. Cut along the thickly marked lines, take the two other corners to the centre and raise the side walls, as in Fig. 920. The other two sides are now taken up and turned down, so that the uppermost corners come to the centre of the base of the box (921). Lid and base are folded similarly, except that the sides of the square for the lid should be about ⅜ in. longer. The folds round the edges of a flat box should be slightly narrower (922).

Japanese Paper Bird

Up to Fig. 925, everything is done exactly as for the shopping basket (see Figs. 910 and 911). The paper is then opened and creased along the dotted lines. It is then folded as before, but the other way round, so that we obtain the form with the creases outside.

One corner is folded back, then another (928). Back and front are folded together lengthways, so that we get the form in Fig. 929. The two lower points form the tail. One of the two upper points is turned into the feet, the other the head, as shown in Figs. 930 to 932.

A Swan

A swan, another Japanese folding motif, is made from the same basic pattern. We continue as for the bird up to Fig. 929, then we must work differently. The two

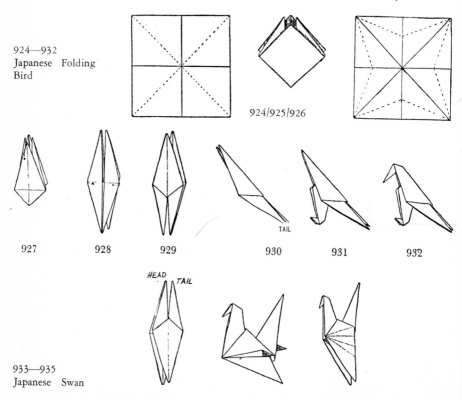

924—932
Japanese Folding Bird

924/925/926

927   928   929   930   931   932

TAIL

HEAD   TAIL

933—935
Japanese Swan

236

936 This bird is made from an old Chinese pattern and can be great fun. Children are particularly happy if he is also giving a feeding trough

tips - the crow's tail - become the swan's head and tail, the two other tips (the crow's head and feet) form his handsome wings. We continue as shown in Figs. 933 to 935: the paper is folded for the head, the tail is pulled in a bit to form an angle, and the paper is folded along the dotted lines like a fan to produce a pair of fine wings.

937 The swan is also based on a Japanese pattern and is a simple variation of the bird above. It can also be made into a stork with outspread wings

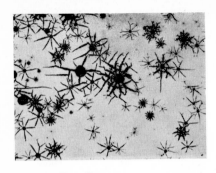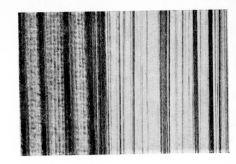

938—939 Paste Papers

COLOURED PAPERS

We can make many kinds ourselves. The most important groups are paste paper, marbled paper, oiled paper, paper decorated with lino, rubber or potato-stencils, batik paper, sized paper and mottled paper.

Paste Papers

To make paste papers, we must either make our own paste or use ordinary liquid paste from a stationery shop.

Apart from paste, we also need a fairly strong white or coloured paper, a wide and a narrow brush, newspaper, and some colours. Drawing inks are generally sufficient for our needs. If not, dyes, coloured tracing inks etc. can be used.

We work as follows: the paper is slightly damped with the brush or sponge and covered with paste. The colour is then applied over the sticky paste. Patterns can be produced with paper combs, the handle of the brush, with the fingers or even with the brush, when it has dried stiff. If we draw these "tools" over the damp paper, covered with paste and colour, the colour will appear lighter in these places and darker where it was allowed to run. A good combination of colours is very important in paste papers.

Another pattern, as shown in Fig. 938, is formed by spraying the damp paste-covered paper with a little colour. The drops of colour form little stars on the paste. Some close-meshed wire, as used for spraying colour on geometrical drawings, is best for this purpose.

We need a lightly glued paper, a strip of stencil, ordinary oil paint in tubes and a flannel rag. A little oil paint is squeezed out on an old plate or a palette, spread

238

940 Potato Print (from one potato stamp used several times)

out and touched lightly with the flannel rag. The stencil is then put over the paper and pressed down hard with the left hand. The paper is rubbed with the flannel in the same direction to a width of half an inch more beyond the sides of the stencil. The colour is much darker near the stencil.

This basic method allows many variations: the stencil can be put down at shorter or longer intervals, a gap can be left and given a different colour and we can go over smaller or larger areas with a piece of cotton wool. Everybody will discover their own method and can improve on it. It is of course essential that pattern and colour should suit the purpose of the paper.

Marbled Papers

We need a square zinc trough, a bristle brush and bowls for the colours. The ground for the colours is made of Carrageen moss as follows: two quarts of rain-water are put into a four-quart saucepan and left to boil. When boiling we put in an ounce of moss and keep boiling for five minutes longer, stirring all the while. As soon as moss and water have boiled the requisite time, the saucepan is taken from the fire and a pint of cold water is added. The size should be left standing for 24 hours and then strained into the trough through a linen bag. Several makes of colours are available on the market. We add some drops of ox gall to the colour - best bought already prepared for use, since fresh gall will not mix satisfactorily - spread it on the marbling ground with the brush and distribute it with a sharp-toothed comb or a little wooden stick. The paper - which should be unglazed, to take the colour better - is damped with alum water and put slowly on the marbling ground, beginning at the bottom left-hand corner. It should be left in the mixture for a few seconds, removed carefully and hung up to dry.

The remaining colour is removed with a strip of newspaper that is slightly longer than the trough. We can also use the same ground for marbling with ordinary oil paint. These colours can be thinned with paraffin or turpentine (not both together) and applied in the same way. Damping the paper with an alum solution is not necessary in this case.

Sized Paper

Size can be bought as a powder and makes paper very durable. It also makes it washable and therefore allows us to use ordinary powdered colours. The technique is similar to making paste paper: the powder is dissolved in water and mixed with a little size. The paper is then covered with this mixture and left to dry. It is essential to let the paper dry very thoroughly. The paper is now covered with another, contrasting colour. It is important to work very fast with a brush, a small stick or a strip of cardboard since the second layer of colour must not be allowed to dry. The first layer of colour will thus be revealed and we can produce a number of interesting patterns. The paper should dry thoroughly for at least a week, or it will easily suffer damage when pressed.

Batik Paper

We first draw a pattern on a sheet of paper with wax pencils or with a brush dipped in liquid wax or stearin. If we now cover the paper with colour, the parts covered in wax will not be affected by it. A white paper, covered in blue, would therefore produce a white pattern on a blue ground. If the pattern is to have several colours, we cover the blue areas again with wax and paint the entire sheet a darker blue. The pattern is then white, blue and dark blue.

When the paper has dried, we put it between two sheets of newspaper and iron out the wax. The newspapers will have to be changed several times. The paper is afterwards waxed and polished.

Mottled Paper

We first make a drawing with a thick layer of flake white.

When the paint has dried, the paper is covered with black tracing ink and dried again thoroughly. Afterwards, we go over the paper with the finest wire wool, until the colour re-appears. The remaining ink gives the drawing a rather attractive, patina-like quality.

For printed papers see lino printing, page 199, and for potato printing Fig. 940.

941 A Simple Folder. The boards are covered in grass paper. A fine present, easy to make. Only paste has been used. For instructions see page 249

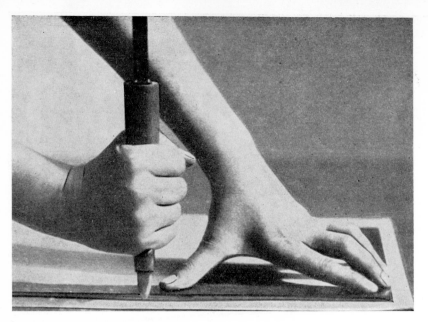

942 Using the Mount Cutter's Knife

CARDBOARD

Working with cardboard is a step towards book-binding. Here, too, our work must be technically perfect. It will help to gain good experience with the materials. Perhaps it will give some of you so much pleasure, that you may even take up book-binding.

MATERIALS

Cardboard, paper and linen are the most important materials and they are easy to work. Yet each type of board, each paper, has its individuality and its own particular needs that we must get to know. Linen and paper stretch more in one direction than in another, boards have their "grain"; in one case we need glue, in another paste. Indeed, we must learn a wealth of rules and century-old techniques.

Let us look at our materials:

Board

We distinguish between different types of board:

1. Grey-board or binder's board, is most commonly used for our purpose. It is made of paper waste and rags, is very hard-wearing and elastic and does not absorb glue and paste as much as softer types of board. It is made in a great variety of thicknesses, indicated by the number of boards to the cwt., such as 24's grey-board or binder's board, 30's grey-board, etc. 24's grey-board is amongst the thickest, 90's grey-board amongst the thinnest kinds. A full board usually measures 40" x 30".

2. Straw-board is generally used for cartons. The better varieties are comparatively flexible and can be used for some of our work.

3. Mill-boards are made from old rope and are very strong and durable, although comparatively thin. Since they are very expensive, they will not be used often.

Paper

The paper we shall use can be divided into three groups:

1. Bank paper (bond paper) is used for lining, for making note books, coloured papers, etc. and for cut paper or folded paper-work. It is best to keep to well-known brands.

2. Single colour paper is often used to cover folders and boxes. It is made in many varieties. For our work we generally use a slightly ribbed and very durable paper, the so-called Kraft paper. It is easily worked and can be had in many colours. Hand-made paper looks rather well, but is very expensive.

3. Coloured papers: We distinguish between paste-papers, lithographed, hand-printed and machine-printed papers. They are used for covering folders and boxes, occasionally also as endpapers. Anyone interested in the book-crafts should learn to make coloured papers. Short instructions are given on pages 238 to 240.

Cartridge Paper (Strong Drawing Paper)

We need the following types of cartridge paper:

1. White cartridge paper, available in several thicknesses.

2. Coloured cartridge paper, available in many shades and colours and also suitable for passe-partout work.

3. Hand-made cartridge paper.

Binder's Cloth, Buckram, Grass Paper

Books, folders and boxes are often covered with binder's cloth or buckram to make them more durable. Sometimes, such treatment is only applied to spines, corners or edges.

Binder's cloth is a specially prepared fabric (today mostly made of cotton or synthetic materials). It is made in many colours and varieties. It must always be worked along the run of the warp (pages 248-249).

Calico is a cotton fabric, made stiff by special treatment. Smooth calico can occasionally look very attractive, the variety with the artificially raised surface less so. Here, too, we must always work along the warp. Glue, never paste, is used with calico.

Japanese grass paper, a fabric made of Japanese grasses and masked with paper,

243

can look very well indeed. Here, we always use paste, as for all Chinese and Japanese papers (941).

Bookbinder's mull (a kind of muslin), as used for backing maps, is also widely used.

Adhesives

In our first steps, we will generally use paste. Later we will need both paste and glue. The type of adhesive needed for a particular job is mentioned throughout the book.

A good flour paste can be made as follows:

One cupful of white flour and a teaspoonful of ground alum should be mixed in one cupful of water and beaten into a smooth cream. It should then be put into a double saucepan with two more cups of water. We then stir the paste all the time and allow the water in the outer jacket to go on boiling until the paste has thickened.

This should be about five minutes after the water has come to the boil. The paste is then taken off the stove and covered with a little cold water to prevent the formation of a skin. Paste is best preserved in wooden jars.

Usually, we will find a cold water paste more convenient. It is made of a powder, obtainable in most handicraft shops and mixed according to the instructions on the packet.

For making glue see page 284.

A good cold flexible glue will save a lot of unpleasant work and can be obtained from most handicraft shops.

TOOLS

A good workman is judged by his tools. This also applies to us. Below are listed the most important tools.

A board cutting knife (943). There are board cutters with small and with large blades. A small blade would be more suitable for us. Large ones are made for bigger hands.

A steel try square (945).

A bone folder (946), used for folding paper, etc.

Scissors (947). Bookbinder's shears are best, but a good pair of ordinary scissors will do.

A paring stone, for sharpening the knife.

Thick strawboard, as a base for cutting.

A press (a few large books, weighed down with a stone, a flat iron, etc. will suffice). Ordinary bricks, wrapped in paper, are very suitable for this purpose.

Paste pot and brush.

The following articles would prove very useful:

A guillotine. Small cardboard scissors would be even better.

A mount cutter's knife (948), used for cutting and marking boards. The handle is designed to allow for strong pressure, the adjustable blade is double-edged at one end.

A pair of spring dividers (950).

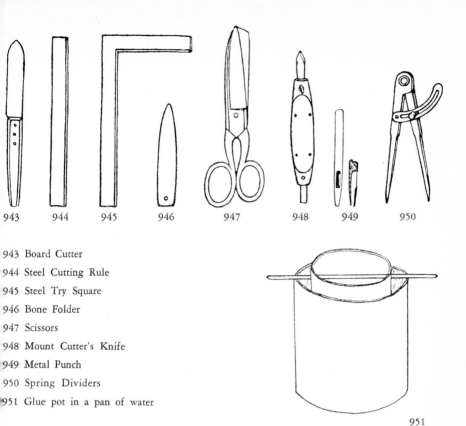

943 944 945 946 947 948 949 950

943 Board Cutter

944 Steel Cutting Rule

945 Steel Try Square

946 Bone Folder

947 Scissors

948 Mount Cutter's Knife

949 Metal Punch

950 Spring Dividers

951 Glue pot in a pan of water

951

A metal punch (949) used for making holes in albums, etc.

A steel cutting rule (944).

A glue pot (951). A kind of double saucepan. It can also be improvised from two carefully cleaned old tins. The smaller tin is pierced with a piece of wire or a long nail, which will also hold it in position within the larger tin. The smaller tin is for the glue, the larger for water, exactly as if we were using a double saucepan.

A sandpaper holder, i.e. a piece of wood, with sandpaper glued to it. It must be large enough to be handled comfortably and is used to file down the edges of the boards.

Pressing boards. Smooth wooden boards for pressing.

Pieces of chipboard. These are put between the pressing boards and our actual work, so that the latter should be protected. The chipboard may have to be cut to the appropriate size.

SIMPLE FOLDERS

How to make folders for Documents, Pamphlets or Single Section Books

See Fig. 952. We place the fully opened notebook or pamphlet on a piece of board of the appropriate size and make three holes from the inside. We then take the thread from the central hole to the outside, then through the upper hole towards

245

the inside down to the lower hole, and again to the outside. The thread returns to the inside through the hole in the middle. Both ends are then finished in such a way that the folder will hold really tightly. The folder can also be given a cover, preferably of a coloured paper we have made ourselves (see page 238). This cover would be trimmed to the size of the folder at top and bottom, but folded at the sides.

Making Folders for Single Sheets

We take two pieces of cardboard of the required size, and make a crease in each about ¾ in. from the edge. We then take the sheets to be bound, smear them at the back with glue or paste, place them in the folder and put some weights on top. Having dried, folder and paper are pierced with an awl in three to five places - according to size - (953) and sewn together with a strong hemp thread. A strip of binder's cloth - it should come as far as the crease on each side - is used to cover the spine. (The binder's cloth must be cut lengthways).

Lacing-up Note-Books in the Japanese Manner

This method is shown in Figs. 956 and 957. We need a strong paper of good quality for the cover. This paper will form a long strip, which has to be folded as shown in Fig. 954. We put in the sheets, close the folder and punch the holes at equal distances as shown in Fig. 953. A punch (949) is best, but a single-hole office punch, a nail or a strong needle can also be used. Finally, the folder is sewn together with a thin cord or some raffia, as shown in Fig. 955.

The folder shown in Fig. 958 is made similarly. It consists of real vellum. The two separate covers have been punched together with the manuscript. A strip of parchment has been used for sewing.

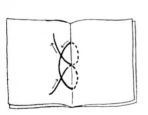  

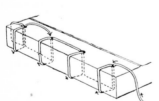

952 Sewing

953 Sewing Single Sections

954 A Folder for Laced-in Sections

955 Japanese Lacing

MOUNTING MAPS

We need a piece of fine cotton cloth called jaconet. It should project about four inches beyond the map on all sides.

The jaconet is first covered at the edges with paste to a width of not quite an inch and stuck to an old drawing-board or an old table-top. When it sticks properly it should be damped all over with a sponge to make it quite taut.

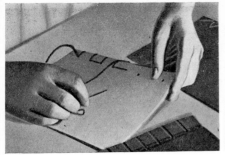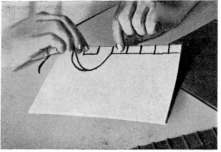

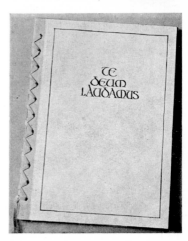

956—957 Japanese Lacing

958 Lacing up with Parchment or Vellum (right)

959—960 Finishing the corner of a map

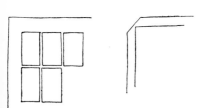

The map is then cut into sections of equal size. These should be numbered immediately, so that they do not get mixed up. Maps are generally folded twice sideways and five times lengthways, so that there will be eighteen sections.

We now mark a right angle at the top left-hand corner of the piece of jaconet about 2½ in. from the edge. The six sections of the first row are then covered at the back with paste and stuck on along the lines at distances of slightly less than 1/8 in. The other sections are stuck on similarly, row by row. Each section must be pressed down carefully under a sheet of paper. Having mounted the entire map, we press it down with boards and heavy books. Next day, when everything has dried, we carefully detach the jaconet from the board, trim it to a margin of about 3/16 in. cut off the corners, and fold the edges inwards over the map (959, 960).

Finally the map is carefully pressed down, having been first folded lengthways and then sideways.

THE ELEMENTS OF BOOKCRAFTS
AS SHOWN IN INDIVIDUAL EXAMPLES

The basic principles are best studied in connection with different types of work. This book has been arranged to show how the more difficult techniques follow those of a simpler nature, so that all can gradually be mastered.

Before dealing with various techniques, we would like to mention some fundamentals.

Warping

If we stick a piece of paper to one side of the cardboard only, it will always warp after drying, i.e. it will contract or bend towards the papered side. We must therefore paste or glue paper on both sides. This is a basic rule.

Another point to be noted to avoid warping is the grain of the paper, cardboard or cloth, as already mentioned earlier on.

The adhesive is also of great importance. At first, we use only home-made paste or cold water paste, but we should know of the effect of the adhesive on the boards from the very beginning. If we use paste, the paper must be coated thickly to stick well; it gets very damp, expands and contracts accordingly when it dries. In the case of thinly applied hot glue, the paper absorbs less humidity and stretches much less when it dries. We therefore use paste.

If we cover a piece of cardboard, the side covered first is exposed to considerable stress, since the covering material is stuck down on the other side. We therefore use both, paste and glue, for larger folders and take glue for the outside, and paste for the inside. This also applies to boxes, albums, etc.

The Grain of Cardboard, Paper and Cloth

The grain of binder's cloth or calico must be considered carefully, when we make the spine of a book or folder. Like all fabrics they will stretch very little along the warp, but considerably more between the selvedge. Cloth is always cut to stretch sideways, i.e. from front to back-cover. Otherwise we shall get a lot of creases. The grain of paper and board must also run parallel to the spine.

The grain of cloth and paper is discovered by stretching them along the edge

961

between thumb and index finger. If the material remains flat, it will have been stretched lengthways; if it turns wavy it will have been stretched sideways. We can also cut off a piece of paper and damp it on one side. It will curl in a horizontal direction.

In the case of cardboard the grain can usually be seen from the run of the fibres. To make sure, we can bend the board slightly horizontally and vertically. It will bend much more easily in the direction of the grain.

The grain of paper and cardboard depends - like that of fabric - on the method of manufacture. They have been run through the machines lengthways, i.e. they have matted much more in that direction.

CUTTING AND COVERING BOARDS

Cutting

Fig. 942 shows how boards are cut. Having marked the exact size, we put on the try square and press it down with the left hand, while the right cuts along its edge, holding the knife absolutely straight. Before we start cutting, we must make quite sure that thumb and index finger are well out of the way of the knife. The first cut merely marks the route the knife will take, the following cuts must be made firmly. And we must not forget to cut along the grain of the board. Afterwards, the rough edges are smoothed with the folder.

Paper used for covering should be cut to project ⅜ in. beyond the boards on all sides.

Covering Boards

Having cut the paper to size, it is put on a sheet of newspaper and covered with paste. This is done as follows (961): the left hand holds the paper down with thumb and index finger, while right spreads the paste with the brush from the centre towards the edges. We must take great care to cover the paper evenly to avoid air bubbles and ugly wrinkles. We now place the cardboard on top of the paper. There should be a margin of ⅜ in. on all sides.

Having done this, the corners of the paper are mitred to a distance slightly in excess of the thickness of the cardboard (962). Now we fold down the two opposite ends of the paper (it is advisable to pull across the newspaper as well, the paper for the cover will then lie flat much more easily). Afterwards the small upright folds at the corners are turned down (964) and the two remaining margins are again pasted and turned over. Everything must be done very quickly.

When the boards have been covered on the outside, we line the inside. This lining must be about ½ in. smaller all-round than the board.

TIME-TABLE, CALENDAR, ETC.

For a time-table or map we simply paste on these instead of the lining.

LEPORELLO, OR ACCORDION-STYLE, PHOTO-ALBUM

For a Leporello photo-album (941) we fold a strip of cartridge paper as illustrated on pages 275-276, cut and cover boards and paste these to the ends of the strip.

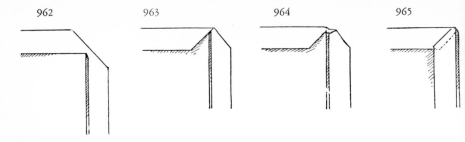

ADJUSTABLE FOLDER

An adjustable folder (966) is very useful. We take two boards of equal size and cover them as described on page 249 except that we do not line the inside of one board. Having covered the boards, we make three cuts in each as shown in Fig. 966, and pull parchment strips through them. The ends are left to project for about an inch on the inside of one cover, while two cuts are made on the unlined cover to take the parchment strips. These are pulled through and glued down. The lining is then pasted over boards and strips.

A READING CASE

For a reading case two pieces of board are joined by a cloth spine. This can be done in several ways. We can either have a flexible spine by simply lining it with cloth, or we can reinforce it with paper or even cardboard to make it a stiff spine, as shown in Figs. 968 and 1005.

Cutting the Materials

First of all we cut the two boards to size, then we cut out three pieces for the spine as follows:

966 Adjustable Folder.   967 Reading case with flexible Spine.   968 Stiff-backed Reading Case.

1. The so-called gauge. It is made of the same material as the boards and must be of the same height and as wide as we want the spine to be.
2. A piece of cloth for the spine. It must be about an inch longer than the boards and about two inches wider than the gauge.
3. A piece of cloth for lining the spine. This should be about ⅜ in. shorter than the covers and about an inch wider than the gauge.

Different Types of Spine

a) Flexible Spine (967): The cloth for the outside is covered with paste and the gauge is put on it very lightly, so that the distances at top and bottom and to the left and right of the gauge are equal. We then put the boards against the gauge, taking great care that they are exactly in line. This is best checked with a ruler. The gauge is then removed and the cloth turned in at head and tail. It must be pressed down carefully with the folder. Now we paste on the lining (970), press it down with the folder, put the gauge on it with the clean side (969) and leave our folder to dry for a few hours under some evenly distributed weights before we continue. (The gauge is removed after drying).

b) A stiff back (968): For a hard spine we incorporate the gauge. The cloth for the outside is covered with paste or glue and the gauge is placed in the middle. The boards are then put on each side of the gauge, only this time not directly against it, but at a distance of about twice their thickness. Now the cloth is turned in and pressed down. We then paste down the lining for the spine, crease it firmly with the folder in the gaps between gauge and boards and leave the folder to dry for a few hours, as above. The two grooves will be much more marked and regular if we put two narrow strips of board against them when we are pressing down the lining for the spine.

c) A Reinforced Spine: Apart from the three parts mentioned above (spine, inner strip and gauge) we also need another inner lining of strong paper. It is cut along the grain to exactly the same size as the gauge. We work as if we were making a flexible spine: the cloth is covered with paste, the gauge is placed on it, the boards are put against the gauge. Then we remove the gauge and replace it with a cloth interlining. This interlining is stuck down with glue. Now we continue as for the flexible spine: the strip of cloth is covered with paste, stuck on and smoothed out, the gauge is placed on it and pressed down.

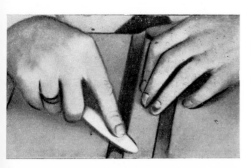

969 (left) The back must be lined before it can be pressed down

970 (right) Lining the back

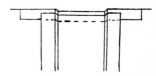

Covering the Boards

The paper for covering the boards is cut to overlap the cloth by about ⅛ in. and to fold in at the top and sides by slightly under ½ in. It is covered on one side with paste or very thin glue - beginning from the end where it meets the cloth towards the other edges. We must take care that the margins are equal on three sides. On the fourth, the paper will be joined to the cloth. The folder is now opened and the overlapping paper turned in and pressed down We then line it with paper as described on page 249.

Corners and Bound Edges

If the folder is used often, the corners should be reinforced with cloth. It also looks very nice if we bind the edges of the cover. We distinguish between visible and invisible corners.

The visible corner is shown in Figs. 971a to c. We take a strip of cloth, about two inches wide, and cut the corners out (it is best to use a paper-pattern) as shown in Fig. 971a. The cloth-corners are covered with glue, put on the boards and treated otherwise exactly as if they were paper. The lining is cut off at the corners, as shown in Fig. 971a.

The invisible corner only projects for about $^1/_{16}$ in. or even less. We cut small squares out of a piece of cloth no wider than half an inch and paste them round the corners (972). The paper used for covering is also rounded to follow the outline of the corners (973).

In the case of 'round' corners, the cardboard is rounded as well. The paper or cloth is turned over (974) and gathered in small folds (975).

Binding one edge with cloth (976). If we want to bind the entire edge with cloth, we have to cut a strip about an inch wide and long enough to project at each end by about half an inch. It is covered with thin glue, placed against the edge of the board and treated like an ordinary corner.

Bound Edges (977). We cut a strip slightly less than an inch longer than the circumference of the board. It is covered on the side with thin glue and put round the edges of the boards as shown in Fig. 977. A piece of the strip is cut out at the corners (see dotted lines) and the cloth is turned down.

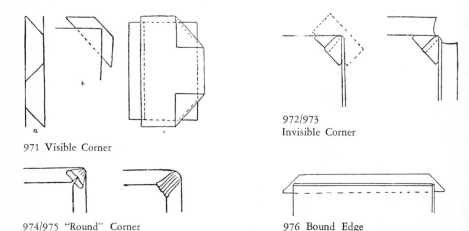

971 Visible Corner

972/973 Invisible Corner

974/975 "Round" Corner

976 Bound Edge

A Folder bound in Full Cloth

A folder bound in full cloth can be made with a flexible, a hard or a reinforced spine. In place of a strip of cloth for the back we will have to cut a piece large enough to cover the boards and gauge as shown in Fig. 978. It should turn in ½ in. all round. The grain of the cloth should run along the direction of the spine. Otherwise we work exactly as described above.

A VARIETY OF USEFUL FOLDERS

Our basic design can be adapted to many purposes. It can be turned into an album for photographs, for documents, for newspaper cuttings, a scrap-book, a guest-book or travel diary.

Photo-Album and Portfolio

We make first of all a stiff-backed folder. On the inside on the left we paste an ordinary end-paper, on the right a piece of hand-made paper, in place of an end-paper. This has to be folded along the dotted lines, so that the flaps can be turned back (979). For the photo-album we shall need a number of boards (cut preferably with a small guillotine) to mount the photographs.

Photo-Album

First we make an ordinary folder, preferably with a stiff back. Then we cut out the boards for the pages which must be slightly smaller than the folder. These are crossed about an inch from the spine, so that they can be turned over better. Afterwards they are tied to the back cover with parchment strips or with a cord. They must have two or three holes made either with the metal punch or with an ordinary office-punch.

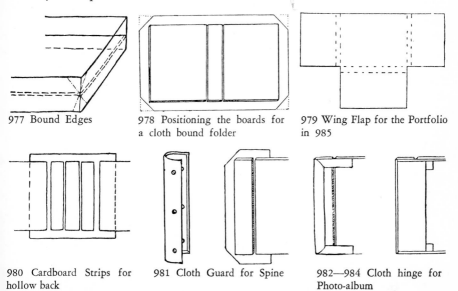

977 Bound Edges

978 Positioning the boards for a cloth bound folder

979 Wing Flap for the Portfolio in 985

980 Cardboard Strips for hollow back

981 Cloth Guard for Spine

982—984 Cloth hinge for Photo-album

Since the album will be very much thicker, once the photographs are in it, we shall have to insert narrow strips of cardboard or carton - to be punched and bound with the rest - after every other page, to prevent bulging.

Portfolio for Newspaper Cuttings, etc.

Such a portfolio is made like an ordinary album, except that large, punched envelopes for the cuttings take the place of the pages. These envelopes should be folded double for strength where they are punched and can have a list of contents written on the outside

Portfolio for Documents

A simple portfolio for documents can be made like the portfolio described above, except that we use a larger size, and try to make our own envelopes of a good quality paper. Our portfolio will look even better, if we make a guard for the spine of the same material as the cover (981). It is put round the boards and punched and bound with them. It is made as follows: a piece of strong paper of the appropriate size is covered with cloth. The cloth is turned in and pasted down, a cloth lining is stuck on and the finished guard is made to curve slightly.

Photo-Album with Japanese Lacing

Having had the pages cut to the appropriate size, we crease them with ruler and folder as for an ordinary photo-album.

We now cut half as many strips as we have sheets, of the same material and height as the latter and about $3/4$ in. wide. The sheets are interleaved with these strips to prevent the album from bulging.

Now we cut out the boards for the cover. They must be about $1/8$ in. wider than the album at the fore-edge and $1/16$ in. at head and tail (foot). The back-cover is made of one piece and covered and lined in the usual way.

The front cover is given a cloth guard as follows: we cut a strip $3/4$ in. wide from the narrow side of the board and another twice the thickness of the board in width. This narrow strip will be needed for giving the cloth a proper crease. Fig. 982 and 984 show us how to cut the strips of cloth for the outside of the guard and the smaller strip for the lining.

The guard is now made like a narrow spine, except that the crease is made from the outside, and not from the inside. Finally, the narrow strip is pasted in as a lining.

The edges of the upper cover are now bound all round with a strip of cloth or reinforced with invisible corners (see page 252). Then we cover the boards and fix end-papers of the same material as the pages. Finally, the whole album is punched and tied with parchment strips or a cord. The lacing is shown in Fig. 955.

An Album with hollow back

This is made like any other album, except that we use an additional lining for the spine. This extra lining must be as wide as the entire album is thick. All the parts are now glued to a wide strip of cloth, as shown in Fig. 980: the lining for the spine goes in the middle, two narrow strips of board are placed to the right

985 Portfolio with Wing
Flaps for Single Sheets

and left at a distance equal to the thickness of the covers, which, in turn are put next to the strips not less than $^3/_{16}$ in. away. The cloth is turned in with the folder. Now we stick a strip of cloth along each of the gaps between boards and spine and press them in very firmly, so that there should be no stress when the folder is opened. Finally, we stick on the corners, cover the boards, line them and punch and lace up the album. The correct way of lacing is similar to the lacing shown in Fig. 952.

Guest-book or Diary

The guest-book is made like the album with Japanese lacing, except that white writing paper is used instead of board.

When we have finished the covers, we should have some paper cut to the required size. We then punch the holes through boards and paper (949) at a distance of about $^5/_8$ in. from the left and tie the book up with raffia, cord, leather or parchment strips as shown in Fig. 955.

Folder with Wing Flaps (992)

A stiff-backed folder is made as described on page 251. The boards should be about $^1/_8$ in. wider all round than the drawings or reproductions for which the folder is intended, the hinges for the flaps should be about $^1/_8$ to $^3/_8$ in. wider than the contents will be thick.

The flaps can be made of fairly thin board and covered, or of a high-grade white board and left uncovered.

The hinges for the flaps are made as 'hard', i.e. inflexible spines with cardboard lining. The pieces of lining are as long as the respective flaps. In the case of the smaller flaps, the lining is slightly under $^1/_{16}$ in. wider than the height of the contents

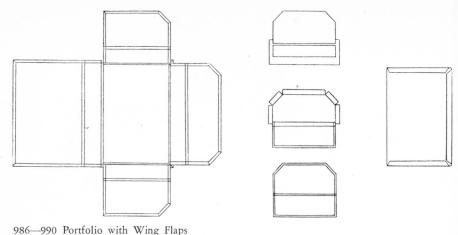

986—990 Portfolio with Wing Flaps

of the folder; the hinge of the long flap is about ¼ in. wider. The cloth is cut for spine and lining, the spine being 1¼ in. wider, the lining one inch wider, than the cardboard inter-lining.

The flaps are first completed separately as shown in Figs. 986 to 989, i.e. the piece for the hinge is covered on the inside with paste or glue, the inter-lining is put on to project about ¾ in. on one side, but only about ½ in. on the other (987). The flaps are placed against the board at the narrow sides at a distance of twice the thickness of the boards, the cloth is pressed down and the lining for the spine stuck on. To accentuate the crease, we put in a strip of cardboard for pressing and we also put a strip of cloth on the outside, where flaps and board will join.

All the flaps are made in the same way. If they are made of cardboard, they are also covered with paper (988, 989).

The flaps are best attached as follows: we cut the lining for the cover that is to take the flaps of white cardboard and then place first the projecting strips of cloth of the two shorter flaps against the back of the lining, then that of the longer flap. The cloth must be cut diagonally where the flaps meet and the cloth must be creased properly against the edge of the lining. Having made certain that every-thing fits properly, the strips of cloth are glued on. Now the back of the entire lining is covered with glue and stuck to the inside of the cover. Finally, the folder is opened out fully and pressed.

A COMPOSITE BOX

Cutting to Size

If we want a box in the dimensions of 5 ins. x 7 in. x 3 in., we first of all cut out the base in the proportions of 5 in. x 7 in., then the two long panels and finally the two short panels in the proportions of 5 in. x 3 in. To get a neat edge, the two emall panels will be slightly wider than the height of the box. In fact, they should be twice the width of the board. Thus if the board is 1/16 in. thick these panels must be 5⅛ in. x 3 ins.

991 Photo-album with Cloth Hinge and Japanese Lacing (left), and with Cloth Spine (right)

992 Portfolio with wing flaps for photographs etc.

Assembling

Before the box can be assembled, we have to cut some strips about ⅝ in. wide from thin paper (typing paper, etc.). These are stuck round the edges, as soon as the box is put together, to fix the panels in position.

We need an absolutely even surface for assembling the box, preferably a board kept for the purpose.

The bottom panel is now placed on a flat surface and the four panels are put against it. We now smear the edges, where the longer panels join the base, with glue to a distance twice the thickness of the cardboard and do the same to three edges of the smaller panels (993). This has to be done very quickly, or the glue will soon be cold and hard. Fig. 994 shows the shape of the box.

Reinforcing with Strips of Paper

If the edges are to be bound with cloth, as shown in Fig. 995, we must cut strips of cloth about half an inch to an inch in width and stick these round the edges like the paper strips, except that the strips joining the long and the short panels must project about half an inch at top and bottom. They are cut along the middle and turned down.

Covering the Box

Once the edges have been bound, the box can be covered with paper. The panels should be covered separately to show a narrow piece of cloth. The paper for the side panels is cut to be turned in at the top for an overlap of about ⅜ to ⅝ in.

The Lining

We first cut the lining for the bottom of the box. It should be about ⅜ in. wider and longer than the box. To make neat corners, we cut into them to the size of the box at an angle of 45 deg. When the lining is pasted down, the paper at these corners will close and must be pasted over.

The lining for the longer panels is cut to be ⅜ in. longer but of the same width as the panel; the pieces for the smaller panels are cut to fit exactly. Paste is always used for the lining.

Having lined the lid in the same way, a rim is now glued to the outside of the bottom panel, to make the box stand properly.

There is no need to reinforce the edges of small boxes with cloth. It is enough to cover them with paper, after they have been assembled and stuck together.

BOX WITH A FLAT HINGED LID

The box is assembled and bound as decribed on pages 256-8. The lid must be flush with the box on three sides; on the fourth - where it opens - it should project by slightly under ⅛ in. so that it can be opened more easily. It is attached to the box with two strips of cloth as follows: We cut two strips of cloth about an inch wide. One of these strips must be the exact outer length of the box, the other the exact inner length, i.e. the length of the box less the combined thickness of the two side-panels. The first strip is pasted against the outside, the second against the inside

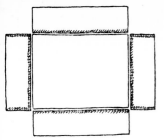

993 Gluing the parts of a Box

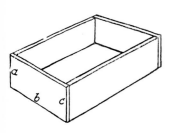

994 Placing the Sides against the Bottom of the Box

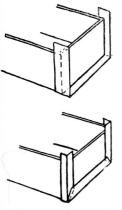

995/996 Reinforcing the Edges with Strips of Paper

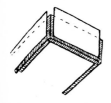

998 Covering the Box

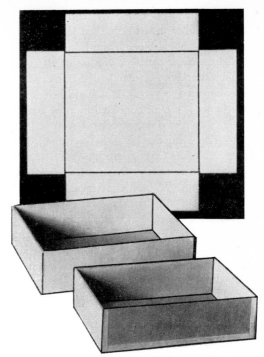

997 A Box. a. the parts, b. assembling, c. reinforcing the edges

999 The Box Completed

1000 Composite Box with Hinged Lid

of the same edge. The inner strip is immediately pressed hard against the cut edge of the cardboard and only then joined to the outer strip. Fig. 1001 shows how the two strips should look. If the lid is not to be bound with cloth, it should be covered and lined with paper on the inside. It must be dried under some weight before it can be attached. Meanwhile, the box can be covered and lined. The paper for covering the panel to which the lid will be fitted must be cut to tuck in at the lower edge only since it cannot be tucked into the box on this side. If the edges are to be bound with cloth, the paper is not cut to tuck in at any side. So that the lid should close properly, when the hinge has been fitted, we stick on the inside a piece of cardboard that fits exactly into the box. It can be of the same thickness as the lid and is lined with paper. If it is cut to be about 1/16 in. smaller all round than the opening it should fit exactly, after it has been covered. The projecting corners of our hinge are now cut as shown in Fig. 1002. The cloth is covered with glue where it will be attached to the lid, and the latter placed against it, so that it is entirely in line along three edges of the box. The box is then placed against the hinge and the lid adjusted very carefully, until it rests on the box entirely flat. The cloth is now pressed hard against the lid. When this is done, the cardboard lining mentioned above can be glued on, but before it is placed in its final position, we must make sure that the lid will close without pulling. We then put the opened box on the bench or table and place a weight board on the lid or simply use the press.

PORTFOLIO WITH A FITTED BOX

Such a portfolio is very useful for keeping letters, photographs or documents. A box is fitted to a stiff-backed folder as shown on page 251. The previous pages describe how such a box is made. We simply glue the finished box to the inside in place of a lining. The width of the folder must be calculated very accurately. It should exceed the height of the box by slightly more than twice the thickness of the cardboard. So that we can take out our letters easily, we place a piece of stiff paper with a fixed ribbon on the bottom of the box.

1003 The Cloth Hinge

1004 Attaching the Lid to the Hinge. The Hinge is first glued to the lid, which is then given its paper-covered cardboard lining

1001
Attaching the Hinge

1002
Cutting off the Corner of the Cloth Hinge

1005 Portfolio with Fitted Box for Letters and Documents

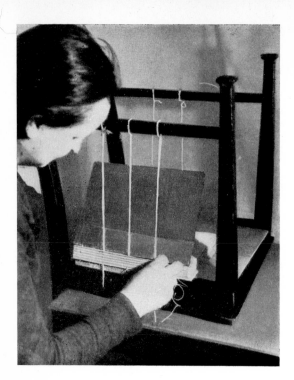

BOOKBINDING

TOOLS AND MATERIALS

Apart from the tools and materials for working with cardboard we shall need:
Linen thread and whip-stitching needles.
5-ply hemp cord for the sections and for sewing on tapes.
Linen tape.
We could easily make a simple sewing-frame (1007) ourselves. The illustration
shows how the frame is assembled. A kitchen chair turned upside down (1006)
is often quite sufficient.

Very few of us will have a press. But we can make one quite easily from two
stout pieces of wood and two adjustable screws (1015). Or we could improvise
a press with two smooth, even boards and a vice.

WORKING PROCESSES

1. Taking a book apart

First of all we carefully separate the individual sections. This process is called 'pulling'. We do this by cutting the sewing thread section by section - it should always be cut in the middle of the page - and then pull away the section with the left hand, while the right holds the next section. If the book is not sewn, but stapled, we have to unbend and remove the staples carefully. Finally, we remove traces of glue and ends of thread carefully with a knife.

2. Repairs

The pages are often damaged near the spine and therefore must be repaired. We take a strip of thin, but strong, typing paper or Japanese vellum, paste it on the inside of the fold and leave the pages to dry between books or boards under slight pressure. After an hour they are folded again and re-assembled.

3. Pressing the Sections

When the sections have been knocked up square and true they are put into a press overnight. Large books should be assembled in sections, since the boards of the press might slip otherwise.

1007 A simple home-made Sewing Frame from Boards and Battens

4. End-papers

When we open a bound book we see that the first and the last sheets are the same type of paper. This also lines the inside of the covers. These sheets - sometimes in colour - are called the end-papers. There are many ways of fastening the end-papers to the sections. We only show the most common form: a piece of paper the height of the pages, but 2½ times their width is folded according to Figs. 1008 and 1009, so that the folded end-papers are still at least ⅜ in. wider than a single page. The paper used for this purpose is cut to stretch sideways. We then make a crease in the folded paper along the dotted line (see arrow on Figs. 1009b and c and 1010) at a distance of ³/₁₆ to ¼ in. from the left edge. It is best to do this with the bone folder held against the straight edge.

When the two end-papers have been folded, one is placed round the first section as shown in Fig. 1011, the other round the last and they are then sewn together.

5. Marking up for the Tapes

Before we begin to sew, we must mark up the spine for the tapes on which the sections will be sewn. According to size and thickness, a book is sewn on two, three, four, five or even six tapes. Fig. 1012 shows a book marked up for three tapes, a number usually considered adequate for medium-sized books. In addition, we also mark the so-called kettlestitch kerfs at head and tail (foot), as the bookbinder

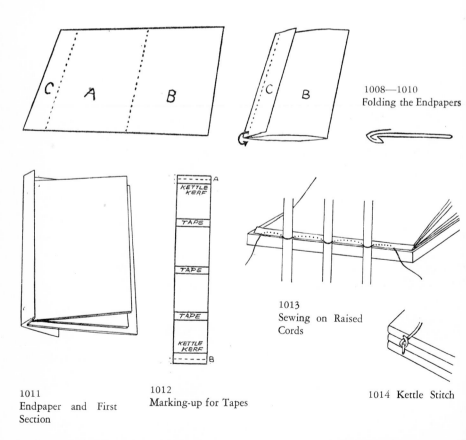

1008—1010
Folding the Endpapers

1013
Sewing on Raised
Cords

1011
Endpaper and First
Section

1012
Marking-up for Tapes

1014 Kettle Stitch

calls it. (At the head ¼ in., at the tail ⅜ in. from the dotted line). The kettlestitch kerfs are marked lightly with a worn saw and must only be deep enough to receive loop stitches when sewing (1014).

6. Sewing

a) S e w i n g o n T a p e s : When the sewing press is set up we can start work.

We begin with the last section, which is placed on the board, with the end-paper folded round it, the fore-edge towards the sewer. The left hand is inserted where the sewing is to be and presses the section against the tapes. A waxed thread is passed through the kettle stitch kerf (1013), through the crease in the end-paper into the centre of the first section, out again close to the right of the first tape, round the tape and back to the left until we come out at the outer kettle stitch kerf. Although the needle enters on the outside, the holes must always be marked first from the inside. When the first section has been sewn to the tapes the thread is pulled tightly and the sheets are pressed down with the bone folder. This must be repeated after each layer. On no account must the tape be sewn in.

The second section is sewn from left to right. The thread is now tied to the thread left hanging from the previous section. This is called the kettle stitch. The third section is again sewn from right to left, and the thread pulled through the loop formed by the previous kettle stitch (1014). We repeat this process until the whole book is sewn together. Finally, the thread is tied up and the book is taken from the frame.

If a fresh piece of thread has to be joined, it must always be done on the *outside*. A useful knot is described on page 96.

b) S e w i n g o n S a w n - i n B a n d s : We first have to saw kerfs into the sections for taking the cords (fully- or half-bound books have so-called raised bands, but these are rather beyond the scope of this volume).

For sawing the kerfs, the book is placed into a press without the first and last sections - the end-papers must not be sawn into, or the holes would show - so that the back projects by about ⅜ in. We then mark the places for the cords, moving the saw to the right and left, to produce a small groove that will only just take the cords. The kettle kerfs are marked very lightly.

The first and last sections have no grooves and are treated exactly as for sewing on tapes, i.e. the needle goes in to the right of the cord and comes out on the left. From the second section onwards, we sew as follows: after the needle has entered at the left kettle kerf, it comes out at the first hole on the left of the cord, and is then taken round on the right, again passed through the same hole and brought to the middle of the section (1007). We continue as for sewing on tapes.

7. Pasting down the Fold of the End-paper and the Tapes

Having taken the book from the sewing frame, we open it behind the first section, fold back the end-paper where it has been creased and stick it to the back of the second section. The two last sections are treated similarly.

The tapes are then cut to within about an inch on each side, frayed out carefully and pasted down between cover and end-papers.

8. *Gluing up*

After the book has dried, the back is knocked up square on a bench. The book is then placed between two strips of cardboard exactly in line with the back, which is covered with thin glue or paste. The left hand holds the book firmly in position. The back should project slightly beyond the edge of the table. We must rub in the adhesive very quickly with the finger, so that the sections will form a solid volume. The strips of cardboard are now removed and the book is left to dry between two wooden boards for an hour. Again, the back should project slightly, so as not to get stuck to the wood.

9. *Cutting the Fore-edge*

The fore-edge should be cut with a guillotine or paper cutter. If we do not possess such an implement, a bookbinder will do it for us. But we can leave it uncut, which can look rather well.

10. *Rounding*

To round a book, it should be held with the left hand pressed against the fore-edge, while the right taps it gently along the back edge of the end-paper. The book is then turned over and the process is repeated.

11. *Backing*

After the book has been rounded, we place it between two pressing boards, leaving the back to project by an eighth of an inch or slightly under, depending on the thickness of the covers. Having screwed the boards together very tightly, we tap with a hammer against the back of the sections so that they fall equally over the edges of the boards (1015 and 1017). Backing must be done with great care, since it determines the shape of the book. The depth of the grooves, caused by backing,

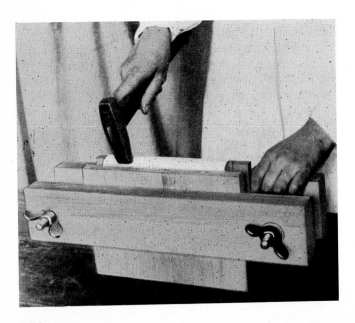

1015

Backing in a Home made Press

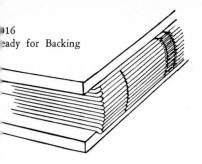

1017 Making the Grooves

should correspond to the thickness of the covers. The pressing boards can be damped
: the edges to prevent slipping.

The grooves must be of exactly the same depth.

After backing, the back is covered in paste and again rounded, this time, how-
ver, by holding the hammer at a slant. We then cover the back with a soft, but
strong, paper - this should be cut along the grain - and cover this paper and put
n it a little paste. The paste should be worked in very firmly with the fingers. Now
the book can be left to dry until the next day.

2. Trimming the Edges

The next day, the pages are trimmed at head and tail (foot) (1020). To prevent
the grooves from getting flattened, we must place two pieces of cardboard against
them, one on each side. The cardboard should be as thick as the grooves are deep,
e. of the same thickness as the covers are going to be. A bookbinder will do the
trimming for us, if we do not have a guillotine or paper cutter.

3. Gluing on the headband

Head and tail of the book now have the so-called headband attached (it can be
bought in shops for bookbinding accessories). We cut two pieces to the necessary
width, put some glue on head and tail (foot) and fix the headband into position.
The edges can be touched with glue to prevent fraying. Originally, the headband
was sewn by hand. This is much nicer and much more professional, but would be
too difficult at this stage for our simple books.

4. Cutting Boards and Spine

The boards are cut out of greyboard and must be of such thickness that they
it exactly into the groove of the spine. They are cut to project slightly under $\frac{1}{8}$
n. at head and tail. For the time being, the boards are not cut at the fore-edge, where
they should now project by slightly less than $\frac{1}{2}$ in. In addition to the boards, we
eed a so-called hollow back. This is made of a piece of stout paper, preferably
good cartridge paper, a little longer than the book and at least four times as
wide as the spine, and of a piece of brown paper of the same length, but $2\frac{1}{2}$ in.
wider. The lining is pasted carefully on the brown paper, then we turn over the
brown paper and go over it with the folder, so that the edges of the cartridge paper
should stand out clearly. Now we turn it over again, fold the paper over the lining
and draw a line with the folder and ruler at a distance of $\frac{1}{8}$ in. from each edge, as

shown in Fig. 1018. The hollow back should be rounded while it is still soft to fit the book exactly. It is best done with the folder or on the edge of the table.

15. Attaching the boards and Hollow Back

We thinly glue the piece of paper forming the hollow back to the first groove on the inside. The lining and the two folds are left free from glue. The left hand now takes the hollow, while the right places the book with the spine against it. Great care must be taken to ensure that an equal piece of the hollow will overlap at head and tail. When the hollow fits exactly, we rub it down with the folder very firmly to make it fit like a glove.

Having attached the hollow, we cover the boards with glue one side to a width of about an inch, and place them against the groove (1020). To protect the end paper, a piece of newspaper should be placed against the grooves. Now the book is put into the press in such a way that the boards of the press are flush with the cover along one edge and fit exactly into the groove. Only the back will project. The book must be left in the press until the next day.

16. Preparing to Cover

Next day, the book is taken from the press and prepared for covering. First we trim the boards. They should exceed the dimensions of the book by about $\frac{1}{8}$ in. at the fore-edge and slightly less at head and tail (foot). The parts of the hollow back, which have not been glued to the boards, are now carefully detached, having first marked the limits of the glued area with a knife.

The ends of the hollow at head and tail must now be carefully cut off or torn away.

To allow the cloth to be turned in properly the hollow is cut into for about $\frac{3}{4}$ in. at head and tail along the boards (1019). We must take great care to cut only into the crease and not into the back.

17. Covering

a) Half Cloth. We speak of half cloth, because only the spine is covered with cloth, the rest with paper.

We cut a piece of cloth an inch longer than the book and sufficiently wide to cover a third of each side. The cloth is covered with paste on one side and the back of the book is put against it exactly in the middle. Then we place the book with the attached cloth on the table, so that the back projects beyond the table's edge, and we rub the cloth against the back with the fingers. Now we press the cloth into the grooves, and only then can we attach it to the boards. The book is turned round and the process repeated on the other side.

The cloth is then turned in. The book is put on the table, so that the side, where the cloth has to be turned in, projects slightly beyond the table edge. The covers are fully opened. The left hand holds the book and forces the board back slightly to assure a clean turning-in. We now turn the cloth in, first at the back, then round the boards, always taking care to avoid creases. The boards are then closed, the book is stood up and the cloth is straightened out at head and tail. The boards are covered as described on page 252. The corners can be finished in cloth round or "invisibly", or we could also bind the covers at the fore-edge (see page

252). When the book is covered, we can paste in the end-papers, as described below.
b) **F u l l C l o t h.** For a full cloth binding, the material has to be cut sufficiently large to cover the entire book. When the book rests on the cloth, there should be a margin of half an inch on each side. The cloth should be cut along the warp.

Having covered the inside of the cloth completely with glue or paste, the opened book is placed against it, leaving a margin of half an inch all round. It is then closed, so that the covered board faces us, and the cloth is smoothed out with the folder and the fingers. Special care must be taken to ensure that it will fit neatly into the groove between spine and board. The book is turned round, we give a gentle tug to the piece of cloth on the other side, and repeat the process. Now we trim the corners and continue exactly as for half-cloth, first at head and tail, then at the fore-edge.

If the cloth tends to pull and causes the boards to curve, we must paste a lining inside the boards before pasting down the end-papers.

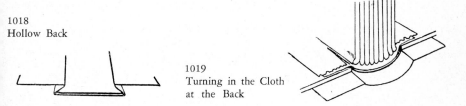

1018
Hollow Back

1019
Turning in the Cloth
at the Back

18. *End-papers*

Before pasting down the end-papers, we must trim the turned-in cloth and paper. A board the thickness of the book should be placed under the cover to have proper support when cutting. We guide the knife carefully along a metal ruler at a distance of about half an inch from the edge and then remove the cut-off strip with the knife. The end-paper is now pasted on the side facing the cover. A piece of newspaper, slightly larger than the book, must be put between book and end-paper. After the end-paper has been covered with paste the sheet of newspaper is removed again and we quickly wipe off some of the paste along the fore-edge with the fingers, so that it should not come out during pressing. Then we close the book, treat the other cover in the same way, and place it in the press - where it is left for twenty-four hours - between two pieces of brown board. Now our book is finished.

1020 Boards and a Cloth Binding. The volume above has been trimmed and backed, the other has had its headbands sewn on and its hollow back attached. It rests between two strong pieces of board. The fore-edge is still uncut

1021 Completed Bindings: Two books are bound in boards, the third in full cloth

LAMPS AND
LAMPSHADES

A home-made lampshade or, better still, a lamp, will give joy to the whole family. There are many ways of making lamps.

LAMPSHADES

Simple, Elegant Forms

The best material for plain lampshades is vellum paper, but we can also use cartridge paper (or construction paper) and treat it ourselves with linseed oil, having first cut it out. It is advisable to make a pattern before cutting.

Synthetic raffia is very suitable for tying, since it is soft and can be cut to any length.

Ceiling Shade

A simple, flat shade can be made according to Figs. 1023 and 1024. A strip of paper will have to be stuck along one of the edges of the segment for tying up or gluing (see dotted line). Holes are punched into the paper at regular intervals (the holes should be approximately a quarter of an inch from the edge and slightly under half an inch apart). We then paste the shade together with Uhu or any good paste, or tie it up and reinforce it at the outer edge with a fairly strong cane or metal ring. The latter can be soldered as described on page 227.

The finished shade is fitted to cords and hung up. It will give an even, indirect light.

A Flat, Hanging Shade

The same shade can also be used for a table-lamp, so that the light will only fall on a limited surface. To soften the glow, we can fit a disc with a portion cut out, as shown in Fig. 1026.

The shade must be reinforced at the top with a sort of hat, (see Fig. 1026). This hat can be bought ready made or cut from metal foil and fixed with Uhu or a good paste.

Shades For Desk Lamps, Etc.

If the shade is to be symmetrical along one axis only - for instance, for a desk or a bedside lamp - it should be cut to the pattern in Fig. 1028. This basic form allows many variations. The shade is either tied or pasted together and strengthened with wire or cane at each end.

1022 A Lamp from a Chianti Bottle

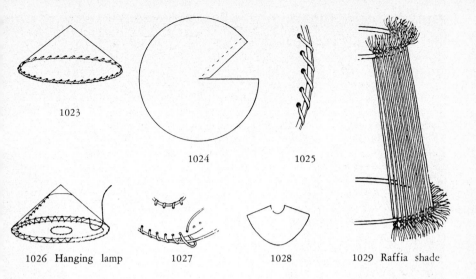

1023

1024

1025

1026 Hanging lamp

1027

1028

1029 Raffia shade

Renewing An Old Lampshade

If an old lampshade is to be renewed, it is best to repeat the old pattern - but only if it looks really nice. The old wire frame can be used for drawing the outline along a piece of paper. We merely have to roll the shade along the paper and follow with a pencil. In the case of a very large shade, we can cut the pattern straight away, but we must continue fixing the paper to the frame with small clothes-pegs, clips or clothes pins, while we cut.

PLEATED SHADES

A lamp-shade can be pleated from good-quality paper. The paper must be neither too thick, nor too thin, so that it can be creased properly and will stay pleated. Good writing paper, vellum paper, oiled paper, thin drawing paper are all suitable. We can also use translucent Japanese rice paper for simple shades, but we would have to pleat it together with a stiff paper, since it would otherwise be too soft. There are various ways of pleating.

Shade With Simple Pleats

We need a strip of paper two and a half times as long as the shade's circumference at its widest point. If the sheet should not be large enough, we can stick two pieces together.

The pleats are best made as in Fig. 1033 to 1037, i.e. the strip is folded in two and all the creases are made towards the *centre line,* so that the outer edge always falls where the next crease but one is to be, as the arrow indicates (1034). First we make all the pleats on one side, then we fold the others in exactly the same way.

The shade having been pleated evenly, we punch the holes for the cord 2½ ins. from the upper edge. To make the shade fit properly to the frame, we also punch another hole through the inward-facing pleats at a distance of 1 in. from the top (Fig. 1032).

1030 A useful Table Lamp that is easy to make

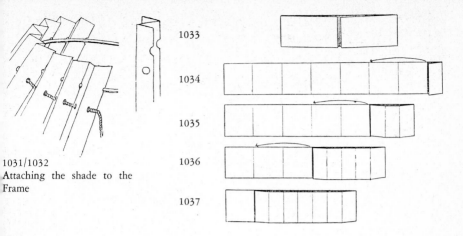

1033

1034

1035

1036

1037

1031/1032
Attaching the shade to the
Frame

Hanging Lamp - Pleated Shades With Double Creases

The shades in Figs. 1022 and 1030 give a pleasant, evenly distributed light and are not so very difficult to make. All we need is some suitable paper.

It is a characteristic feature of these shades that the pleats are afterwards creased at a certain angle. There are two completely different ways of doing this. While the pleats in Fig. 1043 have been pulled out and refolded at the point of the new crease, this is not necessary for the method shown in Fig. 1040.

It is advisable to take two pieces of writing paper and try each method.

1038—1040

A Hanging Lamp
Method I

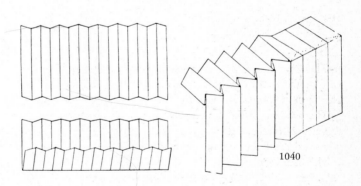

1040

Method I (1038 to 1040). The paper is first folded, as for an ordinary pleated shade and then folded across while being pulled out (1039). We then stand up the paper at an angle (1040) and turn the first two hollow creases inside out. The other creases will not be difficult; the paper will almost fall into position by itself.

Method II (1041 to 1043). The problem of changing the fold of the creases can be overcome, if first we fold the paper over and then pleat (1041, 1042). Afterwards we stand it up as before (1043), and fold the first two creases at the angle we want. Again the paper will fall into position quite easily.

Method III. If the paper is very thin and the shade is to be very small, we can fold the paper at the angle we want in one operation. The pleats will thus be easy to make, because they are already outlined.

A Hanging Lamp
Method II

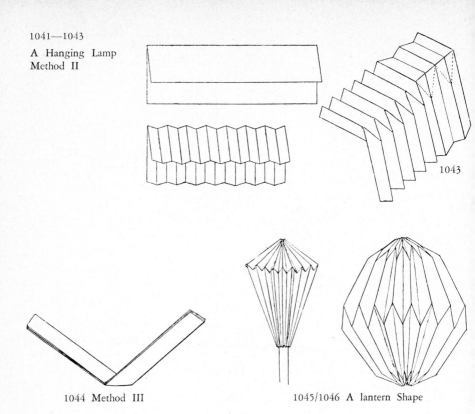

1043

1044 Method III   1045/1046 A lantern Shape

Lampshade shown in Fig. 1022

This shade is made of an oiled, yellowish paper. The strip is 44 ins. long and 18 ins. wide. It is pleated according to the first method, the widest circumference has been obtained by folding the paper lengthways 4¾ ins. from the edge.

The shade is fitted to a frame, obtainable in handwork or hardware stores. The socket and bulb are also fitted to the frame. The pleats are punched at the upper edge and are held together by a fine cord.

This shade can also be turned upside down, with the shorter pleats at the top and will then look like the shade in Fig. 1045, which is very suitable for table lamps.

TYPES OF LAMPS

Lamp Made From A Chianti Bottle, Fig. 1022

A Chianti wine bottle, with its green glass and curving lines, will make a good base for a lamp. We can, of course, fit socket and cable ourselves, but could thus easily lose the bottle or cause a short circuit in the house. It is therefore much better to buy a fitting that can be screwed in at the top of the bottle - since we can, in any case, not make beautiful fittings - and involves no risk to bottle, life or domestic comfort.

Table Lamp With Pleated Shade, Fig. 1030

We shall need a strip of lampshade parchment, roughly 44 ins. x 18 ins. folded into pleats, and make another pleat roughly 3 ins. from the horizontal edges as shown in Fig. 1040. The vertical edges of the strip are then glued together and a ring of cane or white flex is inserted. A bakelite fitting used for attaching lamps to the ceiling can be used in reverse as a base. It should be slightly under 5 ins. wide.

ATTACHING THE FLEX
OR ELECTRIC CORD

This is not very difficult, but it must be done with great care, so that the wires do not meet, or a short circuit occurs. Figs. 1051-1054 show how it is done. The two bare wires, each separately insulated in the flex, are exposed at the ends (to a length of roughly half an inch). Each end must be slightly twisted. We then unscrew the bottom of the bulb socket and screw it into the threaded end of the adaptor. Then we thread the flex through the adaptor and insert one of the bared ends in each of the holes in the porcelain core of the socket (1051), tightening the screws so that the wires are held firmly in place. Afterwards, the socket is re-assembled. That is all. The other end of the cable is similarly attached to the plug. It is advisable to ask an expert's help if we have never fitted a flex before. Fittings for converting vases and bottles can also be bought ready-made.

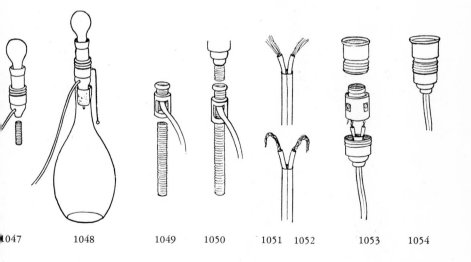

1047   1048   1049   1050   1051   1052   1053   1054

1055

This handsome Giraffe with the fine "antlers" was made of Twigs, Roots and Fir-cones

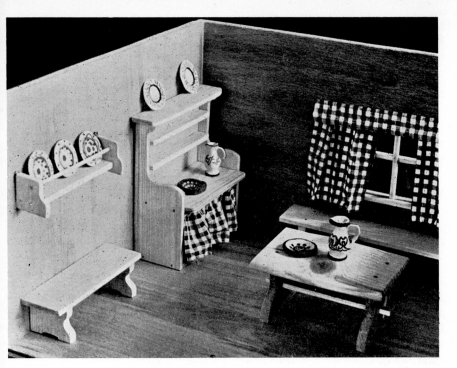

1056 All Children love Dolls' Kitchens

WOODWORK

Woodwork for girls? Why not? Admittedly, girls will do less woodwork than boys. But is there a girl who would not like to furnish her room? This requires skill with wood, paints, hammer, saw, rasp and drill. And would not any girl love to make toys for her younger brothers and sisters and, perhaps, one day, for her own children?

Future teachers will need to do woodwork with their classes. Youth-leaders, architects, designers and interior decorators all need to be acquainted with the fundamentals of woodwork.

279

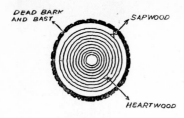

1057 Cross section of a Tree Trunk

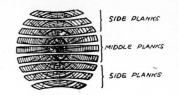

1058 Cross section of a Tree Trunk sawn into Planks

WOOD

Structure, Annual Rings

Wood must be treated as a material that lives if we are to do justice to its beauty and its potentialities. Let us first take its growth and its natural characteristics, as apparent in the section of a tree. The heartwood is surrounded by the annual rings. The cambium lies underneath the bark. Each year produces a new layer of wood, a so-called "annual ring". The annual rings are not of uniform width or colour, since the tree grows faster in spring than in autumn. We can discover the exact age of a felled tree by counting the annual rings.

Indeed, the annual rings reveal a good deal more. They also tell by their unequal size whether the seasons were good or bad, whether the years were wet or the winters long.

WOOD AS A LIVING SUBSTANCE

The tree is cut into boards at the sawmill. You have probably heard that carpenters value wood according to heartwood or sapwood. Heartwood is at the core of the tree, sapwood on the periphery (1057, 1058).

Heartwood is older and therefore drier and closer grained. The younger sapwood is more loosely grained and has larger pores. Its cells are still alive and form the tubes for moisture. Boards taken from the outside of a tree therefore warp more easily, since the pores shrink in drying. These changes are called the working of the wood and must be allowed for.

Each board, each single piece of wood, has its cross-cut and its length-cut. The length-cut runs along the grain, the cross-cut across, as the name indicates. Both cuts have their own characteristics.

THE MOST IMPORTANT WOODS

a) Deciduous Trees

L i m e, L i n d e n or B a s s w o o d : Soft, white woods, very suitable for carving.

A l d e r : Reddish-brown and fairly light and soft. Very good for our purposes and suitable for fretwork and for carving wooden bowls.

Sycamore: A hard timber, of a white and very pure colour. Used a lot for fretwork; it is not really suitable for children because of its hardness.

Elm: Heartwood, light brown, sapwood, yellowish white. It has a fine, natural colour and is very suitable for carving bowls.

Oak: One of the most valuable timbers. It is very hard and has a distinctive grain. In the past, wood-carvers made chests, wardrobes and elaborate pieces of furniture from it. The heartwood is light brown, the sapwood is lighter and difficult to work. There are several varieties. The Common White Oak is the hardest, the wood of the Turkey Oak is very brittle; the Japanese Oak is somewhat softer, but still much harder than lime or elm.

Pearwood: On younger trees light brown, on older trees reddish or dark brown. Suitable for smaller carvings.

Birch: A light, reddish-white wood. It has a pleasant grain, but warps rather badly if not carefully seasoned. Not very hard and suitable for carving and turning.

Poplar: A straight-grained, dense wood, pleasant to work.

b) Conifers

Spruce: Widely used and one of the cheapest woods on the Continent, since the tree grows very fast. Poorer grades are coarse grained, with many knots. Suitable for simple work.

Pine and Fir: Much stronger than spruce. Yellowish wood with clearly marked, light brown annual rings. Also used for furniture and very suitable for toys.

c) Plywood and Laminboard

We distinguish between plywood and laminboard. Plywood is usually made in thicknesses from 1/32 in. to an inch, laminboard from $\frac{1}{2}$ in. to 2 ins.

Plywood consists of several layers of wood, which have been glued together with the grain always lying at a right angle. It is therefore very durable and hard to break in any direction.

d) Battens and Canes

We use ready-made battens and canes a lot in our work. These can be bought in great variety and are especially useful for toys.

e) Scraps

We also use old cigar boxes and old boxes from the grocer wherever possible. They can be taken apart and the boards used separately. They are often ideal for dolls' rooms, toy boxes, etc. and save a lot of time, if we can exploit their form properly. Workshop scraps are also very useful and can be transformed into a great many things.

THE TECHNICAL ASPECT

THE TOOLS AND HOW TO USE THEM

Essential Tools (Plate N)

a good penknife	pincers	screw-driver
back-saw or tenon-saw and mitre box (1059) fret saw (1062)	hammer	file, half-round (1088)
		G, or C, clamp (1091)

a) Saws

The tenon-saw (1059) is used for cutting battens and fairly thick boards.

The mitre box makes sawing battens very much easier. They can be cut at a right angle or at an angle of 45° (1059). The mitre box is attached to the bench with a clamp. We put in a small piece of waste timber to avoid cutting into the mitre box itself. The batten is then put in and is pressed against the back of the box with the left hand during sawing.

The fret-saw has one great advantage: we can saw with it along curved lines and can even cut out pieces of wood. The blade should be stretched very firmly, since it easily breaks, yet it should not be too taut. The teeth must point downwards while sawing. A medium blade is best. If the wood is thicker than $\frac{3}{8}$ in., we use a so-called coping-saw.

How to use a fret-saw: The saw should not be moved up and down too fast. The left hand holds the wood and keeps it adjusted to the saw, so that we can always work at the same angle. The blade should be at a right angle to the wood. However, the angle of the frame will be no guide, since the blade is not always fitted in the same position.

A small table is useful for finished parts.

The hand-saw has stronger teeth than the back-saw and is used for cutting larger boards for boxes, etc.

There are several types of hand-saw. The best known are the rip-saw and the cross-cut saw; the former cuts with, the latter across, the grain. In both, the teeth are set alternately to the right and left, so as to cut a kerf, i.e. a groove wider than the saw is thick to prevent it from binding. A medium-sized saw 24 ins. long with fine teeth (12 point) and a blade that is not too wide will suit us best. An expert will no doubt show us how to use the saw properly, if we ask him.

The compass saw is built like an ordinary hand-saw, but has a narrow blade for cutting curves.

b) Drills

The bradawl (1063) is used for making holes for nails and screws and for marking lines on wood.

The gimlet (1064) is used for drilling holes for screws, etc.

The push brace, or push drill, (1065) is suitable for more intricate work. It will take a variety of bits.

The hand-drill (1066) is slightly more expensive than the hand-brace, but is extremely useful. It will take twist drills (1068) of varying thickness. Twist drills will not suffer damage if they come into contact with nails and can also be used for metal. They are ideal for precision work.

The bit-brace or hand-brace (1067) is used for boring large holes. It will also take different bits, such as:

1. Centre Bits (1070). These drill large and accurate holes and can be used near the edge of the wood. Using a centre bit takes rather a lot of strength.

2. Augers (1069). The tip of an auger is formed like a screw and therefore makes boring very easy.

3. Countersinks (1071-1072). These are used to drill holes for taking a countersunk screw head.

c) Chisels for Cutting Wood and Carving Tools

There are chisels for cutting wood and for cutting metal. Only chisels for cutting wood concern us here.

The f i r m e r c h i s e l (1078) is used for making grooves, letting in hinges, etc. It is available in many widths.

There are chisels and gouges made especially for carving in relief. The gouges are called quick (1082), medium (1083), flat (1084), according to the depth of the curve. Figs. 1085 and 1086 show bent shank gouges.

We also need an oilstone for sharpening. It is best to watch an expert before venturing to sharpen tools ourselves.

d) Measuring

We shall first of all need a metal rule or a steel tape.

D i v i d e r s are used for picking up measurements and for marking small circles or semi-circles on wood.

The t r y-s q u a r e (1090) is needed for marking and checking right angles.

e) Rasp, File and Sandpaper

Rasps and files serve for smoothing down.

We first use a wood rasp (1089), which has a very rough surface. Afterwards, we finish with the smoother file. The type of file used will depend on the edge we have to treat. We will use the flat side of file (1088) for a straight or curved edge; for making round grooves we shall take the curved side. A triangular file will serve for cleaning up V-shaped grooves, a round file for small openings. Anyone who works to a very small scale would be well advised to buy a set of keyhole files. This consists of six files of different shape.

A metal brush will be necessary for cleaning rasps and files. If they are very dirty, they can first be wetted with paraffin and boiled in water afterwards.

Emery cloth, glasspaper or sandpaper serve for rubbing down surfaces, and should be attached to a small block of wood or cork. They are graded according to the fineness of the grit. The usual grading starts from fine, i.e. Nos. 0 to 3. Black emery cloth should not be used on wood. It is much harder and more effective when used on metal.

f) Shooting Board and Plane

Saw, file and sandpaper are not sufficient for smoothing large planks or blocks, and we therefore have to plane them on a shooting board (1060). A shooting board is either attached to the bench or fitted to the table with G cramps (C clamps). A long plane, the so-called jack plane, will prove more useful than any other and has to be used as shown in Fig. 1060.

P l a n e s : The basic types are block plane, smoothing plane and jack plane.

The b l o c k p l a n e produces the biggest shavings and is used on rough surfaces and edges. It has a single plane iron, in contrast to the smoothing plane.

The s m o o t h i n g p l a n e is mainly used for giving the finishing touches. It has a double iron consisting of a sharp and longer part, the actual iron, and a shorter part, the cap. The cap is adjustable and is fitted with a clamping screw (1092). Its purpose is to prevent the iron from entering the wood too deeply.

The j a c k p l a n e (1060) has a double iron, exactly like the smoothing plane, and is used in the same manner.

A b l u n t i r o n is sharpened on an oilstone. Again, it is best to get an expert's advice.

One plane will be enough for us. A jack plane will be the most suitable kind, because it is easiest to handle on a shooting board.

g) Glue

We shall generally use cold glue, since working with hot glue can be rather difficult. There are a number of prepared liquid glues on the market. Any wood shop, ironmonger or hardware store will have a fairly wide selection.

Glue in tubes or small jars, such as Uhu (hard) etc., is suitable for small models.

A n i m a l g l u e is generally sold in sheets. A broken-up sheet is first soaked in cold water for 24 hours and softened, and afterwards melted in a double boiler. Animal glue must always be used hot, since it will otherwise not be sufficiently liquid to penetrate the wood thoroughly to produce a joint. Keeping glue warm causes some evaporation and water must therefore be added from time to time.

Granulated glue is useful, if we want some glue very quickly, since it only has to soak for about half an hour. Otherwise we use it like animal glue.

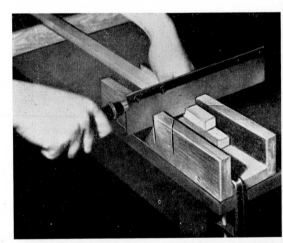

1059 Battens etc. are sawn in a mitre box

1060 Lining up the Wood on the Shooting Board

Wood-working Tools

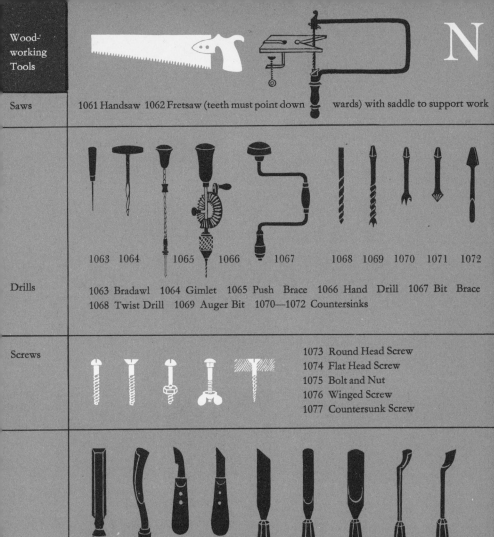

N

Saws

1061 Handsaw 1062 Fretsaw (teeth must point down   wards) with saddle to support work

Drills

1063   1064   1065   1066   1067   1068   1069   1070   1071   1072

1063 Bradawl 1064 Gimlet 1065 Push Brace 1066 Hand Drill 1067 Bit Brace
1068 Twist Drill 1069 Auger Bit 1070—1072 Countersinks

Screws

1073 Round Head Screw
1074 Flat Head Screw
1075 Bolt and Nut
1076 Winged Screw
1077 Countersunk Screw

Knives, Gouges and Chisels

1078   1079   1080   1081   1082   1083   1084   1085   1086

1078 Firmer Chisel   1079 Bent Gouge   1080—1081 Knives 1082—1086 Chisels

Files, Rasps Try-square Clamp Plane

1087   1088   1089   1090   1091   1092

1087 Finishing Rasp 1088 Wood File 1089 Wood Rasp 1090 Try Square 1091 Clamp
1092 (a) Single Plane Iron (b) Double Plane Iron

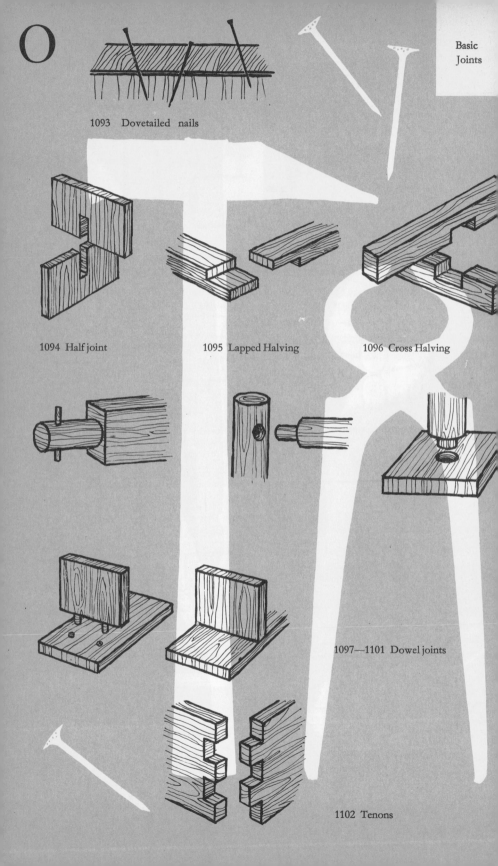

O

1093 Dovetailed nails

1094 Half joint

1095 Lapped Halving

1096 Cross Halving

1097—1101 Dowel joints

1102 Tenons

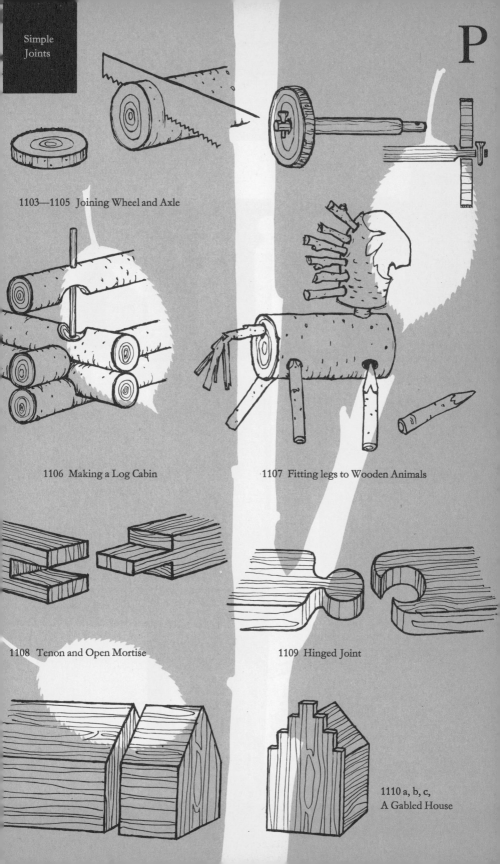

1103—1105 Joining Wheel and Axle

1106 Making a Log Cabin

1107 Fitting legs to Wooden Animals

1108 Tenon and Open Mortise

1109 Hinged Joint

1110 a, b, c,
A Gabled House

Q

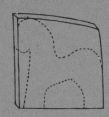  

1111—1113 Board into Horse

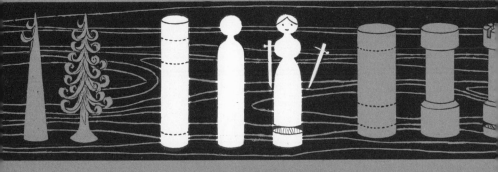

1114—1115 A tree from a Pointed Wedge

1116—1118 A Doll from a stick

1119—1121 Carving Chessmen

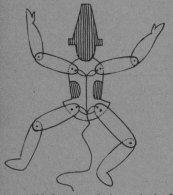

1122 Jumping Jack: method of joining sections with string.
1123—1124 How to make wooden bolts

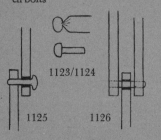

1123/1124

1125

1126

1125 Fastening with wooden Bolts
1126 Making a 2-sided Jumping Jack

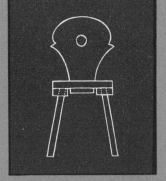

1127 A Chair

1128 Fitting the cradle to the post

1130 A Wooden Peg

1129 Fitting the rockers to the posts of the cradle

SAWING AND FINISHING INDIVIDUAL PARTS

Before settling down to detail, we should know the most important recurring operations.

If we break up a wooden box to make something out of it, the inscription will first have to be removed. It is best to use a scraper, a very useful tool which we can buy from any ironmonger or hardware store. We finish first with rough and then with smooth sandpaper. As already mentioned, sandpaper should be wrapped round a small piece of wood to obtain a better result.

Never saw directly on the marked line, but on the waste side very *close* to it. The line must remain, since it will be the only guide for the file afterwards. But the more accurately we saw along the line, the easier the next stages will be.

If we want to cut out a piece of wood, for example a window for a doll's house, we drill a hole with the hand drill, detach the blade of the fret-saw at one end, push it through the hole, fix it again and saw along the marked line.

The sawn wood is planed smoothly on the shooting board (1060). If we have no shooting board or plane, we first smooth the edges with rasp and file and then go over them with emery paper or sandpaper as follows: An entire sheet is pinned on an even surface, i.e. an old table or drawing board, with the rough side up. The part we want to smooth down is then rubbed against it for as long as necessary. But we must hold it at a right angle, or we shall get a bevelled edge.

JOINTS

Joining two boards with nails at a right angle.

We mark the width of the second board on the first. The nails are driven in along the marked line after we have first marked the holes with the bradawl. It is better to drive the nails in obliquely, as shown in Fig. 1093, since they will hold better that way. If the heads are not meant to show, they can be beaten flat on an iron block. We can also use so-called 'lost heads' or 'cut heads' (brads, finish nails and cut nails). These are types of nails with a head that is practically invisible when driven below the surface of the work.

In the case of very thin wood, the nail points should first be flattened with a hammer to avoid splitting.

Glue should be used in addition if we want our work to hold particularly well.

Strong boards can be joined with screws. The holes are marked as for nails, but they must be drilled with a twist drill of nearly the same thickness as the screw. We also must widen the hole for countersunk screws with a countersink to take the head (1071, 1077). The hole in the second board has to be as deep as the screw it has to take is long. Finally, the screws are put in with a screw driver.

For a cupboard with shelves and partitions we first make the parts separately. They are then put into the cupboards and nailed in from the outside.

If two boards cross in the cupboard, we saw a slit the thickness of the wood to the middle of each board (1094). The boards are then joined. We call this a halved joint or crosslap joint. Care has to be taken not to make the slits too wide.

BASIC JOINTS (CHART O)

Real craftsmen never nail wood, but join it. These joints have been used for centuries. They allow the wood to shrink and expand since they are adapted to its structure, in contrast to nails and screws.

It is not the task of this book to describe the different joints in great detail, but we hope to awaken an understanding for good craftsmanship in young people so that they will be able to distinguish between a well-made piece from the hands of a conscientious craftsman and poorly made work.

We therefore list a few simple joints. One of the simplest is the half-joint or crosslap joint, already mentioned above (1094). A lapped halving or end lap is used to join battens at a right angle for frames etc., (1095). If they are not joined at the ends we speak of a cross halving (1096). To make a lapped halving or end lap, we cut halfway through the board with the tenon saw. It is best to cut first with the grain from above and then across it until the unwanted piece of wood comes off. The battens are then glued together. For a cross halving the wood is sawn to half its width and the waste removed with the chisel (1078). On many occasions, dowel joints can be used (1099). Dowels can be bought ready-made, but we can also make them ourselves. First we mark the diameter on the end grain. We then make marks around it with the saw, gradually split off the waste and work out the shape of the dowel. Cogs for the wheels of dolls' prams are made the same way (1097). Figs. 1100 and 1101 show a dowelled joint used in place of a dove-tailed or halved joint. Both boards have had sockets cut out to take the dowels.

Hingeing

a) We mark the width of the hinge, having first placed the lid on the box. Now we take lid and box apart again and chisel away enough wood to take the hinges, but no more. The holes for the screws are then marked on lid and box with a brad-awl and the hinges can be fitted.

b) For very thin wood, i.e. cigar boxes, dolls' wardrobes etc., veneer pins are often used in place of screws. Also, the hinge is not fixed on the inside of the lid, but against its edge, since the panels would be too thin to take the veneer pins. It is quite safe to use fairly long pins. If they are driven in at a slant they will hold much better.

c) A full-length hinge lasts particularly well. It is bought by the length and fitted like an ordinary hinge along the lid. It can also be screwed to the lid and thus makes cutting out the waste unnecessary. But the height of the box would have to be calculated accordingly.

FINISHING THE SURFACES

Sandpapering

When we have finished, we go over the surfaces again with sandpaper, as described on page 284. Occasionally, the edges have to be gone over with a file. Small holes etc. have to be filled in with plastic wood, which can be bought in various shades. It can be treated like real wood.

Usually, we will want to give the surfaces some further treatment. There are several possibilities.

Waxing, Varnishing, Staining

If the wood has an interesting grain, we will want to make the most of it. The following methods are all suitable:

W a x i n g. The wood must be warmed first to allow the pores to open, so that the wax should not harden too quickly. We then coat the wood with a good, slightly warmed, furniture polish and leave it until the next day, when we rub it with a soft brush or a rag until it has a mellow glow.

B e e s w a x is not really suitable for amateurs, since, having to be mixed with paraffin, it is highly inflammable.

L i n s e e d   o i l brings out the grain quite well, but causes the wood to darken. It should be applied very evenly with a clean brush.

Since the waxed and polished surface is easily spoiled by liquids, it should be coated with colourless varnish some time after polishing.

V a r n i s h i n g. A great variety of varnishes is available. It is possible to varnish wood without affecting its natural shade. Any handicraft shop will recommend a suitable brand.

S t a i n i n g. If the wood is to be given a colour that will not hide the grain, it has to be stained. Stains are available in many shades and can be bought as a powder or crystals by weight or by the packet. We mainly use a stain soluble in hot water. It is applied evenly to the wood with a flat brush.

We must let the wood dry for twenty-four hours after staining. It is then either waxed, oiled or varnished.

Solutions of stain can be kept in bottles and will last indefinitely. The brush has to be cleaned with soap and hot water.

W a x   s t a i n. A stain with the wax already added gives the wood a better finish and saves a lot of time and work. It is applied with a brush and brushed and polished twenty-four hours later.

Painting

Poster colours can be used for small surfaces. Being very bright and clear they are especially suitable for toys. Coated with stainless varnish, they will not wash off.

1131 These Chessmen were made with a pocket knife from Hazel Sticks. Cuts and Colours indicate the names

Oil paint can be had with a matt (flat) or glossy finish. It must always be put on thinly, or it will not dry properly. It is better to have two thin coats than one thick and uneven coat. Turpentine is used for cleaning the brush. If, for some reason, the brush has not been cleaned immediately, it can be soaked in a paint solvent or one of the soapless washing powders. It will lose its hardness and can then be easily cleaned with turpentine.

All painted surfaces are improved if we go over them with fine, used sandpaper after each coat. It gives a more even and less glossy finish.

EXAMPLES

1. CARVINGS FROM BARK AND ROOTS:

Bark Boats

A little boat, made from a piece of bark, is often a child's first carving. The bark of conifers - it must, of course, only be taken from felled trees - is ideal for such efforts. A simple pocket knife is all we need to cut out the basic form. A little groove is made in the middle and the boat can then be carefully hollowed out in narrow strips.

A Bird from Fir Cones

Young fir cones, still firmly closed, can be made into all kinds of birds (1133). To prevent the cone from opening later, we can first dip it into a thin mixture of glue and water. Small branches provide head, neck and legs. You will discover a wealth of forms and will soon develop a feeling for the kind of animals that can grow out of them. The most important thing is that head and legs should be properly socketed in the cone. Having made the necessary holes, the limbs are fixed with glue. The birds can be placed into a small box with sand to make them stand properly, or they can also be glued to a base of bark of a small split twig.

The Root Giraffe

Odd-shaped twigs and roots can be an inspiration to make all kinds of weird animals, prehistoric monsters and snakes.

The giraffe (1055) with the lovely 'antlers' and the gentle expression was made of such bits of wood. The legs are formed by three branches, the head is a root, eyes and mane are small fir cones.

Whistles

When the sap rises in spring, the time has come to make whistles. We take a straight, smooth piece of willow as thick as a finger and make a cut around it just

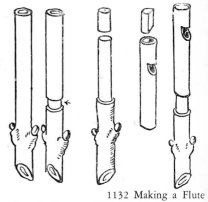

1132 Making a Flute

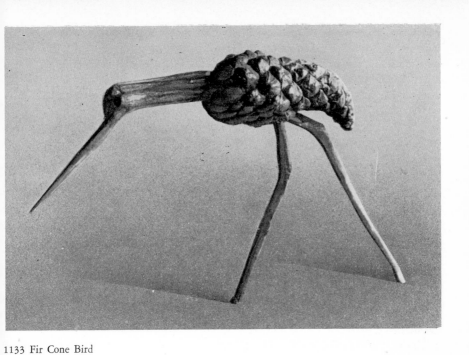

1133 Fir Cone Bird

1134 Toys from Twigs

above the place where it branches out. We then tap the part above the cut with the back of the knife and keep turning it until the bark is ready to be detached. Great care must be taken not to damage the bark. To complete our whistle, we cut a hole into the bark, saw off a small piece of the peeled wood - to be flattened and used as a mouth-piece - and insert the remaining piece in the bark (1132).

2. TWIGS (CHART P)

Tree prunings are wonderful material for carving. Fruit trees, beeches, ash and other deciduous trees all provide excellent wood that does not need any further treatment. The young twigs of the hazelnut are very suitable, but beech, ash or any other wood of a deciduous tree is just as good.

The contrast between the bark and the light wood makes carving from twigs very interesting and can inspire us a great deal. The beauty of the bark should therefore be brought out as much as possible. A farmyard with cows, sheep, horses, carts, human beings and wooden sheds or indeed the contents of a whole Noah's Ark could be carved out of small twigs. Again, we could make useful things like tent pegs or canes for tying up plants. Even nutcrackers and chessmen should not prove too difficult.

The only tools needed are a sharp knife, a fret-saw or a tenon-saw and a drill. Small figures are best carved on the twig and cut off afterwards.

Wooden bolts and pegs will be used in place of glue. They should be cone shaped and should fit very tightly, since young wood still warps and contracts. Raffia should be tied round the joints to strengthen them. Partitions will be made to join like the sides of log cabins (1106), i.e. a semi-circular section will be cut out of each twig, so that the pieces can interlock.

These are just a few of the infinite possibilities:-

Chessmen (1131): As much of the bark as possible is left on the wood for black chessmen, while it is removed for the white ones. The figures are carved on the branch and cut off afterwards. Fig. 1135 shows examples of carving on sticks, canes, etc.

Animals, figures and carts (1134) are held together as shown in Fig. 1099. The holes are made with a simple twist drill, the wheels are cut from the branch (1103), pierced to take the axle, and secured to the latter with a small wooden peg. Figures, as always, are first cut on the branch.

3. CARVINGS FROM FIREWOOD

The powerful mask in Fig. 1136 was made by a girl from a log of wood found in the yard. She merely put it into the vice and used a carving gouge. As on most really good pieces, one can see how it was made. Try it for yourselves!

4. COCONUT SHELLS

The coconut shell consists of a fine hard wood of a dark colour with an interesting grain. But it is hidden under thick brown hair and is only revealed if

1135 Interesting patterns are not hard to make

we can clean and sandpaper the surface first. It can afterwards be waxed or oiled. The wood can be carved into ash-trays, spoons, salt-cellars, buttons, or clasps. We shall need a fret-saw, although a tenon-saw can be used for rougher work. Of course, we must open the coconut and drain the milk - which has a nice fla-vour - before we start sawing. This is done by making a hole in the marked spots at the base with a tin-opener or a bradawl.

5. SMALL FIGURES AND DOLLS' HEADS

Simple figures for a Christmas Crib etc., can be cut from fairly thick stakes (1116 to 1118). A wood file (1088) and a sharp knife are all we need. For easy working, the stake should be slightly longer than the figure. It is marked as shown in Figs. 1116 to 1118 then carved. The arms are made separately and glued on. Finally, the surplus wood is sawn off and the doll is painted.

The little tree in Figs. 1114 and 1115 was made from a small cone-shaped piece. The wood-fir is most suitable - it was damped first and the branches were afterwards peeled off (1114). The tree also has a small base.

Lime, linden or basswood are the most suitable woods for figures, chessmen, etc. It is advisable to make the figure in clay before we start carving. But the form must not be followed slavishly in wood. The clay model merely serves as a guide for the proportions. The wood should again be slightly longer than the figure, although of the same thickness and width. This will make it easier to hold it in the vice (1119 to 1121).

If we have no bench, the wood can be cut in a vice on the table.

The outlines are first marked on the figure in pencil. The wood is then gradually split off in layers. Great care must be taken to avoid splitting. Occasional damping may help. We first carve the figure in rough outlines and then work out the detail.

The finished carving is waxed (see page 287) and brushed until it has a mellow shine. Linseed oil should not be used on lime or basswood, since it darkens the wood and brings out the grain so much that the form almost disappears. But colourless shoe polish or furniture polish can produce very pleasant effects.

Wood for the heads of marionettes should have a shape that already contains the essential features and therefore only requires little carving. An auger bit can be used to drill the hole for the fingers. Everything else is done as described above.

6. DECORATIVE CARVING

Many old tools have carved decoration, often of a symbolic nature. Old buildings, too, sometimes show such carving. It was only lately that this art degenerated. As a result, we find wood covered with meaningless decoration. But used sparingly, it enhances a piece of furniture or a building.

It is not essential, although desirable, to have special carving tools. Most sharp knives and gouges will also prove useful for other purposes. An oilstone for sharpening is most important. It can also be used for board-cutters.

Not all woods are suitable for such decoration. The wood has to be fairly soft, finely grained and yet firm, must not splinter and must give a clean surface when cut. Lime or basswood is especially good.

The piece of wood in question must be fixed to the table with two G- or C-clamps to leave both hands free.

Some basic rules:

We start cutting where the grooves are to be deepest. All cuts must be made deep enough the first time. Corrections should be avoided. The design is drawn on the wood, the upper and lower limits especially must be marked very carefully.

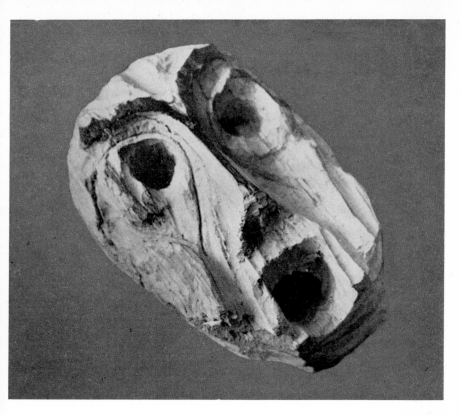

1136 Mask from Firewood

1137 Coconut Bowl and Ash-tray

For a simple jagged outline we mark the triangles with the gouge to the necessary depth and then lift them out with a knife. The knife must be set on diagonally. If the wood splits, the cut must be made in the opposite direction.

7. CARVING MOULDS FOR CAKES AND COOKIES

Cake moulds we have made ourselves are a fine present. Cakes, cookies and biscuits can be made in them for festive occasions, as used to be done in the past.

Pear or box is the best wood. We draw the outline in reverse on a board about ¾ in. thick, retrace it with a knife and gouge out the wood. To see what the cakes will look like, we can press Plasticene into the form. This will also show what corrections might still be needed.

1138/1139 Old Baking Moulds. Such Moulds, usually designed by their maker and preserved through many generations can make baking really exciting

A Recipe

We shall need 1 lb. of self-raising flour, 1 lb. of sugar, four eggs, one tablespoonful of butter and a little aniseed. All the ingredients, apart from the flour, are then mixed thoroughly and stirred for a quarter of an hour. The flour is then mixed in and kneaded. The dough is rolled out to ¼ in. thickness and lightly dusted with flour. Then we press the mould - which has previously been dusted with flour on the inside - onto it, cut out the forms and put them on an aniseed covered board. They are then put on well-greased cake tins and baked in the oven to a light yellow.

8. BOWLS

Suitable woods have already been

mentioned on page 280. Elm, lime, basswood, birch, oak or pearwood can also be used. We cut out the basic shape with a hand-saw from a board of the required thickness. Anyone not too conversant with the hand-saw should ask a more experienced friend to do it, since it needs quite a lot of skill. Having traced the outline on both sides of the board, we fix the latter to an old table with a vice (1140). We then remove the wood with a gouge (1079 and 1085), always working from the edges towards the centre. Care must be taken to cut always with the grain and remove equal quantities of the wood with each stroke. To make this possible, the prospective bowl will have to be removed and replaced in the vice many times. All good carving depends on making the most of the characteristics of the particular piece of wood.

1140—1142 Carving a bowl

Fig. 1141 shows how the depth of the bowl is marked on the outside. We mark it first on the board and then drive a nail into a piece of wood until it projects a distance equal to the depth of the bowl. The nail is then slipped off and can be used for measuring. The line marking the thickness of the bowl should not be removed in the course of the work.

Having hollowed out the wood, it is turned round and carved to shape from the outside. An ordinary chisel will do this better than a gouge. The finished bowl is sandpapered and waxed or covered with a clear varnish.

If the bowl is to have a wide, flat rim we must saw round the block after it has been hollowed out. The surplus wood is then removed with a chisel or gouge.

1143 A handsome carved Animal

9. TOYS FROM SCRAPS OF WOOD (CHART Q)

It is important to *think* in wood, even when we only make very small objects. That means, that we must choose forms that are clear and simple, in the nature of the material. A toy must be firm and must look it. The spidery fret-saw animals with their thin legs - as we see them so often - do not suggest wood. They are like paper patterns, thought out on paper, and have merely been applied to wood. They do no justice to the material they were made from and are no pleasure to look at.

Building Bricks

Building bricks are often a child's first toy. Smooth, sturdy blocks, well finished and neatly arranged in a box (1144), are most suitable for children between one and two. There should not be too great a variety to confuse the child.

They are cut from square pieces of wood, preferably with tenon-saw and mitre box, and are then sandpapered. The corners should be slightly rounded so as not to be too sharp for small children. Other forms such as prisms, cones, etc., can be added gradually (1145) as the child grows older.

Toy Village

Children love toy houses for reconstructing their street, their village or even entire cities. Houses can be made in different ways.

We need a moulding profiled as shown in Fig. 1110c. The houses are simply cut out with a tenon-saw in the mitre box. Roofs, doors and windows can be painted, after the wood has first been sandpapered. We can also fix a layer of wood with a gable (see Figs. 1110a, b and c) to the front of a house.

296

1144
Small wooden blocks, well finished, give great joy to small children

The houses in Fig. 1145 were not cut out of one piece, but from square and triangular battens. The roofs are simply put on in the course of the game.

Jumping Jack

A jumping jack should have bright colours and should be made to last. He will give pleasure to small children for a long time and will be in their thoughts for years after their childhood has passed.

The five separate parts - seven, if there is to be a joint in the knee - are drawn on paper, transferred to wood, cut out, painted and varnished. Fig. 1122 shows how the parts are joined. Arms and legs must be able to move. They should therefore be attached to the body with small wooden pins, made out of hard wood (1123, 1124). They must move in the body, but must be glued firmly into the limbs. Arms and legs are connected with thread. Finally the vertical thread is attached to the horizontal threads, and if we tug at it the jumping jack will bounce up and down with joy.

Our jumping jack will look even better if he is finished on both sides. The piece for head and body will have to be cut out twice in this case. We will also need three additional pieces (see shaded parts in Fig. 1122). The wooden bolts must be fixed into the body; the holes in the limbs, however, must be large enough to allow movement (1126).

297

1145
Children betwe
four and five c
be given more
elaborate forms
Houses make f
toys

Jointed Toys

Fig. 1146 shows a toy with great possibilities. It can be used for towing, building and making sand pies. It is made so interesting by the way it interlocks. The flat joint has been cut with a coping-saw (1109).

Sailing Ship

A beautiful present for a small boy. First we cut the hull, then the rigging. The hull is made of one piece, rather like the outside of the wooden bowl on page 295, first with the gouge, then with file and sandpaper. The sails have been correctly soaked with linseed oil, the masts are let into the hull. Everything has to be balanced properly, or the ship will not float.

A Piglet

The basic form has been cut with a coping-saw from a piece of lime or bass-wood, the outlines are afterwards smoothed out with a pocket knife. The ears are little pieces of leather; a piece of string was glued on for the tail.

Doll's Bed on Wheels

We need a brace and an auger bit (1067 and 1069) for our doll's bed on

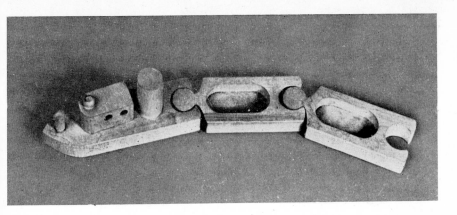

1146 A toy with many uses

1147 A present for a little brother

1148 Wooden pigs

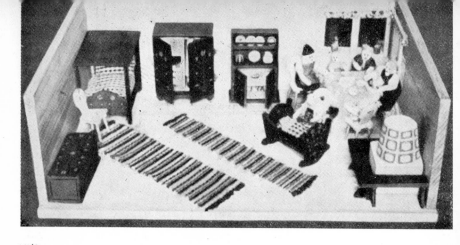

1149

wheels (1150). The bit must be the diameter of the stakes. Dowel joints can be used as shown on Plate O. We first cut the bars and battens. The battens meant to hold the mattress must be given an inner ledge for this purpose. The corner posts are slightly flattened at the top and are given a hole to take the axle for the wheels. These are fitted to dowels (1097) and are fastened with small pegs of beech. The sides are made first and fitted into the posts later. A little frame with webbing will hold the mattress. Clear varnish will protect the bed from scratches.

A Dolls' Room

A dolls' room (1149 and 1151) with painted furniture gives joy to every little girl. It is a wonderful toy! There is a linen press, full of sheets, a dresser with coloured plates, and the whole family sits in the corner near the window with their porridge bowls.

The furniture has been made from small boards and was cut partly with the fret-saw and partly with the tenon-saw in the mitre box. It is very durable and made with real joints wherever possible. Chairs and tables have been left in natural wood. The rest has been stained and painted afterwards with poster colours and colourless varnish. Note how the decorations follow the shape of the individual pieces.

Figs. 1127 to 1130 give instructions for making the furniture. The table has been pegged (1130), the backs and legs of the chairs have been let into the seats (1127). Chests and wardrobes were made like boxes, the partitions for the wardrobe were made separately and then fitted (see page 284). Doors are fitted with hinges (see page 286). Figs. 1129 and 1128 show how the components of the cradle were made to fit into the posts.

The plates were made of clay, glazed and fired. The small spoons have been carved in lime with a pocket knife. The tiled stove, too, has been fired properly. The rugs are hand woven, the origins of the doll family are described on page 302. All their joints are flexible and can therefore move.

Dolls' Kitchen

The kitchen is made like the dolls' living-room, but the furniture has been left unvarnished and can thus be scrubbed like real kitchen furniture. The gingham curtains and the coloured plates stand out nicely against the plain wood. The making of the window is described on page 284.

1150 Doll's Bed or Cot on Wheels

1151 A Doll's Living Room

DOLLS AND ANIMALS

DOLLS

Dolls

The two dolls shown in Fig. 1152 (opposite) are just right for a small child

The B o d y : It is best made from a pattern. We must allow some extra material for the seams. The sections are sewn by machine on the *wrong* side, turned right side out, stuffed with cotton wool, rags or sawdust and joined.

The H e a d : We make a little ball from flock or cotton wool, put a piece of mull round it and tie it up (1153). Next we make a dent between nose and forehead with a few strong back stitches (1154), and attach little pads of cotton wool for forehead, cheeks, chin and nose (1155). The head is then covered with a piece of flesh-coloured stockinette, though this should first be done provisionally with a few pins to make sure that it will fit. If it does fit, it is first sewn at the back of the head (1163) and then at each end. Eyes and mouth are embroidered with coloured silks. The nose can be brought out a little more with a few extra stitches, the cheeks can be dyed with a little rouge.

The W i g : Teased (ravelled) cotton, wool, hemp or old stockings can all be made into wigs. Each material has a character of its own. If the doll is to have a crew cut or urchin cut, the hair has to be sewn to the crown in small tufts (1157) If there is to be a parting, the hair will have to be sewn along it with chain stitches. (1159). For a pony tail, the hair will have to be sewn in long strands on the hair line (1161), with a few short additional hairs for the fringe (1162). Everything must be sewn on very thoroughly.

Dolls' Clothes. "Clothes make the man', for dolls as much as for human beings We therefore use bright colours. Every doll must be made for dressing and undressing. Buttons, buttonholes and ribbons must be made properly. Instructions for sewing dolls' clothes are given on page 71.

DOLLS FOR THE DOLLS' HOUSE

Twisted Dolls

We take a small bundle of thread, tie it round the middle, place the ends against each other and tie up a piece at the top for the head (see Fig. 1165). We now place this on top of a second bundle - for the arms - and tie on the latter in a criss-cross fashion (1166). Finally, we tie some string round arms and legs and cut off any surplus threads (1167).

A Doll from a Duster or Handkerchief

We make a small ball from soft paper or rag, wrap it up in a square piece of

1153—1156 The Making of a Doll's Head

1157—1160 Urchin Cut, wigs with and without parting

cloth and tie it up (1168). The sides are then turned in half-ways (1169) and the hands are tied off as shown in Fig. 1170. We then make the feet (1170) and use another piece of coloured rag for the skirt (1171).

A Flexible Doll on a Wire Frame

We take two pieces of wire, a longer piece for head, body and legs, and a short piece for arms and hands. The long piece is twisted into a loop at the top for the head, the shorter piece is wound across underneath the loop. The ends are bent to make hands and feet (1173).

When the wire frame is completed, we take a small rag for the head and cover it with pink silk, jersey or stockinette, etc. (1174). We then wrap some material round arms and legs (1175), pad the body a little (1176) and cover the doll with jersey or ordinary material.

Dolls from Tissue Paper

If we cover the wire frame (1173) with tissue paper instead of fabric, we have dolls that are very suitable for a little theatre. The paper should first be lightly coated with paste.

First we screw up some paper for the head, put it through the loop and paste two or three layers of pink tissue paper over it. The paste makes the paper soft and malleable. Arms and legs can be formed while the tissue paper in the colours of the skin or suit is pasted on.

The most suitable dress is a simple smock, but we must have enough courage to try other patterns as well. Woman dolls need no legs, since they can be made to stand with their long skirts.

Movable Dolls from Beads

The dolls shown in Figs. 1181 and 1182 can make all kinds of movements. They can be made to sit down, to have fights and to make it up again. In winter, they

304

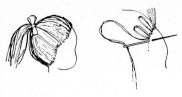 

1161—1162 The Pony Tail   1163 Invisible Stitch

1164—1167 A Doll from Scraps of Wool

1168—1172 A Duster Doll

1173—1177 Made of Wire and Bits of Rag

1178—1181 A doll from beads with a special hair style

1182 Though made of beads he can ride a scooter

1183 A cheerful donkey and a contented pig

go skiing and tobogganing, in summer they do exercises and roll along on their scooters. They can be dressed and undressed and can even be made to endure the hairdresser's art.

We need a large wooden bead for the head, a small button or press button, and some thin wire. Hands and feet can be carved from scraps of wood. They must have holes, made with a small hand drill, to take the wire (1180).

Figs. 1178 to 1180 show how the frame is made. Both ends of the wire are pushed through the largest bead, which is to form the head. The material for the hair is then pulled through the loop at the head (1179) to keep the wire in position. Now we fasten the legs and take another piece of wire - to be fastened immediately under the head - for the arms and hands.

The "skeleton" is either padded with white cotton or with small strips of material. Bits of yarn or felt etc., are used for the hair (1152). They are pasted on and can be given a more definite shape. Finally, the doll has its face painted and is dressed.

The scooter is made from bits of wood, the wheels are flat wooden buttons or discs fastened with wire.

Two thin, shaped boards will make a fine pair of skis, if we soak the tips in boiling water and keep them bent in position until they are dry.

WOOLLEN ANIMALS

Animals from rags, American cloth (oil cloth), raffia, straw and felt are some of the most attractive inhabitants of the nursery. They are not difficult to make. We can use our own patterns and can give full rein to the imagination.

Animals made in two sections (1183 and 1195)

First a few basic rules. We draw the required form in profile. It is then cut out twice, once for each side. It must be realized that the animal will be somewhat fatter on the back, at the flanks and near the head. We must allow for this when cutting out.

Two more pieces are then cut for the inside of the legs and the stomach (1185). Both pieces can be cut at the same time. They must fit the part for the back *very close-ly*. Having been sewn together as shown in Fig. 1186, they are sewn to the main sections. Head and back are then sewn up, except for a small opening, so that our animal can be stuffed with wood shavings, cotton wool, sawdust or flock, etc. We must not forget to sew up the hole, since a small child, however appreciative, would undoubtedly pull out all the stuffing. Some coloured wool or a strip of felt for the mane can be sewn in. The donkey and the piglet in Fig. 1183 were made that way.

Animals with Separate Legs (Fig. 1195, left)

Rump and head and the legs are sewn separately. The legs are afterwards sewn firmly to the body. If they have been stuffed really tightly, the animal will stand on the ground firmly.

Animals on Wire Frames

Animals on such frames can be bent into many positions. The frame is made as shown in Fig. 1190, built up with strips of material (1191) and covered in bright cloth.

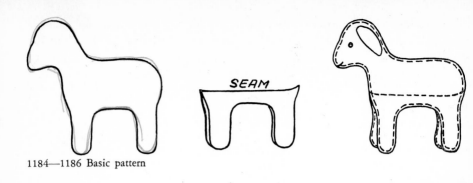

1184—1186 Basic pattern

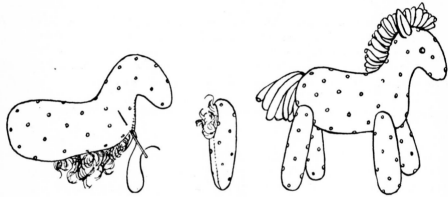

1187—1189 Legs and body are worked separately for this horse. The finished legs are sewn to the horse

1190—1191 The wire frame for movable animals is first covered with strips of rags

1192—1194 A bench covered with strips of rags and with a coloured material makes a fine horse or donkey

A Comfortable Horse (Fig. 1194)

A horse, to be really comfortable, must be built on a frame, rather like a bench. The frame (1192) is padded with flock or wood shavings. Strips of linen are then wound tightly all over it. The head must not be raised too high or taken too far forward, or the horse will not balance properly. Finally, it is given its hide. Body and legs should be covered separately. The material must be stretched very tightly. For the seams see Fig. 1163.

MASKS

We can make a great variety of masks ourselves and, with experience, will dis-cover new ideas and new forms.

The simplest mask is made from an old nylon stocking. The children merely sew bits of wool on to it and pull it over their faces. What joy, if someone does not recognise them! They also like to disguise themselves with painted paperbags, having first cut out holes for nose, eyes and mouth. A piece of cardboard can also be trans-formed into a face (1199 to 1205).

Paper Mask

(Fig. 1203). A mask from a square piece of cartridge paper (construction paper) or brown paper can be great fun. The paper is folded at the sides (see dotted lines) to fit the face better. It can either be pasted down or held together with paper clips (1205). Small clothes pegs (clothes pins) will also do. The eyelashes can be cut and folded back or stuck on (1202), the 'hair' is cut out in strips and rolled across the knife to give a more ferocious expression. We can also make it separately and glue it on like the beard in Fig. 1201. A triangle can be cut out for the nose (1204). A really good long nose has to be made separately, creased and stuck on with narrow strips of paper from the inside.

A Birdmask (1198)

This mask was made in a country school. Its feathers recall American Indian masks. The basic form was made over a clay base, as described on page 314. Finally, the mask was painted and lined with buckram. The feathers were glued to the lining.

A Hedgehog Mask (1197)

This mask is made of wire netting covered with brown paper. The spikes made of straws can easily be fitted to the wire.

Wire netting is used a lot in the theatre since it lends itself as the base for many interesting shapes. It is particularly useful for making scenery and masks.

A Mask from Raffia and Cane (1196)

This fine mask was made of bent cane, bound with raffia, as described on page 140.

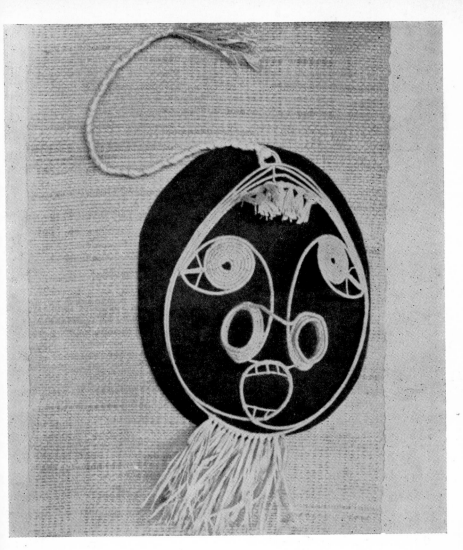

1196 Mask from Cane and Raffia
1195 A Group of Animals

HEADS FOR DOLLS AND MARIONETTES

1. Heads from Corrugated Paper

A piece of corrugated paper (about 6 ins. x 6 ins.) is rolled round the index finger on the flat side. The paper should be dotted lightly with glue. A narrow strip is then rolled round the upper part of the tube until we have the shape of a head (1207). Eyes, mouth and nose can be glued on or painted. It is even more effective to cut small openings and to treat them as shown in Fig. 1211. A small piece of corrugated paper can be the nose, the lips can be filled in with red cotton,

1197 Hedgehog Mask

stars can be stuck on for the eyes, and raffia, scraps of wool, teased (ravelled) cotton, etc. can be used for the hair.

2. Heads from Newspapers

We cover old newspapers with paste to make them soft and malleable and mould them over the left index finger or over a round block of wood (1212). The basic form should be brought out as much as possible at this stage. Butter muslin (cheese cloth) can be used for the more difficult parts, such as nose and chin. Having finished the head in outline, we leave it to dry for a few days. We then apply a layer of thin, soft paper in small pieces and later put on another layer of flesh-coloured tissue paper.

When the head is finished and completely dry, it is painted in water-colours. Coloured paper can also be used for eyes and mouth. Crumpled tissue paper, or some flock or fur will make a nice wig. The opening for the index finger is finished properly at this stage. Some paper or cardboard can be stuck in to make it smaller if necessary.

The hands are made of newspaper or tissue paper on a wire frame. We then stick small paper cuffs round them and stitch them to the clothes of the marionette. The clothes can be sewn like a sack, with a small opening for the head.

3. Papier Mâché Heads

Newspaper is torn into small pieces and soaked in hot water with a little washing soda for about half an hour. A handful of sawdust is then added to the water and

312

1198 Birdmask with Coloured Feathers

the whole mass is left to boil. It is then cooled and mixed with plaster of Paris and cold glue in powder form until it is suitable for modelling. We never make more than we need for one head at a time. The opening for the finger must not be forgotten. The dry heads can be carved or finished with sandpaper. They are then covered with paste and, having again dried completely, painted with poster colours.

They should be given a protective coat of clear varnish when the colours have dried.

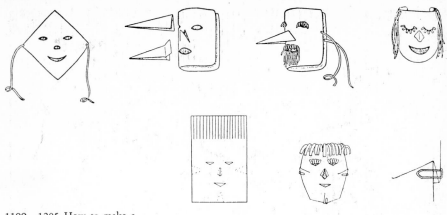

1199—1205 How to make a
few simple masks

4. Heads modelled over Plasticene or Clay

This method is more complicated, but can give very satisfactory results. The head is first formed of clay or plasticene. When it has slightly hardened, we glue small pieces of paper - about the size of a shilling, or a twenty-five cent piece - all over it. It will need about six or seven layers like this to become really firm. A coating of glue should be put on after every second layer of paper. When the head has dried, the clay is carefully removed bit by bit. The head can be sawn open for this purpose and stuck together again with strips of paper or adhesive tape. We would also have to cover the seam with pieces of paper. The head can be painted with poster colours when it has dried.

5. Marionette Figures from Lead Weights

A marionette theatre is one of the most pleasant memories of childhood. One can remember the little figures with their rather stiff movements very vividly. Small marionettes can be made quite easily.

We shall need a large round wooden bead for the head, a small piece of fur for

1206—1210

314

1211 Even Small Children can make Marionettes from Corrugated Paper

1212—1213 A Head from Paste and Old Newspaper can have great character

1215   1214

the hair, about half a yard of lead shot (these are small lead weights sewn into a piece of material so as to form a chain, and these may be difficult to obtain in England, but are widely used for weighing down curtains on the Continent), a cardboard star, or a similar piece of cardboard, and a few coloured rags.

We first finish the head, paint on the face, glue on the piece of fur for the hair, or simply paint the hair on. We shall need a piece of lead shot for the arms and a long piece for body, legs and feet. The two pieces are sewn together in the middle - as shown in Fig. 1215 - the thread is inserted in the wooden bead and left dangling for the time being. For the feet, we fold the lead shot twice in such a way that it will form a right angle to the legs, and stick each foot together. Then we glue some black tissue paper over them. The hands are dipped into watered red ink to give them the colour of skin, and the doll can then be dressed.

CHRISTMAS CRIBS AND DECORATIONS FOR THE CHRISTMAS TREE

STARS

Stars From Straw

Straws are split open, flattened and cut up into strips of slightly under 3 ins. in length. Eight of these strips are then glued together crossways with Uhu or another patent glue (paste is useless for this purpose). Finally, the point where the straws cross is strengthened with a small piece of gold or metallic paper on both sides.

A more beautiful star can be made by tying the straws together with raffia (1223-1224). It is better not to split them in this case to preserve their natural beauty.

Golden Wheels

These can be made from metallic or coloured paper. A strip of gold paper, about 3 ins. x 12 ins. - if the paper is coloured on both sides, the strip only has to be half as wide - is folded lengthways, so that the gold should show on both sides. It is then folded in the manner shown in Fig. 1217.

Having drawn two threads of cotton through the folds of paper (1218), we pull it out into the shape of a disc. The first crease is fitted into the last and another thread is pulled through to hang up our little wheel. The paper can be turned in at the edges (1216) or left as it is.

Pointed Stars

A strip of bank, or note, paper, about 2 ins. x 14 ins. is folded as for the wheel. A large portion of the paper is then cut out (1221). We can also make our own pattern. The points of the star must be trimmed with the scissors after cutting out. Two threads for hanging up are taken through all the points. A narrow strip of paper is pasted over the first and last points to connect them.

Double Star

A square piece of gold paper is folded as shown in Fig. 1225, cut at the four

1216 Golden Wheels from Tinsel make a simple and worthy Christmas Decoration

marked places and made into a star (1226). If two such stars are pasted against each other, we have an eight-pointed star.

A similar star - with, however, three dimensions - is shown in Fig. 1228. It is folded as in Fig. 1225, but instead of folding both parts inwards, one is always folded under, so that it looks more substantial (1227).

Plaited Star

We cut four strips about ½ in. wide and between 12 ins. and 14 ins. in length from gold or silver paper. If the paper is only coloured on one side, it has to be taken in double width. The strips are folded lengthways and plaited (1229 to 1237) as follows:

The strips are placed at right angles, forming loops, and pulled through each

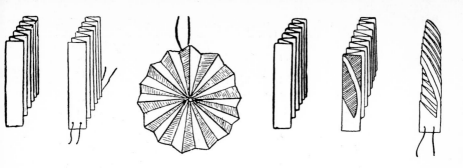

1217—1219 Golden Wheel   1220—1222 A Pointed Star

other (1229). The four upper ends are then turned in the opposite direction, starting at the upper right (1230), and then at the bottom left. The end of the last strip is pulled through the loop of the first (1231). The lower strip is then turned under to the right (1232), folded again, turned upwards (1233) and pulled through the loop (1234). The other three loops are formed in the same manner (1235). The four ends will then project as in 1235. They should be folded across and pushed through the next strip to form an upright point. The end is then cut off (1237).

CANDLEHOLDERS

Candleholder from Interlocking Chains

We make an interlocking chain (1239 to 1243). This requires two strips of paper, each slightly over ½ in. wide and about 2 ft. in length. Silver foil is even better. The ends of the chain are then stuck together, so that the candle can stand in the middle.

Candleholder from a Paper Square

A square piece of paper about 4 ins. x 4 ins. is folded as shown in Figs. 1247 to 1250. The corners are then taken up (1251), and interlocked (1252). Finally, the whole structure is slightly rounded from the inside with the help of a pencil.

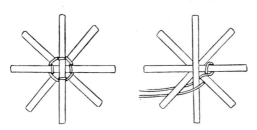

1223-1224 A Star from Straw

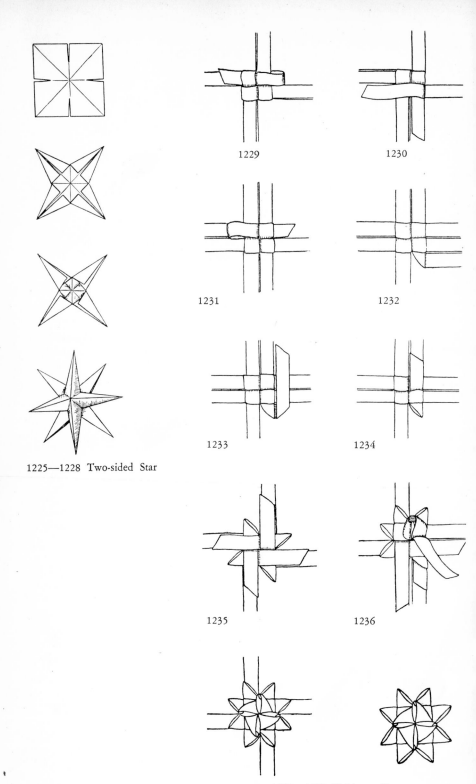

1229

1230

1231

1232

1233

1234

1235

1236

1225—1228 Two-sided Star

1229—1238 Plaiting a Star

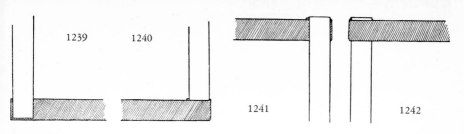

1239—1244 A Star-Shaped Candleholder

1245/1246 A Candleholder from two strips of paper of different widths

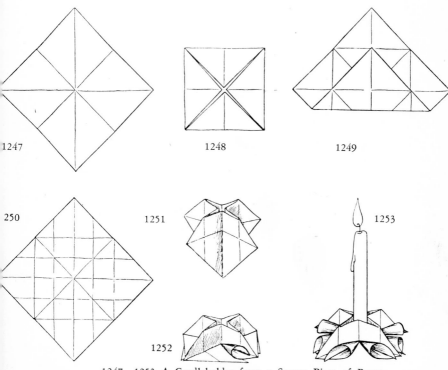

1247—1253 A Candleholder from a Square Piece of Paper

1254 A Star-shaped Candleholder

CHRISTMAS CRIBS

To make a good crib is not simple. We need patience, perseverence and, above all, devotion to our task. Indeed, joy and devotion are needed in all handwork, but never more than for a Christmas crib.

There are many ways of making a crib. The figures can be cut out of plywood, painted and supported with small blocks of wood glued to the back. But children do not like such flat cribs generally. They seem to lack the character of three-dimensional cribs. Figures carved in wood are very beautiful, but they are not easy to make.

1255—1256 Frames for the Figures of a Christmas Crib

1256 Frame for a Sheep

We therefore suggest making figures on wire frames. They can be coated with wax and dressed.

Translucent modelling wax (such as Glitter Wax) gives soft outlines and has a mellow glow that seems very suitable for our purpose. Children find it an easy material.

The Frame

The figures in Fig. 1255 were made on a frame. A thin copper wire is sufficient for figures up to 6 ins. in height, those of a larger size will need wire of a thicker gauge. We need two pieces of wire for each figure, a longer piece for head, trunk and legs, and a shorter piece for arms and hands. Having made a loop in the longer wire for the head, we fasten the shorter piece just under the loop by twisting the two wires together (1255). It must be remembered that the distance between the fingertips of the outstretched arms is equal to the height.

Head and Limbs

The frame is now covered with the slightly warmed, skin-coloured Glitter Wax. The final outlines are slightly modelled. The figures in Fig. 1216 were made in this way.

The figures are either dressed in crêpe paper or in cloth. A simple tunic is most suitable. Raw wool can be used for the hair. The frame for the child has been made with special care, and the child itself was then formed entirely of wax.

The sheep in Fig. 1216 were made of paste and paper over a wire frame. A little wax was put on the tips of their noses, finely shredded paper provided the fur. It was wrapped round the form - slightly coated with paste - and 'shorn' afterwards. The sheep in the last illustration were covered with nylon fur.

Joseph's wand is a piece of wire, covered with brown tissue paper over paste.

INDEX

The numerals in *heavy* type denote the figure numbers
of the illustrations

A

Adhesives 244, 284
Album, Photograph 249: **941, 982, 984, 991**
    with Japanese lacing 254: **955**
Animals
    Maize-straw 155: **684-691**
    Paper 228: **890, 894, 896, 897, 936, 937**
    Raffia 156: **697-700**
    Root and Bark 288: **1133, 1134, 1143**
    Rush 155: **681**
    Wooden 298: **1143, 1148**
    Woollen 307: **1183-1195**
Annealing 224
Appliqué 60: **288**

B

Baby's bootees and mitts, knitted 35, 37:
    134, 135
    jacket and bonnet 30: **126, 127, 129**
    matinee coats 29: **126**
    pants 34: **130-133**
    romper suit 38: **136**
    shoes, Crochetted 47: **153**
    Felt 85: **406**
Bags, Beach 83: **393, 394**
    Newspaper 150: **673**
Basketry 129 et seq
    Broom and raffia 131: **588**
    Cane 159: **701-784**
    Chip 130
    Maize leaf 129, 146: **653-662**
    Palm fibre 130
    Paper 235: **910-913**
    Raffia 129, 141: **633**
    Rush 130, 176: **778-784**
    Straw 130, 143: **645**
    Willow 131, 174: **770-784**
    Wood-based 173: **766-768**
Batik 205: **846-853**
    Paper 240
Beach bags 83: **393, 394**
Bead chain pattern 23: **114**
Beadwork 97: **476-489**
Bibs, Child's 347-349
Binder's cloth 243
Binding, Bias binding and facing 70
Birdmask **1198**
Birds, Chinese **936, 937**
    Japanese paper 236: **924-935**
Blocking (metalwork) 224
Blouses 56: **281, 282**
Book-binding 262: **1006-1021**
Book covers, Raffia 153: **152**
Bookcrafts 247: **961** et seq

Borders, Basketwork 165: **728-754**
Border trimmings 56: **289**
Bottle, Lamp from a 276: **1022**
Bowl, Carving a 294: **1140-1142**
    Hammered copper 224: **876**
Box, Composite 256: **993-1004**
    Paper 235: **903-907, 919-923**
Bracelet, Wire **860**
Bread basket, Cane 162, 168: **701**
Brooch, Wire 222: **860-867**
Brushes, Paint 219
Building blocks, Toy 296: **1144, 1145**
Buttonholes 71, 78: **314-317**
    Knitting 10
Buttons, Leather 183: **800**

C

Cable-and-rib pattern 23: **112**
Cable pattern 22: **111**
Candleholders 319: **1239-1254**
Cane basketry 159: **701-784**
    sizes 704
Canoe, Bark 156: **696**
Card or Tablet weaving 106: **511-540**
Cardboard 242: **942-1005**
Cardloom weaving 101: **497-501**
Carving, Decorative 292: **1135, 1136**
Carving moulds 294: **1138-1142**
Carvings from bark and roots 288: **1055, 1132-1134**
Castle, Paper **889**
Cellophane 180
Chamois leather 180
Chessmen, Hazelwood 290: **1131**
Chevreau 180
Children's clothes 53, 54, 67, 72: **48-67b, 198-200, 289, 333-353**
    Knitted 29: **126-136**
Chinese Plait 96: **458-461**
Christening robes 60: **286, 286**
Christmas cribs 322: **1216, 1255, 1256**
    decorations 317: **1216-1254**
Coat hangers 81: **389**
Coatee, Quilted 74: **344, 350**
Coconut bowl and ash-tray 4: **1137**
Coffee cloth in drawn threadwork 277
Coffee cosy 55: **202, 376-380**
Coiling (pottery) 210: **854-858**
Colours, for porcelain 219
Cording 95: **449-461**
Cowhide 180
Cribs, Christmas 322: **1216, 1255, 1256**
Crochet 44: **146-188**
    Stitches 155-172

Tunisian coloured 48: 174-184
Cross stitch 52: 147
Cushion, Handwoven 572
Cutlery holder 81: 387

D

Dolls 302: 1152-1182
Doll's bed 298: 1150
    clothes 71: 318-382
    heads:
    paper 311: 1207, 1211
    papier mâché 312: 1212-1213
    plasticine 314
Doll's kitchen 284: 1056
    room 300: 1149, 1151
Drawn threadwork 56: 196, 274-279

E

Egyptian upright loom 492
Electric flex to lamps, Attaching 277:
    1047-1054
Embroidery 51: 145-277
    stitches 203-284

F

Fabric printing 200: 842-845
Fabrics, Raffia 149: 672-675
    Woven 101: 494-496
Filet network 87: 409-413
Filigree work 222: 860-869
Flute, Carving a 288: 1132
Folder, Cardboard 245, 250: 941, 952-960,
    966-984
    Leather 185: 804, 805, 814, 815
Fringes 96: 475

G

Gathering 70
Ghiordes Knot 125: 579
Glazes, Pottery 216
Gloves, Knitted 13: 88-92
    Leather 189: 821-832
Gloving needle 786
Glue 284
Goatskin 180
Gobelin techniques 576, 577
Golden wheels 317: 1216-1219
Grain pattern 19: 104

H

Hairpin work 49: 190-193
Hallstatt Urn, Earliest European weaving
    weaving on 100: 493
Hammered metalwork 224: 870-876
Hammer punch 787
Handbag, Leather 187: 816, 818
Hauswirth, J. J. Silhouette cut by 834
Haversack-cum-bag 83: 394
Heddle and heddle-holder 116: 555-559
Heddle Reed, Weaving with a 103: 502-510

Herringbone pattern 25: 117
Horse, Raffia 157: 697-699
    Toy 309: 1190-1195
Houses, Toy 296: 1145

I

Indian corn: See Maize straw
Inlaid threadwork 56: 278-280

J

Jacket, Lady's knitted 41: 141
Jumping Jack 297: 1122-1126

K

Keyholder, Leather 184: 807
Khelim weave 125: 575
Knitting 1-43: 4-6, 62-145
    Basic Principles 7-47
    Coloured 28: 123-125
    patterns 23: 48-61, 112-125
    stitches:
    Bound 22: 110
    Brioche 20, 22: 105, 106
    Cable 22: 111, 112
    Chain 65
    Double Brioche 111: 106
    Double Moss 102
    Double Overlay 107
    Dropped 20: 5, 100
    Garter 66
    Holed 115, 116
    Lace 23: 116
    Lacing 64
    Ladder 23: 113
    Moss 101
    Mossed rib 103
    Net Brioche 111: 109
    Net overlay 20: 105, 106
    Picot 69, 69
    Pleats 108
    Raglan 67
Knotting 87-97: 408-489
    Maize leaves 146: 662

L

Lamps 276: 1022, 1047-1054
Lampshades 271: 1022-1046
Laurel leaf pattern 25: 122
Leatherwork 179: 785-832
    Buttons and fasteners 183: 796-803
    Folders 185: 804, 805, 814, 815, 817
    Gloves 185, 189: 785, 821-832
    Handbag 187: 816, 818
    Keyholder 184: 807
    Licence holder 184
    Matchbook case 185: 798, 799, 808
    Slippers 189: 820
    Tool bag 188: 819
    Wallet 185: 806, 809-813
Lino-cutting and fabric printing 197: 833,

836-845
Looms, Hand 112: **541-569**
Loops, Sewing 79: **369-375**
Lozenge pattern 25: **120**

M

Macramée work 92: **423-448**
Maize knotting 146: **633-662**
    plaiting 132, 155: **592, 593, 681-695**
Majolica (pottery) 215
Mannikin pattern 25: **119**
Maps, Mounting 246: **959, 960**
Marbling (paper) 239
Marionettes 311, 314: **1206-1214**
    Corrugated paper 311: **1211**
    Lead weights 314: **1214, 1215**
    Paste and newspaper 312: **1212, 1213**
    Plasticine or clay 314
Masks 309: **1136, 1195-1205**
Matchbook holder, Leather 185: **808**
Mats, Cane 160: **708**
    Raffia 153: **674, 676-680**
Metalwork 220: **860-876**
Mittens 13, 36, 40: **93, 134, 139, 201**
Mount-cutter's knife, Using the 942

N

Neckband (Knitting) 11: **71-81**
Needlework 1 et seq.
Net sack 45: **148-152**
Netting 87: **408-489**
    Filet 87: **409-420**
    Fishermen's 408
    with Raffia 148: **663, 664**
Network pattern 25: **100**
Newspaper bag, Raffia 150: **675**

O

Openings (sewing) 77: **356-368**
Osier: SEE Willow basketry

P

Painting on porcelain 217: **859**
Paper candleholders 319: **1239-1254**
    folding 234: **898-937**
    lampshades 271: **1022-1046**
    sculpture 228: **882-897**
Paper work 227: **877-960**
Papers. Coloured 238: **938-940**
    Marbled 239
Photo album 249: **941, 982, 984, 991**
    with Japanese lacing 254: **955**
Piglet, Wooden 298: **1148**
Pigskin 180
Pillowcase 79: **383-385**
Plaiting cord of leather 94: **441-461**
    Raffia, rush and straw 129: **588 et seq**
Plant-holder, Raffia **664**
Pleats, Knitted 20: **107, 108**
Pockets, Knitted 11: **82-85**

Pompoms, Woollen 96: **465-468**
Porcelain, Painting on 217: **859**
Portfolio 254, 260: **986-992, 1005**
Potato prints **940**
Pottery 211: **854-858**
Punches, Leatherwork **788, 789, 791, 793**

R

Raffia animals 156: **697-700**
    basket 141: **638**
    Book jackets 153: **675**
    doll's pram 143: **644**
    fabric 149: **672-675**
    knotting 146: **653-662**
    mats 153: **676-680**
    netting 148: **668**
    sandals 137: **618-625**
    toys 156: **697-700**
    work 129 et seq.
Romper suit, Child's 335
Rucksack, Crochetted 46: **150-152**
Rug, Handwoven **570, 586, 587**
Rush baskets 176: **778-784**
    plaiting: See Plaiting

S

Saddle stitch **794**
Sandals, Maize straw 137: **626-631**
    Raffia 137: **618-625**
Scales pattern 25: **121**
Scarf, Handwoven **584, 585**
Sennah knot 125: **578**
Sewing 67
    frame (binding) 262: **1007**
Ship, Sailing 298: **1147**
Shawl, Knotted mohair **421**
    Woven mohair **571**
Sheepskin 180
Shoe-cleaning outfit 81: **388**
Shoes: SEE slippers
Shopping baskets 176: **778-784**
Shoulder net 45: **148-152**
Shuttle, Cardboard **503**
Silhouettes 194: **834, 835**
Sized papers 240
Skirt. Child's 53: **198, 199, 351**
Skiver 180
Sleeping bags 81, 82: **390-392**
Slewing 162: **719**
Slippers 83: **395-407**
    Crochetted 47: **153**
    Knitted 37: **135**
    Leather 189: **820**
    Maize straw 137: **626-631**
    Raffia 137: **618-625**
Slip-ware (pottery) 215
Smock, Child's 54, 73, 76: **200, 342, 352-355**
Smyrna knot **580, 581**
Socks, Knitted 17, 39: **94-99, 137, 138**
Spiderweb pattern 23: **118**

Sportswear, Knitted 33, 39: **128, 137-139**
Stars, Paper or straw 317: **1223-1229**
Stitches, Embroidery 284
    Knitting 20-23: **5, 65-69, 100-116**
    Sewing 68
Stoles, Crochetted 45: **147**
    Knitted 42: **142-145**
Stoneware pottery 216
Straw-plaiting 130, 134, 135, 137: **596-613, 626-631**
Swan, Japanese paper 236: **933-935**
Swiss drawn threadwork 56: **274-277**

T

Table cloth 54: **194**
    mats, Linen 196
    Straw 596
Tablet or card weaving 106: **511-540**
Tapestry weave 125: **574**
Tassels, Knotted 96: **462-464**
Thonging punch **788**
Tool bag, Leather 188: **817-819**
Toys, Bark 156: **683, 696**
    Maize straw 155: **688-695**
    Raffia 156: **697-700**
    Rush 155: **681, 682**
    Wooden 296: **1143-1151**
    Woollen 307: **1183-1195**
Travelling bags 81: **386**
    slippers 86: **407**
Tray, Basketwork 172: **765**
Trees, Paper **891-893**

Trellis knots **438-440**
Tulle embroidery 57: **264-271**
Twigs for carving 290: **1106, 1131, 1134, 1135**

V

Village, Toy 296: **1145**

W

Waling 163: **721, 727**
Waistcoat, Knitted 41: **140**
Wallet, Pigskin 185: **806, 809-813**
Warp, Mounting the 118: **561**
Warping posts **562-565**
Waste-paper basket 173: **766-769**
Weaving 99-127: **490-587**
    Handloom 112: **541-587**
    Heddle reed 103: **502-510**
    Raffia 149: **665-680**
    Tablet or card 106: **511-540**
"Weberfresken", Early illustration from the **491**
Willow basketry 131, 174: **770-784**
Windmill, Folded paper 235: **908, 909**
Wire work, Bent 222: **560-569**
Woodwork 279: **1056-1151**
    Tools **1061-1092**
Woollen animals 307: **1183-1195**
Work Basket, Raffia 150: **669**

Y

Yarns, Knitting 6